ASYMMETRIES OF CONFLICT

ASYMMETRIES
OF
CONFLICT

War Without Death

JOHN LEECH

With a Foreword by
LORD JUDD

FRANK CASS
LONDON · PORTLAND, OR.

First published in 2002 in Great Britain by
FRANK CASS PUBLISHERS
Crown House, 47 Chase Side, Southgate
London N14 5BP

and in the United States of America by
FRANK CASS PUBLISHERS
c/o ISBS, 5824 N.E. Hassalo Street
Portland, Oregon, 97213-3644

Website: www.frankcass.com

British Library Cataloguing in Publication Data

Leech, John, 1925
    Asymmetries of conflict: war without death
    1. Terrorism–Prevention–International cooperation
    2. International relations
    I. Title.
    327.1'17

    ISBN 0-7146-5298-9 (cloth)
    ISBN 0-7146-8260-8 (paper)

Library of Congress Cataloging-in-Publication Data

Leech, John, 1925
    Asymmetries of conflict: war without death/John Leech.
        p. cm.
    Includes bibliographical references and index.
    ISBN 0-7146-5298-9 (cloth) – ISBN 0-7146-8260-8 (pbk.)
    1. North Atlantic Treaty Organization – Military policy.
    2. Europe – Military policy. 3. United States – Military policy.
    4. World politics–21st century
    I. Title.
    UA646.3.L34497 2002
    355'.031091821–dc21

Typeset in 11/13pt Century Schoolbook by Cambridge Photosetting Services
Printed in Great Britain by MPG Books Ltd, Bodmin, Cornwall

In homage to our American friends, known and unknown, who continue to search for a just and effective response to the ravages visited on them.

Contents

Foreword by Lord Judd   xi
Preface   xv
Acknowledgements   xix

1 **The Wars of Nations**   **1**
The wages of war   1
The causes   3
The frontier mentality   5
The economic cost   7
Adjusting our sights   10
War and the twenty-first century   12

2 **War and Choice**   **15**
The risks of a fractious world   18
A sketch map of risks   20
Living with proliferation   29
The risks in perspective   33
The phantom armies   36
Arms and the man   39

3 **Countering with Other Means**   **43**
The ultra-smart weapon   43
The concept of just war   45
Preventive diplomacy   47

The Harvard techniques		51
Peace-building from below		56
Fear-reduction measures		59
Defence diplomacy		61
If all else fails		63
Interdiction: the physical means		63
Is the UN a credible instrument?		74
Bending resistance without a fight		78
4	**Sieg ohne Krieg**	**82**
	Psywar	82
	Political and psychological weapons	86
	The psytools	90
	Is it ethical?	96
	Elements of a psyops campaign	100
	Technology and the means of delivery	105
	And then the peace	106
	Can psyops really work?	108
5	**A Strategy for Co-operation**	**110**
	How can it begin?	110
	The growth of authority	115
	Co-operation and the Middle East	117
	It pays to be nice	121
	Deterrence revisited	126
6	**Arms Control and its Technology**	**134**
	Superman and supergun	134
	Where are we technically?	136
	Where are we politically?	138
	The policeman will get you	142
	My brother's keeper	146
	Sending the wrong signals	152
	Or doing what we've always done	154
7	**War without Death**	**158**
	The dilemma of force	158
	The new tasks	160
	Non-lethal weapons	162
	Lessons from experience	170

Contents

Are they ethical?   172
The strategic implications   177
The new options   179

8 Taking the Lead   **183**
A political base for the silent strategies   183
Taking the decision   188
A European Security and Defence Identity   190
A transatlantic security structure   193
A new basis for transatlantic understanding   196
To each his own   199

Bibliography   203
Index   207

Foreword

It has been too often said that '11 September changed the world' and that 'nothing will ever be the same again'. I wonder. What certainly *should* have changed on that terrible and cruel day was that nobody – not least the US administration – could any longer play down or ignore the basic realities of global politics.

The world *is* totally interdependent. Society *is* increasingly vulnerable and advanced technology accentuates that vulnerability. Grotesque disparities of wealth, together with the concentration of power, provoke an almost classic pre-revolutionary situation. The millions of destitute, dispossessed and disempowered are ripe for manipulation by highly intelligent – if disturbed and sometimes psychopathic – often well-educated and articulate extremists. These extremists may be resentfully frustrated by their personal exclusion from the power systems, or may reject what they regard as the crude materialism of ideological market economics, or both. Many people with literally nothing to lose, whose lives are one endless struggle to survive, will inevitably sometimes ask whether extremism is not in fact on their side. Most would probably themselves never participate in an act of terrorism, and would be deeply shocked if they witnessed one at close quarters; nevertheless, to exorcise the terrorists is not top of their daily list of priorities. Terrorism thrives in a constituency of ambivalence.

Indeed, how far is fundamentalism in whatever form not

frequently a vehicle, rather than the real purpose or cause? The fight to contain terrorism will eventually be won by a relentless, transparent and, above all, effective commitment to social and economic justice, coupled with at least an equal commitment to the meaningful redistribution of power in the world. It will inescapably be a matter of 'hearts and minds'.

The calculating extremist wants to demonstrate that, when under pressure, all our brave words about human rights are not worth the paper on which they are recorded. That cynical victory has to be denied. It is precisely when we are under pressure that our commitment to such principles becomes more important than ever. In the way we respond to provocation, not least when military or police action is necessary, our unyielding commitment to the values we espouse must be there for all to see. It is not a matter of whether the physical specifications of US military prison cages in Cuba technically meet the requirements of the Geneva Conventions; it is, rather, a matter of what pictures of perceived humiliation beamed around the world do to swell the ranks of the extremists.

John Leech has produced a timely commentary. His fascinating combination of learning and experience in NATO and transatlantic affairs, development assistance, civil engineering and the arts enable him to bring a challenging perspective to his analysis of global security issues. What, indeed, is security? He is right to pose the question and I, for one, completely endorse his conclusion that it will be found not only in conflict resolution, peacekeeping and pre-emptive diplomacy, but also in economic and social imperatives and good governance.

His attractively logical, at times even passionate, approach stimulates the question that if we are preoccupied with the threats of global terrorism, how is it that we continue with a culture in which it is acceptable or even laudable to export arms unless there is an exceptional reason, sufficiently well argued where it matters, that in some specific instance it would be unwise to do so? Surely, the culture should be that arms are potentially so dangerous to stability and security that they should never be exported unless there is an over-riding and convincing case to do so for security reasons? In the meantime, where exactly do the arms we export end up? On occasions, alas, confronting us!

But the writer takes us much further than this. Is war as we have understood it any longer relevant or likely? If not, what are the scenarios that already confront us and where will they lead us in the future? Are we muscle-bound into our existing military technology? If international peacekeeping and anti-terrorism are to be the real demands, what changes of mindset will be necessary? What of 'psywar' and 'psyops', and what of the ethical concerns they rightly generate?

If we are defending a decent society based on integrity, responsibility and similar values, there is a danger that playing fast and loose with the truth cannot be limited to the tactics of conflict situations. It could too easily infect our social mores as a whole, thereby becoming self-defeating. Means not infrequently erode the ends. This book does not resolve the dilemma, but it does us a service by encouraging debate and setting out the criteria.

And then we come to non-lethal weapons. Here, perhaps I can be forgiven for saying, the text becomes agonisingly controversial. Initially, many readers will be filled with misgivings. Frankly, I am myself. But if we are moving into an age of international policing, these questions do have to be asked. Is it a matter of traditional military mobilisation or nothing, when smart sanctions and the rest are inappropriate or have failed? What clearly needs very careful consideration is how far, freed from the inhibiting restraints of well-tried military techniques, the adherents of 'might is right', in a disturbingly simplistic upsurge of 'we're good' and 'they're evil' politics, might be enabled to extend their omnipotence unchallenged across the globe. In the end, do we see human destiny fulfilled or not by unipolarism; and what are the implications of 'psywar', 'psyops' and non-lethal weapons in this consideration?

Whether or not we opt – if opting is any longer a practical possibility – for a multipolar world, brings us to John Leech's thoughts on Europe and the transatlantic equation. He nails his colours to the mast as a European with a profound transatlantic loyalty. As with so much of the rest of what he writes he honestly, if not always with the outcome he would himself favour, provokes thought. But is he altogether too sanguine, given the new realities of the US leadership – and, for that matter, of the Israeli – and what they represent? While, tellingly, his plea is to be ahead of the game, in these respects the game may have got ahead even of him.

I have myself always until now been an Atlanticist. That has meant that, however vitally important I believe European developments to be, when it comes to the crunch, I have seen the Atlantic link as pivotal. Notwithstanding the nuclear implications, I am no longer quite so certain, as increasingly it seems that what is required of us is, in effect, no more than unquestioning subservience to Washington. In the strategic cause of humanity and its future it is the positive endorsement of pluralism which is imperative. Pluralism is the God-given richness of creative potential. A European 'balance' is becoming indispensable.

Yes, the world is totally interdependent; but to meet that reality we need co-operation, mutual recognition and effective global institutions. Viable order will grow out of a freely shared and developed sense of responsibility and common purpose: whether that be the Kyoto Agreement or a sustained campaign against terrorism. Unilaterally imposed policies and order will, in the end, fracture, as they have always done. In the meantime they will diminish the species. We need a new imperialism of the self-perceived 'good' like we need government by the zealots! International co-operation is more difficult, more frustrating, more complex and more hazardous, but it is about the fulfilment of human potential.

John Leech has made me think, and think hard. For that I am immensely grateful. I take heart from the words of Jefferson he quotes at the head of Chapter 8: 'I hope our wisdom will grow with our power, and teach us that the less we use our power, the greater it will be.'

FRANK JUDD
Hon. Senior Fellow, Saferworld
February 2002

Preface

Asymmetrical conflict is defined as the imbalance of opposing forces. From David and Goliath to Troy, wherever battles have been fought, human ingenuity has further sharpened the basic asymmetries of strategy and equipment. Nowhere were these more marked than in the campaigns of colonial conquest; and, later still, with the panoply of superior powers facing native insurgents, the barefoot armies of the Long March, Vietnam, now once more Afghanistan. The emergence of China as an increasingly crucial factor in global strategy has given new currency to the ancient meaning of the term, that of asymmetrical response or Alternative War. Yet none of these interpretations fully encompasses the dilemmas of modern conflict and its demands for new and inventive responses.

The nature of warfare and the impulses it activates have fundamentally changed. Today's asymmetries present a greatly more complex array of choices than the one-time simplicities of attack-and-defend. Many of them pose paradoxes demanding to be resolved with urgency before the world can be assured of the security which most of it desires. This book is therefore primarily concerned with the techniques of resilience and restraint; that is, the fielding of effective asymmetrical responses, other than war, to the challenges of conflict.

The nineteenth century consolidated the nation-state and its global dominion. The twentieth century had to combat, then to redress its excesses. The twenty-first century has now to repair the fractures which the power politics of the previous two inflicted on the global society. War between nations has become a more distant prospect: the new threat is war by individuals against people. Classic warfare between mighty armies of roughly equal opponents has all but passed into history. The West and its varying coalitions now represent an overwhelming force which can be challenged only in its outlying provinces, or with terrorist acts in its homeland. But any power system exerts psychological pressures on those outside it, which can still turn individuals and groups to the violence of impotence.

In 1905, Einstein's formula $E=mc^2$ changed forever our perception of physics and finally of warfare. A similar transformation has overtaken our security environment. Where Einstein showed that trivial amounts of matter can release vast energy, the formula can equally demonstrate the accessibility of huge destructive forces to even insignificant groups with small material resources but ferocious ingenuity. Quantum physics can become quantum security in a new paradigm to explain twenty-first century conflict.

For over a decade, the Western intelligence community has warned with increasing urgency of the coming risk of terrorist attacks. The West's concern with its own affluence and dominion was creating disparities and resentments. The tools of subversion, both human and material, became easy to accumulate. Disintegration of the Soviet edifice caused a discernible leakage of raw materials and technology for weapons of mass destruction, including their progressive miniaturisation. But military establishments continued to be transfixed by weapons systems with ever greater firepower, and politicians by the size of defence budgets.

Most of today's challenges come from those unwilling to adjust to a global society. Such an asymmetric 'people's war' has to be fought with strategies, tactics and equipment fundamentally different from those of classic warfare. It has no front line, no battle plan, no carpet bombing, no invasions nor massed assaults. Instead, it will be played out substantially in civilian life, by the intelligence community, policing, fraud squads and – where a target has been laid bare – groups of special forces. Aircraft carriers, cruise missiles and all the fearsome ordnance of classic wars will serve a subordinated role in support and as a show of strength, a signal to enforce a basically civilian and political compliance. In his speech to a joint session of the US Congress on 20 September 2001, following the events of 11 September, President Bush himself indicated the place that the tools of war are likely to occupy in this order of battle:

> We will direct every resource at our command – every means of diplomacy, every tool of intelligence, every instrument of law enforcement, every financial influence, and every necessary weapon of war – to the destruction and the defeat of the global terrorism network.[1]

This book examines the history of warfare and its limitations today. In the West's security concerns, territorial defence – including protection from the incursions of terrorism – must remain paramount. But the costs of weapons development are rising inexorably, while we have become less and less prepared to put our fighting personnel at risk. The West can no longer squander its costly armoury in conflicts which more often need the weapons of crowd control and the tools of intelligence and policing. A great deal more should now be invested in scientific strategies to prevent conflict, and to bend the will of an adversary without crippling ourselves in waging war. Our wits must serve as our first protection, in a holistic sequence of economic, diplomatic, psychological and non-lethal actions, as well as the improved technology of arms control: soft power, but always with a hard edge.

Taken together, Europe and the USA exemplify this combination of diplomacy and might – psywar and technowar – but do not as yet fully comprehend their different roles within a common defence. The US economy thrives on the fruits of incremental defence. Americans are prepared to underwrite the cost and take pride in seeing the symbols of US might. By contrast, the economies of its European allies are disparate, unable to follow and reluctant to be drawn into a friendly arms race. They have their own concept of security, complete with military underpinning of its essentially civilian ambitions. Both share a global vision; but what one sees as a military mission, the other regards as pre-eminently political and economic. The NATO alliance – the USA and Europe – must arrive at a sensible recognition of these functions, acknowledging the global investment which each is already making to ensure a common security.

Conflict inevitably commands attention. The 30-odd wars in progress at any time foster the impression of a world in flames, of conflict as the natural state of humankind. Yet the smoke of those battles masks the fact that the very opposite is true: the last half-century has seen the 'zone of peace' steadily enlarged and still growing apace, even in the wake of the wars of ideological decolonisation. Not only have former combatants been pacified, Germany and Japan effectively demilitarised, dictatorships in Europe, Africa, Latin America and elsewhere fallen, and interdependence asserted its claims, but, most significant of all, the world's political map has been completely redrawn. The European Union, Atlantic partnership, economic and political communities elsewhere have created zones of peace and co-operation across the continents. The chart on p. xx traces that history and demonstrates that these zones are now essentially democratic. Albeit with some mighty exceptions, war between them has become unthinkable.

Instead, as every new peacekeeping operation proves, most countries are concerned to quell the conflicts of others before they can disturb the peace. Whether as members of the United Nations or of a plethora of other multilateral bodies, maintaining peace has become a common endeavour. Negotiation, between states or communities, has taken the place of envy and aggrandisement. The entire framework of international relations has become transformed. In the process, a range of tools has been developed with which effectively to inhibit conflict. From negotiating techniques to psychological pressures, from arms control and defence diplomacy to the use of non-lethal weapons to check hostile elements, they form the fundament of an effective, all-embracing strategy of dissuasion and compelling compliance. By not choosing warfare as the symmetrical response to war, we find that there already lies to hand an appropriate set of defences to resist the new assaults upon our society.

Note

1. The White House, Office of the Press Secretary, 20 September 2001.

Acknowledgements

My thanks are due to David Owen and our late and devoted friend Ivo Lederer for their early encouragement for the message of this book, and to Peter Unwin for his invaluable guidance in bringing it to publishable form. Also to Ken Aldred, Paul Schulte, Martin Smith and Roberto Zadra for the trouble they took over more detailed and factual criticism; and to my copy-editor, Penny Rogers, for her constructive and helpful challenges. My particular appreciation to Charles Swett who, as an early believer in non-lethal weapons, introduced the relevant sections to the Pentagon; and to Ben Schemmer of the US Strategic Institute, who published a synopsis in his *Strategic Review*.

A book can have no greater friend than an eminent man who applies his precious time and experience to writing an authoritative foreword. Such is Lord Judd, and I am deeply sensible of the compliment he has bestowed on both book and author. Another is the distinguished sculptor Oliviero Rainaldi, who has kindly allowed me to use an image of his powerful mural in Rome on the jacket.

Beyond that, I am indebted to those many, distinguished in a multiplicity of fields and disciplines, whose ideas became the thread which stimulated me to write this book. And to my wife Noretta, who with great patience represented the uninitiated reader for whose attention, as citizen and voter, the book is ultimately vying.

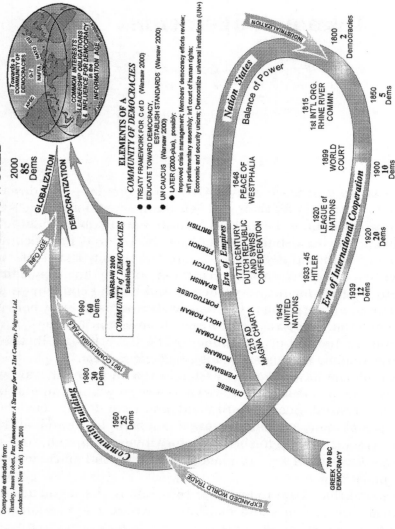

EVOLVING A DEMOCRATIC WORLD

Composite extracted from:

Huntley, James Robert. *Pax Democratica: A Strategy for the 21st Century*, Palgrave Ltd. (London: and New York) 1998, 2001

ELEMENTS OF A
COMMUNITY OF DEMOCRACIES

- TREATY FRAMEWORK FOR C of D   (Warsaw 2000)
- EDUCATE TOWARD DEMOCRACY,
  ESTABLISH STANDARDS (Warsaw 2000)
- UN CAUCUS (Warsaw 2000)
- LATER (2000-plus), possibly:
  Improved crisis management; Members' democracy efforts review;
  Int'l parliamentary assembly; Int'l court of human rights;
  Economic and security unions; Democratize universal institutions (UN+)

WARSAW 2000
COMMUNITY of DEMOCRACIES
Established

2000
85
Dems

GLOBALIZATION

DEMOCRATIZATION

INFO AGE

1990
60
Dems

1991 COMMUNISM FAILS

1980
30
Dems

1960
25
Dems

Community Building

EXPANDED WORLD TRADE

GREEK 700 BC
DEMOCRACY

CHINESE
PERSIANS
ROMANS
OTTOMAN
HOLY ROMAN
PORTUGUESE
SPANISH
DUTCH
FRENCH
BRITISH

Era of Empires

1215 AD
MAGNA CHARTA

17TH CENTURY
DUTCH REPUBLIC
AND SWISS
CONFEDERATION

1648
PEACE OF
WESTPHALIA

Nation States

Balance of Power

INDUSTRIALIZATION

1800
2
Democracies

1815
1st INT'L ORG.
RHINE RIVER
COMMN.

1850
5
Dems

1899
WORLD
COURT

1900
10
Dems

1920
LEAGUE of
NATIONS

1920
20
Dems

Era of International Cooperation

1933 - 45
HITLER

1945
UNITED
NATIONS

1939
12
Dems

James R. Huntley © and Joseph A. Bulger, Jr., 2000

1 The Wars of Nations

'What if doing the right thing not merely
fails to stem the tide of suffering but
actually extends or diverts it?'
Archbishop of York at Gulf Service of Remembrance

The Wages of War

Warfare is bloodshed. Ours, theirs and above all that of civilians.
The last war of territorial aggression was in the Gulf. There, not
even the brilliantly executed Desert Storm was able to prevent
Coalition casualties. A high proportion of those casualties were
Tornado pilots operating the 'smart weapons', the laser-guided
bombs meant to protect them and their machines. Short as that
war was, no one has yet put an authoritative figure on Iraqi
casualties, let alone the civilians who lost their lives. By the time
of the Balkan conflicts, and especially Kosovo, technology and
stand-off bombs had further protected the air crews. Yet, though
'collateral' casualties were relatively few, the cost in human lives
and suffering was still insupportable.

It is a convention that the cost of war is counted in terms of killed
and missing. A historical balance sheet sets out how many of the
enemy were slain and at what cost to ourselves. The former is
normally considered the more significant figure. The latter is
counted in lives, the rest of the effort and sacrifice ignored. In time,
such accounts assume the semblance of a cricket test match score.
The further they recede into history, the more they lose the reality
of blood and gore and instead acquire the aura of a friendly match.

Those who are fascinated by the changing fortunes of test
cricket can consult their *Wisden*. Those who prefer toy soldiers

and the faint echoes of long-stilled bugles can look up their vital statistics in *The Twentieth Century Book of the Dead*[1] or their *Dictionary of Battles*.[2] They will see the steadily escalating numbers; the steeply rising proportion of civilians. The Norman Conquest – 1066 and all that – is thought to have cost a mere 2,000 lives on each side. Some 350 years later, the gloriously remembered battle of Agincourt felled 8,000 French and 400 English. Another 450 years on, the American Civil War accounted for an incredible 204,000 killed in battle and some 413,500 non-battle casualties.

Compare that with the figures for the First World War. The 9 million military casualties in themselves represented a quantum leap; but the war also accounted for 1 million civilian dead. Yet it proved only a mild rehearsal for the carnage of all-out total war seen between 1939 and 1945. The mixture of modern *Blitzkrieg* and carpet bombing, combined with medieval-style decimation of conquered populations, claimed more than 40 million victims. Among the direct war casualties, the proportion of civilians rose from 5 per cent in the First World War to 48 per cent in the Second.

Today it has become more realistic to focus on the civilian casualties as a measure of the havoc wrought by modern warfare. Perhaps it is ghoulish to treat them as statistics. Yet if we are too prudish to learn from their sacrifice, they will really have died senselessly and in vain. The First World War lasted 1,560 days, during which 1 million civilians lost their lives; the Second World War 2,173 days, with 8 million civilian casualties, even excluding the 6 million who died in the Holocaust. The 1990–91 Gulf War was over in 42 days, but not before an estimated 200,000 civilians had been killed.[3] The daily carnage increased from 640 to 3,680 and then 4,800 – without counting the extra millions who perished from prolonged sickness, malnutrition and deprivation. Over the decade since then, 2 million children have been killed by conflict in virtually all continents, including Europe.

The Balkan conflicts added 100,000 fatalities among Croats, Serbs and Bosnians, and a further 16,000 in and on account of Kosovo. The majority, as always, were civilians. Yet numerically the greatest cost was in the suffering, dispossession and displacement of some 2 million people caught up in the fratricides.

Other indirect effects can be equally damaging. The mortality rate of Iraqi children has doubled since the conflict. The Gulf crisis displaced 4 million people, bringing ruin to the economies of neighbouring countries through the influx of returnees and the loss of their remittances. In Western Europe, the costs of maintaining Balkan refugee populations continue to mount, with sad political consequences.

In the face of such evidence it becomes irrelevant to apportion blame for the conflict. Even more unreal is to debate whether a war is a 'just war' or not. Both political and religious leaders become notoriously unreliable at times of national crisis. Nor have 'surgical air strikes' and 'clean weapons' arrested the escalating cost of modern warfare in lives and misery.

Of more immediate relevance than the moral issue is to recall the primary duty of a government: to safeguard the territorial integrity of the realm and the safety of its subjects. After the political failures preceding the two world wars, there was little doubt that they had to be fought. Resistance to prevent the Cold War from developing into a hot one was driven by the same compulsion.

Very different considerations need to be applied to the wars fought since 1945. Some, like Korea and Vietnam, were clearly proxy wars against the hostile communist superpowers. Others were to protect British, French or Belgian interests and nationals during the withdrawal from colonial possessions. Some, like the Malayan emergency, were both. Even if those eras are now at an end, close to 20 million people have perished in hostilities since 1945. It is therefore timely to examine what strategies might be applied to counter the risk of future conflicts.

The Causes

One of Napoleon's generals had little doubt about the causes of war. 'La guerre se fait pour trois choses: pour l'argent, pour plus d'argent, et pour encore plus d'argent' ('War is made for three reasons: for money, for more money and for even more money'), he pronounced with Gallic realism. In the younger countries, particularly in Africa, the motivation is still access to power – and with it to natural riches like the diamond fields. We may

3

prefer our war aims to be more nobly stated, but in essence it is the 'national interest' that is invariably cited – whether its goal is survival or some more material good.

With few exceptions, the national interest centred on possessions – either existing or coveted. Centuries of feuding were devoted to fending off foreign incursions into India. Egypt, the Sudan, the Boer War – all are significant chapters in the annals of British military history. As long as the UK's wealth and commerce rested on such possessions, they needed to be protected with blood.

Only rarely was diplomacy impressed to avoid such campaigns, as for example in the deal in 1890, which recognised a French protectorate over Madagascar in return for concessions in Zanzibar. Otherwise the clash of arms was considered a necessary part of the defence of empire. Every skirmish was a warning not only to today's predator, but to all those with pretensions to feast at our table. Preparedness, and unhesitating alacrity in taking to the field, were the one-time deterrent. The UK's fabled navy, capable of fighting in any corner of the globe from Trafalgar to the South China Sea, was there to lend it credibility.

Both world wars of the twentieth century were provoked in part by a contest for naval superiority. A challenge by German dreadnoughts or battle cruisers to the UK's ability to rule the oceans in defence of its overseas interests could not be ignored.[4] With hindsight, it is often clear that wars were provoked by miscalculation, by an inability to see the lines which could not safely be transgressed. Modern diplomacy has been at pains to eliminate such errors. Monroe doctrines and similar declarations have often delineated a nation's vital interest. Thus Hitler could have known well what he was risking, even if the Kaiser had been unable to comprehend the consequences of his own actions.

In other times, however, the ethos was not avoidance but the joyful acceptance of challenge. The jousting tradition was deeply ingrained in the European soul, and for centuries wars were regarded as knightly tournaments. They were not an exceptional state but a more or less full-time occupation for gentlemen. The concepts of honour, valour, courage and reward were intimately bound to this tradition, not only for knights but equally as an aspiration for commoners. Patriotism was rarely invoked, but mercenaries were freely available for the sport. Others had to be fought because they were there, even if their intent proved to be neither warlike nor evil.

With the arrival of the modern nation-state came establishment wars to consolidate national frontiers. Even well into the twentieth century these continued to be marked by efforts to peg the line beyond disputed provinces such as Silesia or Alsace and the invoking of minority rights to justify periodic annexations. The interplay of the Great Powers was marked by the creation of buffer states, the forerunners of Cold War satellites, among them in 1918 Yugoslavia and Czechoslovakia.

Not until the continental scale of Napoleon's ambitions, until the mounting horror of his losses and victims, until a Tolstoy awoke the European conscience, did the inevitability of war as the primary instrument of foreign policy begin to change. Revulsion from the butchery on the Western Front during the First World War and the loss of a generation of young men allowed a peace culture to develop. Yet even now we are conscious that a substantial defence capability is necessary to protect our interests, and most of our young men would still accept the carrying of arms as an honourable estate.

The Frontier Mentality

The division of the world into friend and foe, civilised and savages, them and us, is as old as humanity itself. Such distinctions helped people through the Dark Ages to identify with their own, to build a sense of community and to develop a social awareness. Less positively, these led to inbreeding, ignorance about the world outside their narrow circumscription, and an irrational fear of what lay beyond. Ignorance was propagated, dragons and witches ruled, heresies flourished, curiosity and scientific enquiry were curtailed.

The dark fringes of our conscious world – the areas of not knowing – breed fears and bitterness. Psychologists tell us that infants start to show fear of strangers in the second half of their first year. This is easily consolidated by fairy stories which have their root in unreasoning imputations of what lies on the other side of the forest, what barbaric customs flourish among those

5

who inhabit the next valley. Ignorance condemned outsiders to savagery. To this day there are traditional communities living in terror of their immediate neighbours because natural obstacles have denied them knowledge of each other. Tribal massacres in New Guinea, ceremonial slaughter in Orissa, and now Bosnia, Kosovo, Rwanda and Sierra Leone, are present-day reminders of what our post-industrial world was like centuries ago.

Such behaviour is evidence of the 'dual code' identified by the social scientist Herbert Spencer:[5] our feelings for our own community are positive, but lend themselves in equal measure to generating negative feelings towards others. This applies as much on the football pitch as on the battlefield. Our potential for negative arousal corresponds to the legacy of Darwinian evolution. Yet there may be hope of eventually liberating ourselves, for the ultimate state of evolution is reason.

It is *un*reason and *un*familiarity that breed contempt. As our horizons widened and our means of transport improved, we discovered that our neighbours were in most respects our kin. That process of discovery has gone on apace. At times we still knew more about Native Americans in Idaho, the fauna of Nigeria and Moghul art in India than about the life of the people in rural France. Discovery was fashionable, still-life was not.

The last step in our liberation from irrational xenophobia came with the peripatetic television crew. All continents, all events, every drama is now instantly accessible to us. Boundaries no longer exist, either in our minds or in reality. As we watch Kurds being hounded across the map of the Near and Middle East, it has become irrelevant to enquire which side of which frontier they are on. The only place for them is called sanctuary. The same applies to the ousting of oppressors, from Panama and Haiti to East Timor and Afghanistan. As television viewers we are right there with the Marines or the Australians. Thus we see on the one hand a world in hopeless turmoil, people visiting brutality and untold suffering on their immediate fellows. And we also see a world in which international arbiters are seeking to impose the rule of law, even if seemingly always two steps behind.

Despite Article 2(7) of the United Nations Charter, which excludes intervention in the domestic affairs of a sovereign state unless they constitute a threat to peace, and despite the protestations of nations still prudish about their own sovereignty, there are significant instances of international policing within states. Transgressors against their own people, like General Manuel Noriega of Panama and Saddam Hussein of Iraq, and threats to regional peace, such as the fragmenting republics of Yugoslavia, have become fields for legitimate intervention by the international community. Enough case-law now exists for actions to protect human rights within states to gain overwhelming backing. The end of superpower confrontation, which once exploited precisely such tensions, has opened the way to a new era of effective defence of human rights – even if transgressions have multiplied.

This is the ultimate retreat of the frontier mentality, the sanctity of borders within which those wielding power could do as they pleased. We shall see that this process will demand changes not only in our view of the legitimacy of intervention but also, more fundamentally, to our concept of armed operations as such.

The Economic Cost

Wars have a cost not only in human capital but even more in economic terms. Gone are the days when booty and plunder amply made up for the investment in warriors and their arms. Then the arithmetic was simple, the outcome a throw of the dice, backed by prowess and numbers.

The figures look startlingly different now. There is the cost of preparedness. The Western world spends approximately US$600 per capita, or 2.6 per cent of its gross domestic product (GDP) for military purposes; for comparison, that is about 20 per cent of what it devotes to health and education combined. Sadly, the Third World feels compelled to emulate this effort – except that it uses an indefensible 4.1 per cent of its slender GDP, in many countries driving social spending into second place.[6] Small wonder that armies tend to be used to maintain law and order among long-suffering populations.

Still, the Western world is rich enough to bear the cost of its own security. Or so we believe. The UK is proud to have been spending about 50 per cent more of its GDP on defence than Germany. Even if defence budgets are coming under unprecedented pressure, that is a cost well worth bearing if its effect is to avoid actual warfare.

The UK's own regression from the most dominant world power to a place among the economically modest serves as a precise indicator of the real cost of war or peacetime military spending. During the whole disastrous period of European fratricidal wars and their aftermath – between 1913 and 1950 – the belligerents condemned each other to insignificant rates of economic growth. In that span of nearly four decades, their real GDP per capita grew at an average of less than 1 per cent per annum (0.8 per cent for the UK, 0.2 per cent for Germany). That compares with the 2.1 per cent achieved even in that grim period by neutral Sweden and Switzerland; and with the 3.8 per cent growth attained by Western Europe as a whole for the next quarter of a century once a durable peace had been achieved.[7]

Although the death and devastation caused by the First World War were greatest in Eastern Europe, the Western part of the continent suffered some of the heaviest fighting and destruction. Western Europe's living standards fell sharply and its 1913 GDP level was not regained for more than a decade. Attempts to sustain that growth were once again thwarted by the Great Depression, one of whose significant contributors was the collapse of Germany's financial system in the aftermath of a ruinous war. The Second World War initially served to take up the slack left by the depression as economies mobilised for war. But all of Western Europe emerged with horrendous casualties and its capital stock depleted. The UK's net foreign assets declined from $21 billion in 1938 to debts of $2 billion in 1947. Inevitably, the aftermath was protracted. It took until 1950 for world trade to regain the level reached in 1929.

We are not, of course, in the luxurious position of being able to reverse history. Nor were we able to avoid having to fight those wars. What we can now do, however, is draw up a realistic balance sheet capable of showing us what such conflicts involve in terms of national sacrifice. It seems astonishing that few such accounts have been prepared. Perhaps no one wanted to know. Perhaps no one thought they would make any difference, given that there was no historical alternative.

Now we may have arrived at a point where alternatives can be called into existence. No doubt we can continue to bear the costs of preparedness. Indeed, they must be the foundation of any valid defence policy. As in all other national expenditures, however, it is legitimate to raise the question of cost-effectiveness. If costs are seen to escalate beyond the availability of national resources, policy changes will become inescapable.

It is the costs of military action itself which are the most substantial element, and which have so far been ignored. And the most crucial aspect of these is what economists call the 'opportunity cost', that is what that money would otherwise have bought. That may be reckoned in terms of relieving social ills, increasing national well-being, or maintaining a stronger currency. It may even be counted in terms of additional ordnance to deter a wrongdoer, so long as that deterrence avoids open conflict.

The point is that today we in the West do have a choice. Unless matters go seriously wrong inside China or Russia, we no longer need to fear a massed attack on our territory. We are unlikely to be invaded other than by mafias and migrants, our peace disturbed other than by terrorists, our lives threatened other than by inattention to social ills.

That means that warfare is not an automatic and inescapable response to the acts of others. With the all-important exception of terrorism, future threats to security will be at longer range. Most will concern not our immediate safety but the proper management of the world in which we have an interest. Should we continue to let any pretender to power in any part of the globe involve us in all-out war which, because of the huge cost of the hardware we need to deploy, will further cripple us economically? If not, would we not be wiser to apply our minds to alternative types of action to curb such transgression?

At present we are tied to the alternatives of inaction or military action. If most threats in future are unlikely to require the military sledgehammer, we need urgently to devise new strategies which will be – even if over a longer time-span – equally effective but affordable.

There is no shame in recognising this, and certainly no cowardice. The shame would be if, one fine day very soon, we found ourselves without the means of countering aggression, of assisting our friends, of defending our values – simply because we had gone into a genteel decline and run out of money to mount the only riposte we know. The agonies of devising a post-Suez defence policy, of drawing in our defence establishments and communications ever closer to home, and finally of finding even the maintenance of bases in Germany too costly – all these should be potent lessons. An honourable stance demands that we search for alternative 'weapons' with which to fight the security threats of tomorrow.

Perhaps Napoleon's general was half-right. Albeit that most wars are no longer fought *for* money, they are still fought *with* money – and ever more money at that. Yet honour demands that we do not yield without a fight. Let us make sure then that at least our wits continue to be a match for whatever enemy thinks of taking the field to challenge our interests.

Adjusting Our Sights

In ages past, society practised self-defence. Each principality had its own force or regiment, vassals for protection against the incursions of predatory neighbours. Communities, even boroughs, looked to their own security. Part watch, part home guard, they fought off marauders and put down whatever threatened their peace. It was they who defended the city walls and repelled those who sought to breach them. Our galleries and local museums are redolent of the days of primitive self-defence.

In time, the towns made common cause. Larger forces fought their battles in the open, to protect their lands and their food supplies. Principalities coalesced to form more powerful units with greater defensive capacity. From alliances grew mini-states; from their mortal trials of strength in the nineteenth century arose, in the end, the modern nation-state.

At each stage the apparently immutable order of things had to give way to a new system. Forces lately hostile or at best suspicious had to be merged into efficient fighting units to defend a henceforth common interest. New doctrines had to be developed and tested, new loyalties accepted, new oaths sworn to new lieges and commanders. Think only of the rough twist of reorientation required to assimilate the fighting Scots into the British forces following the Act of Union of 1707; and, lately, the merging of *Bundeswehr* and *Volksarmee* in the reunited Germany.

Internally, too, the time came when neighbourhood policing was found to have outlived its purpose. The comfortable times when local vigilantes knew each one of the potential miscreants by name had to yield under the pressure of growing and shifting populations. Tensions previously unknown, especially among migrant communities, created new threats to law and order. The time had arrived when policing became a full-time function in its own right. At the same time its acceptance demanded that it had to be non-partisan, and hence subject to a higher responsibility. Here, too, forces became state or county-wide.

Can we imagine the traumas and adjustments involved in these changes? Perhaps the ebb and flow of European military history might have accustomed one to fighting alongside yesterday's enemies. For over a century, from 1714 to 1834, British and Hanoverian forces fought side by side, under the same commanders, for the same king whose regulations they carried in their pockets printed in both languages. A greater step by far was for civilians to submit to new police officers in their midst, with powers to enforce an ever-growing codex of laws. What an infringement of personal liberties they would have represented for most of those on their early beats.

There is only one circumstance which made such imposed restraint acceptable: an imminent breakdown of law and order and the patent inability of citizens themselves to deal with it. New problems, or an unaccustomed escalation, have always demanded new solutions. The only paradox is that, the greater the apparent stability, the more the present order becomes regarded as immutable. Only a few are usually able to see the underlying erosion of that order, and perceive it as a staging post to a yet more advanced form of governance.

We, too, find ourselves at such a juncture. At any time one is able to divide the world into those areas which constitute a potential threat, and those with whom one is no longer in conflict – zones of conflict and zones of peace. The latter are those among whom the use of force has ceased to be a viable instrument. We may henceforth regard them as 'domestic'.

That world which the West can classify as domestic has suddenly expanded out of recognition. Not only are we embarked on making the term a literal reality within the European Union, already embracing virtually all of Western Europe and, within a few short years, most of Central and Eastern Europe. With luck and supreme wisdom, the successor republics to the Soviet

Union may also soon form part of our domestic world. And west-wards, through a hundred organisational links and alliances, the Atlantic world has for most of the last century been the core and guarantor of our own security.

Such states have put aside military, aggressive and territorial ambitions; their new struggle is for a greater share of world commerce. Virtually the whole of the 'northern' hemisphere, including Japan as well as Australasia, has thus become part of the West, 'our' world. Virtually unthinkable that we should resort to arms or fight other than in international fora or on the playing fields. Kant's dictum that democracies seldom fight each other has been proved correct (and see chart, 'Evolving a Democratic World', on p. xx).

Beyond that vast area, however, lies a chequered map of con-tinents and agglomerations of states with whom the West enter-tains a bewildering variety of relations. Most are races distinct from the Caucasian, and ones which at one time or another the West has sought to dominate: Africans and Arabs, Latin Americans, Chinese and Indians, the teeming populations of the East which account for the great majority of the inhabitants of our planet. While representing some of the most ancient nations and civilisations on earth, they also encompass the majority of new states created only in the second half of the twentieth century. Old and new, and with few exceptions, they contain the impoverished and disadvantaged of this world.

But the world is not affected by the behaviour of states alone. Here and there the individuals assert themselves, not as docile voters but in an attempt to re-establish an archaic order. In our midst today, we have Basque separatists, Sinn Feiners, Serb blood brothers, skinheads in neo-Nazi guise and now al-Qaeda and many others who have not yet broken surface. All are seeking to mitigate the perceived exclusion of their present by recreating the imagined glories of their past, or by inventing a more radical future.

War and the Twenty-First Century

In summary, the three touchstones of modern security in the West have become to:

- safeguard our economic – but no longer strategic – interests;
- keep the peace and deal with the grosser violations of human rights elsewhere;
- maintain civil order in our midst.

Meeting and containing these challenges will require a thorough reassessment of their real nature. We are then likely to find that many of the means at our disposal are unsuitable and that we need new tools if such infringements are not to escalate out of hand. Above all, we shall need to readjust our sights to deal with a world changed fundamentally since the invention of gunpowder – even if the claims of many of its inhabitants continue to foster violence.

First, we in the West must conclude that for our domestic world conventional, let alone total, war as experienced in the twentieth century is no longer a usable instrument. Its financial costs are becoming insupportable: such wars have no true victor or vanquished because they lay waste both sides. Moreover, their cost in human lives and misery has become unacceptable. A corollary of the development of a peaceable and domestic world is the proclaiming of an international social and humanitarian consensus reluctant to tolerate such casualties. Real-time newscasts of their horrors both inflame the sense of outrage and carry back its forceful expression. There is a moral revulsion against warfare as such, as well as against the brutality of its consequences.

Second, the political costs of warfare have multiplied also. The support of domestic public opinion can no longer be tested indefinitely. There is a limit to the casualties it is prepared to endure before demanding a halt. Governments, too, operate under a similar ceiling, for the cost of individual warriors and their technology is increasing so fast that losses are no longer affordable. The current fascination with 'virtual war', which keeps forces out of reach of enemy fire, on closer inspection presents an option only against a weaker foe unable to retaliate in kind. More importantly, it is a recognition that war as we knew it is no longer an option, except in the very last resort.

The USA – and its essential leadership in such actions makes its position crucial – has concluded that its troops will not be easily put at risk. It has drawn a distinction between 'obligatory'

13

and 'discretionary' wars. Until it declared 'war' on terrorism it could see none of the former but acknowledged the demands of the latter. Where it chooses to exercise that discretion, normally for humanitarian purposes, it will commit its ground forces only as a last resort. Where it acts on its usually strong impulse to right a wrong, it will use missiles or stand-off bombs. The future of 'warfare' thus lies predominantly in technology, enabling the USA to continue to reap the economic and technical benefits of a strong defence programme while avoiding the political cost of own casualties. A rebalancing of expenditures towards anti-terrorist skills will do little to change that.

Finally, to these dissuasions must still be added the sword of Damocles which hangs over all considerations of conventional all-out war: the risk of an unconventional nuclear riposte.

It is clear that the twenty-first century will demand different solutions from those which ravaged the twentieth.

Notes

1. Gil Elliot, *The Twentieth Century Book of the Dead*, Allen Lane, Penguin Press, London, 1972.
2. David Eggenberger, *A Dictionary of Battles*, George Allen & Unwin, London, 1967.
3. Human Rights Watch USA, *Needless Deaths in the Gulf War*, Human Rights Watch, New York, 1991.
4. Robert K. Massie, *Dreadnought: Britain, Germany and the Coming of the Great War*, Random House, New York, 1991.
5. Herbert Spencer, *The Principles of Sociology*, Williams & Norgate, London, 1896.
6. All figures from International Institute of Strategic Studies (IISS), *The Military Balance 2000/2001*, IISS/Oxford University Press, London, 2001.
7. Angus Maddison, *Monitoring the World Economy 1820–1992*, OECD, Paris, 1995.

2   War and Choice

'Where there is no vision, people perish.'
Proverbs 29:18

We cannot eliminate wars. For more than three centuries, since the Peace of Westphalia put an end to the Thirty Years' War in 1648, states have sought to construct security systems to contain the threats against them. In 1713–14 the Treaty of Utrecht to settle the War of the Spanish Succession, in 1814–15 the Congress of Vienna to dispose of Napoleon's empire, in 1878 the Congress of Berlin to redraw the map of the Balkans in the wake of the Russo-Turkish War, and in 1919 the Treaty of Versailles to reduce Germany and its overseas possessions – all sought to establish a new security order from the moments of sanity and realism following mortal combat. After a false start with the League of Nations, the victors of the Second World War finally saw the need for all-embracing civil institutions to guarantee the peace through prosperity rather than geo-political precautions. The fact that the United Nations (UN) and the 1944 Bretton Woods institutions – the World Bank and the International Monetary Fund – had soon, in 1949, to be joined by a classic military alliance, the North Atlantic Treaty Organisation (NATO), was a sad but possibly final throw-back to an old-fashioned military response.

However, NATO was already different in kind. The obligations of its members were stricter and more far-reaching than former alliances. They represented a cession of sovereignty previously unknown and included for the first time non-European powers for the defence of Europe. Yet as a primarily military alliance

15

NATO remained homogeneous enough to pursue its deterrent purpose in preventing the Cold War becoming hot, and even in real action over Kosovo. That represents an authority and a cohesion which the United Nations still has to find. As a truly global security system, even the UN has not succeeded in stifling conflict, though it has developed means for preventing it – mainly through the painstaking task of economic development – and of dealing with its consequences both politically and through peacekeeping and relief operations.

Thus wars are not of the West's choosing. Conflict today is the choice of others, and we can choose only our response. Expansionist wars, such as Korea and the Gulf, still demand a robust military response. Even though their theatre is not in Europe, there has developed an extension of the NATO spirit which spontaneously produces 'coalitions of the willing' to marshal that response. Mostly with the USA in the lead, such coalitions bring together the European powers with military capability – the UK, France, the Netherlands, Turkey and some others – joined by the countries in the area of action most affected. Whatever the allegations about US 'hegemony', these are not the world's policemen. They fill the void left by the absence of a UN police force, even if they often act more swiftly than the UN's political processes are able to invest them with international authorisation.

Responses to expansionist wars, if notably firm, are also selective. There has been no international action against the events in the former Zaïre (now the Democratic Republic of Congo), or the one-time annexation of East Timor. The real trigger for a campaign, today as throughout history, is the perceived national (or factional) interest. The supply routes for tea and spices or the provisioning of far-flung possessions have been replaced by the flow of oil. Thus the Great Game of the nineteenth century played out in Central Asia over access routes to India has become more serious with the prize of Caspian oil. Deliberate instability fostered in the new republics of the former Soviet Union by those avid to win rights to the oil and pipelines may yet exact a heavy cost.[1] That cost may climb higher still, as many of the world's productive oil resources are in Islamic countries. It then becomes difficult to identify whether fundamentalism or revolt against commercial exploitation lies at the heart of unrest.

The Western world's military superiority has made it relatively immune to challenges to its vital geo-political and economic interests. As empires have shrunk and strategic interests shifted, the means of supply or intervention have also become swifter and less vulnerable. Yet the post-Second World War system of regional stability still represents an unshakeable cornerstone of strategic thinking and a defence imperative. Concerns over North Korean weapons development and the security of Taiwan threaten the efforts to preserve the status quo and the position of Japan in the Far East. There is also erosion on the periphery, especially where – as in Chechnya and Afghanistan – new stabilities have to be established following the crumbling of the old. The risks remain of infringing old-fashioned spheres of influence sacrosanct to more powerful rivals.

The West's response, beyond issuing admonitions, will depend on how crucial is the perceived threat to the national or collective interest. Much of the commercial interest can be safeguarded by the power of wealth, and the political through adroit forms of states- or gamesmanship. It is the large miscalculation, the sabre-rattling carried to an irreversible excess, or the otherworldliness of rogue states which may still lead to serious confrontation.

Much less tractable is the problem of preventing the escalation of conflicts between major regional powers. Disputes between India and Pakistan – both now with some nuclear capacity – could involve China, as could hostilities between North and South Korea. Iran, Iraq and Israel hold out similar dangers. The nuclear dimension, above all, makes a coherent strategy of conflict prevention an imperative.

Beyond these classic challenges are those thrust onto our consciousness by a shrinking world. Prime among them is the protection of human rights and the halting of atrocities. Once the awareness of such problems has been created, a train of reactions is set in motion which will often – but by no means always – lead to some form of intervention. Public opinion, pressures from civil society as well as the horrors of the situation itself will urge action. The international community is swift to react, but slow to act – especially within the UN Security Council; but the conflicts of the 1990s amply demonstrated the likelihood of a call upon armed force. Rwanda, Bosnia and

17

Kosovo (and Northern Ireland) have shown that it is by no means always the minority which suffers; paradoxically, such operations may have to be mounted less to combat insurgency than for the protection of the majority.

Underneath our feet, however, also lies the boiling magma of terrorism, of those unable or unwilling to adjust to a global society. Reaction to their atrocities may justly tempt us into military reprisals whose consequences will be difficult to calculate. To the extent that these confuse the responsibility of states with those of individuals or groups of perpetrators, they risk creating new resentments with unforeseeable consequences.

These, then, form the range of challenges which may still involve the West in mortal combat. Even if the balance appears to have shifted towards humanitarian actions and the restoring of peace, one needs to remain prepared for the worst of them. It is the task of diplomacy and a forward-looking defence policy to ensure that most of them are confronted without clash of arms. If the West does use arms, they need to be tailored to the tasks ahead rather than yesterday's battle doctrines. It is therefore prudent to gauge the modern needs by means of some risk assessment.

The Risks of a Fractious World

Risk assessment is perception and probability, not science or prediction. Like weather forecasting, it is not static but a continuous monitoring of change; nor is the future necessarily contained in perceptions of the present. Even if the process is ambivalent and imprecise, successive defence reviews in the UK and elsewhere since the collapse of communism should have done this job for us. Unhappily, they have been dominated more by financial imperatives; the result has been a progressive scaling down of the West's capabilities. Only now have we begun to see a rigorous questioning of wider security needs and objectives – as distinct from each interested party fighting its own procurement corner – and a re-examination of the weaponry required to meet them.

Any such analysis must come to terms with the problems of change. It is illusory to think in terms of a status quo which has to be defended with strategic and tactical doctrines. The political map of the world knows no state of rest. The point of departure is as much in flux as the future to be anticipated. Our greatest failing is to regard the momentary state of history into which we were born as benign, and thus to see all movement which affects it as hostile.

An analysis is therefore valid only insofar as it correctly identifies the underlying currents of change, seeks to order them as historical processes, and allows for their modification under various forms and degrees of resistance. An added obstacle is that our vision of history is mechanistic, and our quest to interpret it based on extrapolation. Hard as it is for us to discern the vastness of its movements, we find it harder still to look around corners.

Historically, our habits of thought make us trace back a successful outcome in the same way as a punter at a roulette table will analyse a winner's moves to construct a 'system'. In both cases the number of *unrecorded* variables is likely to produce odds of similar magnitude. Encouragement for this approach is provided by the players who have doggedly backed their 0 or 13 and scored before losing all their chips. Yet they are not the apex of a historical process, but only one of the possible outcomes of the theory of probability.

Such a mechanistic approach to history would result in mainlining, that is the retrospective selection of major determinants. This means ignoring or demoting an infinite number of contributories. The result of such an arbitrary process is mostly a matching of a limited cause with an irrational and unrepeatable effect. In any event, the choice of subject and starting point already implies a preferred outcome or direction.

Even more flawed then is the extrapolation of history by the same process of 'logic'. The linear approach will inevitably result in a vision carrying the imprint of a permanently fixed present. This might be called the fish-eye view of history: the virginal unawareness of the fish that there is any break between the water which carries it and the air above. With justification, Peter Allen says: 'We rationalise events by pretending that there was some pre-existing "niche" which was revealed by events,

19

although in reality there may have been a million possible niches and one particular one arose. The future, then, is not contained in the present.'[2]

A Sketch Map of Risks

Bearing in mind such cautions, it is nevertheless possible to construct a sketch map of the categories of risks to which we are exposed. Such a map will be useful only if it is generic rather than geographic, that is if it groups risks instead of attempting to predict the locality of events provoked by them.

The major part of the map will perforce be taken up by the Third World, the vast regions lying beyond the areas defined earlier as 'domestic'. In part through poverty, in part through the aggressive vitality required to catch up with the West – in many cases also through the tensions of being contained within arbitrary borders reflecting the horse-trading of colonial times – this Third World poses a bewildering number of frictions and security risks. Analysis of these reveals a set of distinct categories.

Poverty

Globalisation, that is the involuntary integration of markets and economies across the world, has thrown into sharp relief the endemic poverty of many countries and societies in the South. A facile but telling indicator of that inequality is that the 300 or so billionaires in the world are collectively as rich as its 3 billion poorest inhabitants. This gives rise to a potential 'revolution of unfulfilled expectations'. It is surely no coincidence that the poorest continent, Africa, has also the greatest number of wars and conflicts.

Though Asia has made substantial economic progress, and even cut the rate of its population growth, it remains a tight-run race to avert an increase in poverty. It is calculated that within 35 years even China will be unable to feed its growing population.[3] There are also grave pockets of current poverty: Vietnam, Cambodia and Laos are among the world's poorest countries. Nor, despite its progress to democracy, is Latin America immune. Many of its regimes are weak and the continent has a revolutionary tradition. In poor societies, pockets of riches – be they opium in Colombia, diamonds in Sierra Leone or oil in Angola – become both focus and fuel of conflict.

It is a challenge for the West to address these instabilities and their causes with a recognition that security policy has to embrace trade, aid and economic factors as an integral part of analysis and action.

Remnants of superpower rivalries

African countries such as Angola, Ethiopia, Somalia and other one-time 'front-line states' in the conflict with South Africa, remain the victims of former Soviet and Cuban spheres of influence, established in support of revolution or as part of an anti-apartheid solidarity movement. The communists have now withdrawn, apartheid has been dismantled, and – as in Mozambique – peace has been restored under international supervision. Yet the enmities so cynically inflamed may take generations to subside. As external pressures ease, or the grip of domestic strongmen is relaxed, a whole gamut of feuds may yet take their place.

Slower to respond are the remnants of similar confrontations in Asia and Central America. North Korea still has a long road to travel, and one which Vietnam has only recently begun to tread. The wounds inflicted on the remainder of Indo-China – Laos and Cambodia – are even slower to heal. Cuba meanwhile remains an ideological anachronism, still capable of exerting a disruptive influence in the Caribbean and the isthmus, even if beginning to wane following the withdrawal of Russian personnel and economic support and the influx of curious Western tourists.

Often the political vacuum left by the failure of imported ideologies carries the risk of tribal and ethnic divisions. The retreat of 'African socialism' – a marriage of public ownership, one-party government and the traditional concept of the extended family – has entrained more than moral disillusionment. The sudden reversal of tenets preached for a generation or more, the offering of national assets to the highest bidder – by definition more often than not foreign or non-indigenous – provokes the anger of the common people at being cheated out of their inheritance.

21

In many cases there is a sudden awakening to the absence of a sense of nationhood to withstand the stresses of political change. The legacy of artificial colonial circumscriptions is the lack of a basic unity to protect against a relapse into tribal identities. Economic near-collapse, provoked by withdrawal of 'pay-to-be-good' aid or military support of authoritarian regimes, is creating precisely the social tensions to fuel such fragmentation.

However gloomy such portents, Westerners must guard against falling into the trap of an occicentric perspective. Conditioned by the succession of colonial, developmental and Cold-War interventions in other people's lives, it is still difficult for many to trust developing nations at the controls of their own destinies. The fact is that most have elites which are perfectly capable of organising their own affairs, especially if liberated from superannuated regimes whose authority the West has for decades helped to maintain. As a result, our prognosis vacillates between predictions of chaos without the continuation of our firm guidance, and interpreting developments in terms of the linear evolution profoundly desired by us.

The Chinese enigma

Attitudes towards China are a glowing example of the latter temptation. The Chinese giant has shown itself capable of generating and surviving a series of major political and ideological convulsions. The only certainty is that there is no final state, and that even the present political stasis and rigidity will before long have to adapt to the effects of unremitting economic liberalisation. Only time will tell whether that will mean a return to Maoist orthodoxies or yet another lurch towards a more tolerant system. Normalisation of relations with Russia and Japan, a tight-lipped understanding with the USA, and the far from belligerent contest of wills over Hong Kong may indicate that China is too preoccupied with its impending internal changes to wish for external adventures. Support for 'communist' guerrilla activity in and around Malaysia, Thailand and the Philippines – indeed, for communism as such – has become inactive, while peacemaking initiatives in Korea and Cambodia appear to be genuine.

However, a resurgent China's effort to project power beyond mainland East Asia, where its strategic authority is already widely accepted, to the continent's maritime regions is seriously perturbing. The South China Sea has traditionally been regarded as South-East Asia's 'maritime heartland', while Taiwan has an even wider international significance. It is also not a good omen that China is letting itself be seen to make common cause with Iran, Libya and Syria by assisting them with missile technology. Assuming that the stabilisation process within the Soviet Union's successor republics is satisfactorily concluded, China remains the one power on earth capable in time of challenging the military supremacy of the West. Most likely this would be an exercise of China's inclination towards the age-old Sun Tzu philosophy of not replying to provocation in kind – or what has been called 'alternative war'.

Ethnic and religious tensions

Such problems abound and appear irremediable where they exist. More than half a century after independence and the creation of a separate Muslim state, the Indian subcontinent is still racked by communities and states visiting sporadic violence upon each other. Nor are other countries exempt: similar tensions recur in the islands of Indonesia, the Philippines and the Pacific. Tribal rivalry in South Africa has been added to massacres among Tutsis and Hutus in Rwanda and Burundi, Muslims and Christian sects in Nigeria and Sudan, and the confrontations of coastal and inland peoples in Liberia and Madagascar. Eritreans, Tigreans and mainstream Ethiopians have yet to settle their scores. History is still suspending judgement on the fate of the Kurds. But it is a disease from which Europeans are far from immune. We have no need to be reminded of Northern Ireland, of ETA (*Euzkadi ta Askatsuna*) in the Basque country, of the convulsions of the former Yugoslavia, Cyprus and other flashpoints along the Aegean coast. Tragic as they are, most such conflicts are containable, even where outsiders intervene and borders are violated. The crucial areas – India and Pakistan, Israel and the Arab world – will remain the most alarming and immediate hazards because of their size, potential for nuclear temptation and outside involvement in any conflagration. Kashmir remains a smouldering tinder for one; growing orthodox opposition in Israel sets a potent time constraint for the other.

Bitter and alone

A handful of countries seem intent on isolating themselves totally from the world community. While, as in the former Burma (now Myanmar), the original impetus after independence in 1947 and the ensuing disturbances may have been to wish a plague on both superpowers, in reality total repression soon begins to flourish behind protective walls. Sudan is in a similar category, as Iraq continues to be. For different reasons, Cuba, Chinese-occupied Tibet, Cambodia, Laos and North Korea remain isolated or in a self-imposed outer darkness. Such countries do not necessarily constitute a wider security threat – despite the USA's determination to erect its National Missile Defence (NMD) system against it. But disregard for human rights or violations against their own or subject peoples mark them out as continuing areas of backwardness and instability.

Islam but not Arab

The crescent lining the northern shore of the Persian Gulf, the eastern Mediterranean and the Black Sea represents a zone of turbulence which has historically been the scene of bitter conflict. Even now, there is no respite to the age-old fighting in Afghanistan; conflict, revolutionary and external, still threatens Iran; the newly independent 'stans', the Islamic republics lately freed from Soviet domination, continue to see bitter feuding; and a new aggressiveness is making itself felt in Turkey – with the dagger of the former Ottoman Empire still firmly embedded in the Balkans.

Nationalism, internal divisions and social upheavals have so far been the fuel of these conflicts. More and more, however, there is recourse to religious symbols to enhance the fervour of the warring factions. The Iranian revolution, and secessionist fighting in Azerbaijan, Chechnya, Ossetia, Tajikistan and others follow religious boundaries. A strongly orthodox movement is gathering force in Turkey, which is already presenting itself to the new Islamic republics as their spiritual, and potentially political leader. If Islamic fundamentalism – or 'Wahabism' – were to become their common bond, and it united them in an aggressive xenophobia, it could grow beyond the social-revolutionary dimension and become a threat to their Christian neighbours. Wars need no rationale, only a sufficiently powerful emotional symbolism. If a corruption of Quranic teaching were made to serve that purpose, one might see an awe-inspiring sequel to the Crusades.

This could constitute a vastly more dangerous development than that posed by Islamic fundamentalism in the Arab world. The Middle East continues to be riven by political divisions and its great variety of feudal, revolutionary and despotic regimes. Professions of Arab brotherhood and implacable enmity to Israel are not in themselves sufficient to span those divides. By and large, they also offer a relatively weak alternative to the inexorable pull of modernisation, which has mostly avoided the coarser Western cultural symbols. Yet, imperceptibly, orthodox populations within Israel are multiplying apace and could in time provoke a more severe reaction unless anticipated by a comprehensive peace agreement.

Control of vital resources

Risks to the industrialised world's security continue to be greatest where its remaining vital supply routes can come under threat. Even if the resources no longer originate from its possessions and must in any event be commercially acquired, the danger remains real. The oil crises of 1973 and 1980 showed how exposed Western consumers had become to price manipulation, in part due to increasing US dependence on imported oil. Ten years on, the temporary annexation of Kuwait thus became not only a transgression of international law, but an unpardonable interference in the free flow of strategic resources. Saudi Arabia represents a chapter yet to be written. The political fragility of the West's principal ally in the region is becoming increasingly evident as succession problems and long-deferred internal adjustments draw closer.

Yet oil is only one of the vital materials being exchanged among nations, and the West is only one of the consumers whose supply may be denied. An increasingly scarce commodity is water, upon which the politics of the Middle East are increasingly likely to turn. Others are materials such as wolfram, vanadium and tungsten, vital for hi-tech developments which, *inter alia*, might help the West to become independent of conventional energy – if making it dependent on whoever holds power over their known deposits, currently Namibia, Kenya and South Africa.

The nuclear threat

Perhaps the darkest shadow over the world's post-Cold War normalisation lies in nuclear proliferation. The fruits even of the extended non-proliferation treaty (NPT) remain elusive. Since the original treaty came into force in 1970, between 14 and 16 officially non-nuclear countries are thought to have developed rudimentary devices, though all but a few still lack the means of delivery. Of particular concern is the situation in Asia. North Korea's possession of a nuclear device could provoke Japan to perfect its own, thus altering the balance of power in Asia fundamentally. The seriousness of a nuclear Japan facing a nuclear China would be hard to exaggerate.

Convincing action by the present nuclear powers is hampered by two factors. First, of the five permanent members of the Security Council, only China has so far made an unqualified declaration that it will not resort to first use. Equally equivocal is the USA's stance on the Comprehensive Test Ban Treaty, adopted by the UN General Assembly in September 1996. This is hardly encouraging others to desist, nor to unite the nuclear community behind action to respect the letter and spirit of the treaty and enforce its provisions. The agreement at the sixth NPT review conference in 2000, setting out more firmly than ever the intention to destroy all nuclear stockpiles, is a step forward, but it lacks the commitment of a firm timetable.

In the words of McGeorge Bundy: 'The basic division in the world on the subject of nuclear proliferation is not between those with and without nuclear weapons. It is between almost all nations and the very few who currently seek weapons to reinforce their expansive ambition.'[4]

Instability in the Second World

On the borders of the West's 'domestic world' lies what used to be implicitly the 'Second World', the former Soviet Union and its buffer states. Many of the latter have already been absorbed into our peaceable orbit: Poland, Hungary, the Czech and Slovak republics and Slovenia are firmly embedded; less secure perhaps are Bulgaria and Romania and some Baltic States; while events in the former Yugoslavia require us to suspend judgement on the future stability of Croatia, Serbia, Bosnia, Kosovo, Macedonia, Montenegro and – by extension – Albania. The Commonwealth of Independent States (CIS) itself is, understandably, passing through a prolonged phase of political and economic adaptation, yet extensive hostilities have so far remained confined to Chechnya or are mainly internal. The risks in this area are threefold:

- All the successor republics to the Soviet Union basically accept that they are immune from Western hostility. None of them is either willing or economically able to wage a major war. However, there remain political and economic differences both within the Russian Federation and between Russia and the Commonwealth of Independent States which it would be imprudent to discount. US insistence on national missile defence, and Russia's on the terms of the 1972 Anti-Ballistic Missile (ABM) Treaty, could in turn delay acceptance and implementation of the 1993 START II provisions to reduce each side's stock of warheads from 6,000 to 3,500 by December 2004 and in the long run unravel much of the stability and co-operation with the West. Suspicions surrounding further enlargement of NATO, particularly into the Baltic states, could also provoke a lengthy cooling of relations.
- Second, continuing hostilities between Armenia and Azerbaijan, between separatists and loyalists in Georgia, between the Russian Federation and Chechnya and an array of putative secessionists, and among a host of other potential rivals remain real. To these must be added areas of ethnic fragility such as Kosovo, Moldova, Macedonia and no doubt others not yet discernible. Bosnia and Kosovo will have provided the international community with important lessons in the avoidance of actions which exacerbate such conflicts, if not so far in dealing with them effectively. Yet the risk of any of them spreading, particularly through imprudent international involvement, should not be discounted.

• The third destabilising factor is migration. The most immediate effect of political uncertainty and economic crisis in these areas will be a continued exodus of those seeking a better fortune in the West. Pressures will also come from elsewhere. By the middle of the twenty-first century there will be 10 billion people on this planet, double the world's population in 1987. Even before 2010, it is estimated that more than 60 million people throughout the world will be refugees seeking shelter from war, oppression, natural disasters, environmental degradation, famine or economic collapse. The risk is that increasing human pressures on such a scale will translate into political divisions as well as social instability. Delays in devising sound policies may then also encourage ultra-right factions to occupy the stage.

A common European immigration policy is still not in place. Yet the European interest is not solely to repel all boarders. A UNDP[5] estimate suggests that by 2050 an ageing European population will require an additional workforce of 136 million.

Terrorism

The war of the future could arise between a fundamentally non-violent West and an angry, belligerent South and East. Its causes might be population pressures, access to wealth or living standards, or to water and perceived areas of food security. Such an asymmetrical contest could have racial and religious overtones and find potential recruits among adherents already living in the West.

Terrorism could well be a forerunner as well as an auxiliary to such a contest. It is one of the asymmetrical responses to our well-meaning intervention in the conflicts of others: 'The obverse of intervention is terrorism.'[6] Osama Bin Laden and Egyptian fundamentalists seeking revenge on the USA for perceived wrongs are early examples. Potential causes are legion and do not always need to involve the *locus belli*. The UK and the USA make a fine background for exhibiting grievances from elsewhere with maximum publicity, as witness first the drama of the hijacked Afghan airliner in London in February 2000 and then the ferocious attacks on the USA on 11 September 2001. Nor is there a shortage of means. The nuclear suitcase may still be somewhat fanciful, but chemical and biological agents could be powerful tools for more important political blackmail operations. The real danger is that 'virtual groups' are able to manifest themselves and coalesce through the Internet. Their power rapidly to gain adherents was demonstrated in the street battles in the City of London, Seattle, Washington, Gothenburg and Genoa during 1999–2001, as was the ability of small numbers of agitators to turn them to violence.

An ominous amalgam of all these discontents is already apparent within the anti-globalisation movement. Their numbers are swelled by dozens of civil society organisations espousing a bewildering array of good causes. But the injection of al-Qaeda cells and techniques into these mass protests could produce a murderous cocktail.

Living with Proliferation

Control of heavy weapons and small arms is designed to prevent what happens to others, and what they are capable of inflicting upon each other. Containing the spread of weapons of mass destruction, by contrast, means limiting what can happen to us. Even where not aimed directly against us, sooner or later the effects of such weapons will inevitably reach us. In the end it matters little whether they are detonated among us or carried climatically or by pollution; whether we become involved politically or in a military response; or whether they arrive by terrorist enterprise or blackmail. Once such weapons are in vengeful hands, our safety becomes precarious.

We have noted above that the number of countries which have or are close to constructing nuclear devices is likely to have risen to between 14 and 16. A few also have the means of delivery, on short- or medium-range missiles such as the Scud used by Iraq during the Gulf conflict or North Korea's home-made Nodong missile. The threat posed by proliferation is manifold and varied. Regional adversaries like India and Pakistan, through their respective alliances, could entrain wider concerns involving China, Russia and the USA. A similar confrontation in the Middle East has so far remained one-sided; but Iran, Iraq and Libya are advancing in their efforts to balance the Israeli advantage.

Exhortations and appeals to common sense have predictably achieved little in such cases. Of greater promise are the tools of preventive diplomacy, seeking to remove in the first instance not the weapons but the sources of conflict. Patient Western restraint over Kashmir, and the more effective early interventions in Arab–Israeli relations, have shown that diplomacy has a not inconsiderable role to play.

More ambiguous has been the response to North Korea's bid for nuclear weapons. The 38th Parallel delimits the final Cold War enigma of which an understanding eludes the West. We are still unable to predict reactions based on an unstable amalgam of dogma, indoctrination and the paranoia born of total isolation. Worse, a regime in transition behind an impenetrable curtain made of a warp of domestic secrecy and a weft of obstinate resistance to an understanding of the external world, has meant a game of double-blind diplomacy. The agreement for more than US$4 billion aid to substitute Korea's highly enriched uranium producing reactors is costly and exceedingly long term.[7] It allows for Korean progress to normalcy at stalagmite speed. Adroit and silent diplomacy principally by China and first Italy, then Australia and Russia, but also by the Koreans themselves, has brought the two Koreas into talks; yet confirmation of a real thaw will become visible only step by step.

Meanwhile the scenarios conjured up by the earlier nuclear stand-off were justly alarming. But they also brought a practical lesson: the virtual inability to use pre-emptive means. However tempting may be the notion of a surgical strike to destroy the proliferator's installations, in today's world – and at the hub of such intricate international relationships – it cannot be done in cold blood. US impotence in the face of the subterranean fortress assumed to be the Rabta Chemical plant in Libya presented an example of the dilemma. Such action needs first to be legitimised by the Security Council or an equivalent international authority. By the time that is achieved, one is likely to have entered the 'grey zone' of uncertainty as to whether the proliferator could already be able to reply with nuclear means. However faint, that prospect will further raise the cost of a military option.

The dangers of proliferation of nuclear weapons are perhaps even more pronounced with chemical and biological ones. Their manufacture entails fewer of the hazards of procurement and concealment: their ingredients are freely marketed and arouse suspicion only where large-scale manufacture is involved. Even more convenient is their independence of any specialised delivery system. According to the effect to be achieved (and who is wanting to achieve it) they can be delivered by entirely conventional means, to the battlefield or to hostile populations – or even by civilian messenger for blackmail or terrorist operations.

A look into the past shows only hesitant use of such weapons, even in the First World War which gave birth to them. There are few reliable accounts of the use of either chemical or biological weapons between then and the Iraqi attacks upon Kurds and Iranians in the 1970s and 1980s (unless napalm and Agent Orange, both in part chemical, are classed among them). Perhaps fear of retaliation in kind has acted as a deterrent. However, as with other forms of warfare, the past is unlikely to be a reliable guide to the future.

As nations are released from their traditional need to go to war to increase their wealth – expanding their interests instead by peaceful means within free trade zones and wider political groupings – it is smaller, unrecognised minorities (and conceivably fundamentalists) who will increasingly resort to 'warfare'. They will adopt both the arms and the tactics of guerrillas and terrorists. Low-intensity attacks on high-profile targets would be a first step; achieving specific political goals through blackmail with chemical and biological suitcase weapons could be a logical second.

Another argument runs that, while industrially advanced nations have learned that wars no longer lead to gains, further afield the newer nations in particular still need to complete their rites of passage before being able to live in a stable state with their regional neighbours. Until these trials of strength have run their course – both outside and within their borders – territorial disputes between states or communities will continue. And those tensions can eventually lead to ambitions to possess weapons of mass destruction, possibly of all three kinds.

Strategic calculations cannot afford to neglect either of these hypotheses, the more so as both may well come true simultaneously. It is therefore important to search for means to deal with the threat they pose. What are the prospects of interdiction or containment? We have already seen the sad realities of

31

attempts at physical defence, as well as those inhibiting pre-emptive action. The US 'stellar shield' of the late 1980s 'Star Wars' programme proved patently over-ambitious; but its successor, national missile defence, also has severe technical and protective limitations, as well as political implications in running counter to the ABM Treaty. What other tools can we then perfect to deal with this challenge?

Analysis of decision-making processes leading to the illicit manufacture of nuclear devices indicates that most were the result of an increasing isolation. In some cases, such as South Africa, that isolation was induced by a world community seeking to oust a regime which offended against human rights. Others, like North Korea, had themselves withdrawn from the real world. Having seen their chosen communist universe crumble around them, apparently leaving Korea as its sole heir, the sense of isolation and paranoia was suddenly to increase beyond all reason.

The fear of being threatened by a more powerful adversary acted upon yet others in a similar fashion: a sense of being driven back upon one's own resources through a menacing alliance of supposedly hostile forces. Israel is the exemplar which ignited a chain reaction of retaliatory impulses throughout the Arab world; and so now is Iran.

The South African decision has been traced back to 1974, a time when the Vorster government was still doggedly pursuing its apartheid policies and was forced to leave the Commonwealth and the United Nations. Ruptured relations with the West on the one hand, and its bitter anti-communist stance on the other, saw the end of most of the republic's international links. First reactions to an increasing isolation from the outside world were to pin down potentially hostile neighbours by fomenting unrest in Angola, Mozambique and elsewhere.

Pressure from African National Congress (ANC) bases in Zambia and other border areas served to heighten the self-induced threat. Before long, the leadership had persuaded itself that – sooner or later – one or the other of its adversaries would seek to invade its territory. Whether this would be a vengeful West seeking to dismantle apartheid, a Soviet Union determined to gain a foothold in the rich lands of Southern Africa, or the tens of thousands of Cubans already in Angola, resistance could be guaranteed only with the most powerful of weapons in hand.

Two further aspects of this experience are of abiding interest. The first is the comparative ease and relatively modest cost with which the South Africans were able to produce their devices, and their ability to shield them from detection up to a very advanced stage. The second is the alacrity with which a resumption of relations with the international community led to their dismantling. That final realisation of being safer *without* nuclear weapons is the unique proof that termination of the isolationist laager mentality offers the best means of nuclear defence.

The psychology of withdrawal and self-immolation is well known for individuals, less so for nations. In essence, the psychology of both is identical, since the spiral of intolerance of criticism is the same as that visited upon nations by their afflicted leaders (a need to quell opposition by postulating an external threat, increasing belief in paranoid absurdities). This circumstance gives us perhaps the best and most realistic weapon to counter the impulses towards proliferation: the psychological.

Much of what follows in this book is devoted to the need to outflank conflict with 'soft power' devices. There cannot be a greater necessity to employ these than in order to avoid a nuclear confrontation.

The Risks in Perspective

The common feature of all these risks is instability. Any risk assessment is in itself likely to be less than durable. Nevertheless, on closer examination we can perceive the real risks to be essentially of five kinds.

China

Barring a total breakdown of order in the Commonwealth of Independent States, the one remaining power other than the USA capable at some future point of mounting a large-scale military challenge on a world scale is China. Until it becomes integrated into the international community, that potential threat cannot be fully discounted. Except over Taiwan, any challenge it mounts is unlikely to be directed to the West, but rather to its neighbours in Asia. That could still entrain untold consequences for the hard-won stability of the region; hence any disturbance could also ultimately lead to a confrontation with the West. On the other hand, since the early 1980s China has implemented radical economic and institutional reforms, restricting the role of the public sector and introducing a range of market-orientated policies. As a result, it has for two decades been among the world's fastest growing economies, averaging 8–9 per cent per annum in real terms, though somewhat slower over the immediate past. After a century of turmoil, a yearning for political stability and these long-delayed economic rewards may well provide grounds for a more optimistic assessment. Nor has China's long history cast it in the role of aggressor.

Arms sales and nuclear proliferation

There is outside Europe no other power to confront the West with a serious military challenge. Not, that is, unless we ourselves help it to do so. The days when superpowers intentionally armed their Third-World proxies are hopefully now over. But we are not yet immune from harming our own interests by helping to arm countries which then train our guns upon us. So long as we can devise adequate safeguards on arms sales and nuclear proliferation, there are few foreseeable conflicts in the world which should not now be containable primarily by economic, political and psychological means. Containable, of course, does not mean capable of resolution, only preventable from spreading outside its own theatre. Diplomacy will be the first tool with the offending countries, but also with Russia, whose special standing with Iran, Iraq and North Korea marks it as an important ally. Making its shared interest in limiting nuclear proliferation prevail over its commercial needs must provide the basis for a workable partnership.

Strategic supply lines

The third category of risk – calculated or incidental – is that to our strategic supply lines. The issue is no longer gunboats securing the trade routes but to ensure the stability and goodwill of supplier countries. Too often we seem content with short-term commercial goals, without the stomach to secure our longer-term interests and – as with any sound undertaking – those of our suppliers. Paying our oil bills with sophisticated weaponry is not a durable solution. Assisting supplier governments to modernise, to find stability through the support of their people rather than through Western arms, is better for their security and ours.

Migration

The fourth of the risks, and perhaps much the most predictable, is migration. The disenfranchised communist world has paid the West the compliment of wanting to join a club of free and prosperous societies. In the aftermath of economic disintegration, it wants urgently to be admitted to the West's table. Millions equally desperate in the Third World are longing to do the same. Hundreds of thousands are succeeding. We are encouraging the flow politically by insisting – for ourselves – that freedom of movement be recognised as an essential human right. Economically, too, we abet it by seeking ever greater growth for ourselves without a corresponding willingness to acknowledge and share with others the most fundamental human right, that of requiting basic needs. In the euphoria over the demise of communism we forget that its genesis lay in the dogma that political freedom and democracy were empty terms for those denied the economic freedom to live and eat.

But not only the needy and the persecuted seek our asylum. With them come those for whom the removal of walls and barriers offers rich opportunities. Organised crime and the linking up of mafias are resulting in cross-border operations that can ultimately threaten our own stability. Such threats can become lethal if the goods traded include not only vice and drugs but nuclear materials. They can also begin to rot societies by inducing racial antagonisms.

Terrorism

Such antagonisms can give support to the last category – and now the first to confront us with serious intent – that of terrorism.

The heir of organised crime, using drugs as a source of funding as well as a weapon of attack upon society, it needs no distinct roots but is at home everywhere. In the ten years from 1989 there were over 4,000 attacks worldwide, with perhaps 1,000 casualties a year, mainly in Asia and Africa. Significantly, already in 1999 the majority of targets were businesses.[8] There are deemed to be 18 major terrorist groups. The two in Northern Ireland, as well as the Basque, Kurd and two Colombian ones have well-defined local objectives. The remainder are Islamic groups with cross-border and international targets and intent.

The costs of vigilance, through intelligence, policing and other means, will be substantial. But here, too, there is a psychological dimension. We must not only defend ourselves against their deeds; we have also to counter the resentments which nurture and motivate the Wahabi and others in the Third World and gain them support. The weapons for that will be the sensitivity to recognise their source and diplomacy of a high order to show the world that their perceptions are unjustified.

If this perspective of risks is a broad analysis, it also serves a very essential purpose. It forms the background against which the West can now conduct a practical review of its defence needs. In particular, it should enable us to see to what extent our armed forces – their numbers, dispositions, equipment and doctrines – correspond to these potential challenges. At the same time, it will allow us to judge the extent to which conventional warfare and defence remain an essential option in countering such risks.

The Phantom Armies

Cost-cutting exercises and the cashing in of the post-Cold War peace dividend have resulted in deep cuts in Western armed forces. Across the board, NATO has suffered a reduction of more than 30 per cent of its active armed forces since the Cold War. France is slimming its forces in order to create a more flexible professional army. Italy is following the same pattern, with a projected loss of 60,000 personnel. Germany is embarked on similar reforms, resulting in a further reduction of 100,000. Defence expenditure by NATO's European members has fallen by 22 per cent in real terms since 1992, including 6 per cent between 1999 and 2000 alone.[9] Large numbers of US forces have been withdrawn from Europe and elsewhere, demobilised or stationed in home bases ready to be transported where needed. The UK's forces stationed overseas have undergone a similar contraction.

Since the demise of the all-pervasive Soviet threat, rational troop deployment and targeting have become increasingly uncertain. To station them centrally, and where they are cheapest to maintain, is therefore a logical choice – even where a partial US withdrawal from Europe risks affecting relations with its allies.

However, decisions on the level of forces and their doctrines are made at the political level. They depend not only on current political objectives and perceptions but, to a significant and residual extent, on the image which a nation wishes to project. This factor has for decades served to shield UK and French forces from the full rigours of budgetary prudence. Even if their nuclear capabilities still seem exempt, economic need has imposed reality upon us all.

Already most forces are required to take on dual or multiple roles. In the UK's case, an infantry battalion assigned to the NATO rapid reaction force can be deployed on a peacekeeping mission in Kosovo or an emergency tour in Northern Ireland, then be diverted to Afghanistan. Tornado squadrons on duty in Germany were sent to the Gulf, and then stationed in Italy for action in Bosnia, Albania, Serbia and Kosovo. Only three squadrons and their ground support have since returned to Germany. The fact is that each country has only one set of forces, and these are assigned simultaneously to NATO, the UN, now the European Rapid Reaction Force, or under one such hat or none on active service in the Balkans, Sierra Leone or the Afghan theatre.

The game of robbing Peter to pay Paul can go on happily until a real emergency arises, or a number of lesser ones coincide. In 2001, Britain's armed forces totalled 212,500. The active army had a strength of 114,000. Its core was stationed in the UK, including 13,700 committed to Northern Ireland, while 17,100 were still serving in Germany and 200 were on training in Canada. Support for armed forces overseas in Brunei, Cyprus and Belize accounted for some 3,400, while another 2,100 were garrisoning the Falklands and Gibraltar. At the same time 458 were on loan for training and advisory duties to 26 countries in Africa and elsewhere. The balance were serving under UN command and other peacekeeping missions in former Yugoslavia, Albania, Sierra Leone and similar posts. In the Balkans alone, there were 6,500 troops until large numbers from there and other stations had to be redeployed towards Afghanistan. In the Gulf, the UK has been paying £30 million a year for its military presence of 21 RAF aircraft, two ships and 1,000 personnel from all three services.[10]

The UK's total armed forces, numbering 280,000 in 1992, have since been reduced by 67,000. While the cuts have not fallen equally on all services, it is clear that the strength of the Army has been severely affected. It is currently 6,000 personnel short and labours under severe budgetary restrictions. The situation is basically similar in France, the other major European contributor to peacekeeping and peacemaking operations. France, too, has garrisons throughout the world and is training the forces of other countries. However, around 20,000 of its armed forces of 274,000 are still conscripts who are not normally sent on active service. Some 8,000 are currently serving on UN and peacekeeping attachments and, even if French posts in Africa are being reduced, this may well represent the limits of its capacity. Other NATO members will be equally hard pressed to liberate troops for any multiple peacekeeping operations.[11]

Fortunately, Germany's decision to participate more fully in NATO operations has added significant personnel resources. Yet ongoing reductions in Europe's armed forces will make this a temporary advantage. Overall, it is estimated that perhaps only 2–3 per cent of the personnel under arms in Europe are available for deployment on peacekeeping missions such as Kosovo and Bosnia.[12] In the final analysis, therefore, only the United States will still have the resources quickly to mobilise a force numbering several thousand. Even then, the Gulf campaign showed how long and cumbersome is the process of mustering a complete army which requires the calling up of units of the National Guard. Deployment to Afghanistan, with minimal ground forces required, was accomplished more swiftly.

Even the USA will predictably encounter grave problems in the progressive renewal of its vast military assets. Some insight can be gleaned from the Washington-based Center for Strategic & International Studies' (CSIS) 'Defense Trainwreck Briefing',[13] which assesses ageing assets, closure of bases and alternative expenditures. Taken together, these effects are considered to diminish readiness and modernisation and to constitute a potential threat to US national security.

The conclusion is inescapable: none of the Western powers is any longer ready to fight more than a brush-fire war. Any sustained military campaign could not be carried out with existing force levels and reserves. It would require an extended mobilisation and training period to embark on any significant operations. Moreover, current reductions will mean extended tours of duty and reduced training, which will ultimately be reflected in the efficiency of fighting units.

Much of the contemporary thinking surrounding military intervention is therefore based on shaky premises. It continues to assume that large-scale forces are, or can be made, available at relatively short notice. All our diplomatic, political and defence postures are still conditioned by this. During the Kosovo crisis there was talk of up to 60,000 ground troops to eject the Serb army – two-fifths of the armada assembled for the Gulf operation. Only the generals knew better; but then bluff has always played a leading role in military operations.

Many contingency plans are based on bravura, reflecting the light in which countries wish to display themselves. This has little to do with the reality of having to curb expenditure. Nor is anyone else available to pay the piper. The UN can pay out only what its members subscribe; and most of them, led by the major subscriber of them all (the USA), are reluctant even to pay existing dues. The sad fact is that in future the troops will just not be there, unless recalled from other, often similarly compelling duties.

Arms and the Man

The lessons for our defence and security are clear. First, only in the event of a potential conflagration in the Far East does all-out warfare remain as the ultimate option. However, China is a nuclear power and – because of the size and dispersal of its population – perhaps the only one able to contemplate a conflict with any degree of impunity. For that reason alone, the West will seek at all costs to avoid such a confrontation.

Second, a high degree of military preparedness will still be necessary in the face of the other, smaller potential threats facing the West, or our domestic world. But this will in future have to serve as option of last resort, and hence as back-up for the primary instruments of political and diplomatic suasions, economic pressures, and psychological operations. Conflict prevention will henceforth be the only rational riposte. The new demands for legitimising international intervention require in any event that a traditional military response be deferred to a very advanced stage.

Third, while provision has been made for assigning rapid reaction forces to deal with smaller scale disturbances, no one has yet taken an imaginative and non-traditional look at how they should be equipped. The cuts in force levels make it essential to ensure the full effectiveness of those that remain. If peacekeepers have to rely on the use of rapidly mobile conventional weapons, they will risk both an intensification of conflict and being outgunned. To avoid committing large numbers of ground forces which inevitably become partisans in the conflict, it may be greatly more effective to separate the combatants with a range of the new generation of non-lethal weapons added to the peacekeeper's armoury.

Fourth, it is clear that an essential future role of the military will be in policing. An investment in non-lethal 'weaponry', as discussed in later chapters, promises to be a far less costly method of dominating warring factions and controlling international delinquency. Such devices will be equally appropriate for the protection of threatened minorities, ensuring the safety of relief operations, and intervention on behalf of the International Atomic Energy Agency (IAEA) and the Security Council to destroy unauthorised atomic, biological and chemical (ABC) weapons installations.

Fifth and last, a similarly important role must be accorded to defensive 'software' – that is the development and deployment of all other bloodless means of gaining domination over an adversary. High among these are the psychological weapons which have been used with well-documented success in conflicts large and small from the Second World War, through the Cold War itself to the Gulf campaign and Kosovo. There are some pertinent lessons to be learned from Bosnia. The 1994 success in forcing

the temporary relief of Sarajevo through the threat of air strikes
– rather than their use – was exemplary. The lack of tactical
success achieved by their actual use can only point to the need
for a different generation of persuaders.

The future role of the military should thus be akin to that of
our present nuclear capability: a credible deterrent, readied and
poised for ultimate use, lending force and persuasiveness to all
the non-violent measures adopted in a gradual escalation of
pressure upon a transgressor. As with the deterrent, transparent
doctrines will form an essential part of its power to deter. It
will thus be clear at what point the ignoring of 'conventional'
measures will lead inevitably to the use of force.

Throughout history, weaker combatants have used their
ingenuity to lay low a stronger enemy. From David and Goliath
through Troy to our own psychological warfare in the Second
World War and the bloodless victories of the Cold War, such
methods have scored undeniable successes. Why should not the
stronger for once get smart and adopt them? Or should the West
instead allow itself to be forced to sacrifice the achievements of
its world, as did past civilisations, under the weight of defending its status and possessions?

Notes

1. Geoffrey Kemp, 'The New (Old) Geopolitics of the Persian Gulf',
   Foreign Policy Research Institute, Vol. 6, No. 1, April 2000.
2. Peter M. Allen, 'Evolutionary Theory, Policy Making and Planning',
   Journal of Scientific & Industrial Research, 51, August–September,
   1992, pp. 644–57.
3. Lester R. Brown and Brian Halweil, 'China's Water Shortage Could
   Shake World Food Security', *World Watch Magazine*, July–August,
   1998.
4. McGeorge Bundy, William J. Crowe Jr and Sidney Drell, *Reducing
   Nuclear Danger: The Road away from the Brink,* Council on Foreign
   Relations Press, New York, 1993. Also published in *Foreign Affairs*,
   Spring 1993.
5. Institute of Future Studies for Development, 'Common Currents of
   Power in the Future of Societies and Governance in the USA,
   Europe and Asia', Hoechst Triangle Forum, Frankfurt, 1999.
6. Paul Schulte, 'Is World War Obsolete and Unthinkable?', West–West
   Agenda meeting, Washington DC, October 1998.
7. International Institute for Strategic Studies (IISS), *Strategic*

    Survey 1999/2000, IISS/Oxford University Press, London, 2000, p. 218.

8. IISS, *Strategic Survey 2000/2001*, IISS/Oxford University Press, London, 2001, pp. xxvi–xxvii.

9. IISS, *The Military Balance 2001/2002*, IISS/Oxford University Press, London, 2001.

10. Ibid.

11. Ibid.

12. IISS, *The Military Balance 1999/2000,* Brassey's, London, 2000.

13. *Defense in the Late 1990s: Avoiding the Train Wreck,* Center for Strategic & International Studies, Washington DC, 1995.

3   Countering with Other Means

'To fight and win a hundred battles is not proof of superior
excellence; the supreme achievement is to bend the
resistance of the enemy without fighting him.'

Sun Tzu, The Art of War

The Ultra-Smart Weapon

The really ultra-smart weapon is not the one released furthest
from its target, nor the one we can use to track and disable at a
distance. It is the one that *prevents* the use of all others.

The arts of conflict prevention, management and resolution are
already practised widely by different actors. Intensely valuable
techniques have been developed by individual agencies and some
impressive results achieved among communities and even states
in conflict. The real art, however, will be to find a synthesis
which will bring a well-designed amalgam of their techniques to
bear collectively on a single problem.

In a world where infringements of peace are likely to be almost
exclusively by small players, the West would be foolish not to
develop means of restraint other than at maximal cost to itself.
Once we have adjusted our view to seeing the stilling of such
small-scale aggression in terms of 'domestic' police action, we
realise that our armoury needs to look very different. The
armadas to fight a punitive campaign like Desert Storm, even if
accomplished without casualties, often inflict more economic
punishment on ourselves than the military visited upon the
enemy. That enemy is left without the weapons it should have
been denied in the first place, but with an economy largely intact
if turned to peaceful uses – and even with a still functioning

43

government continuing to exercise internal repression. After 10,000 bombing missions over Serbia and Kosovo, the political result there remained similar, until Serb voters themselves threw out the tyrant.

What has the West gained which it could not have either prevented or achieved by other, less costly means? Mostly the satisfaction of having answered an aggressor in kind, of having vindicated national honour and expunged the bitter memory of Vietnam. 'By God, we kicked the Vietnam syndrome once and for all!' declared the first President George Bush (to the American Legislative Exchange Council) in the flush of victory on 1 March 1991. What was the Vietnam syndrome? Was it merely the absence of victory for a proud nation after a prolonged war of attrition? Far more likely, it was the inability to achieve victory in a most patently unequal contest between a few hundred thousand Viet Cong and the most powerful nation on earth. Euphoria over attacking 14 million Iraqis with an array of 28 nations may not, on closer inspection, be the great catharsis that it seemed at first. In Kosovo, the West failed to prevent the ethnic cleansing – though later alleviated the situation through the return of approximately 800,000 of the 1 million displaced. Yet in the end the bombing campaign had to be undertaken to safeguard NATO's credibility, put at stake because the US threats of it at Rambouillet had, quite improperly, pre-empted NATO's own policy making.

But wars are always fought on two fronts: in the field and in the domestic political arena. There are undeniable political dividends in mounting such gladiatorial contests. A show of strength impresses the electorate; its successful outcome heaps shame upon the doubters and the opposition. Others gain too. Defence budgets can be increased and sales of newly tested hi-tech weapons systems improved. And we may all feel morally better, until the effects wear off and the limits to our war aims are revealed. The bombing of Serbia introduced a new factor: a resiling of public opinion in several NATO countries from the rawness of action, which put heavy strains on the Alliance as time wore on.

After a while, we probably need to start all over again, to worry about the growing might of the 'defeated', about closing the stable doors through which a mass of powerful arms has again bolted, about the human rights violations, and about putting together the next armada. Well before our historians start the process of debunking, time has a way of cheating us of our victories. Already we see signs of the post-war malaise (PWM) syndrome, that hollow feeling which succeeds euphoria. We count the cost and ask ourselves what we have really gained.

The Concept of Just War

Before we examine how we can better achieve our aims than by waging such wars, we must analyse what those aims are. In general, they will be a miscellany of reactions, based on righting wrongs, requiting slights, standing up for decency, rescuing others in distress or in danger of annihilation. Concepts such as territorial integrity, sovereignty, humanitarian principles, the rule of law, a new world order will form the basis of judgements and reactions. Most of us will, as usual, judge the issues by our own principles, rooted in the Judaeo-Christian ethic. According to temperament, our preferred remedy will derive from the Old or New Testament.

St Thomas Aquinas gave previously pacifist Christians a moral justification for participating in war with the concept of the 'just war'. Suitably amended, this has become the basis of relevant international law. In the end, we are therefore likely to apply the test of the just war to confirm our decision to act. The six traditional tests are widely quoted before every campaign. In effect, they are:

- just cause;
- proper authority;
- right intention;
- discrimination between combatants and non-combatants;
- proportionate response; and, significantly,
- minimum force.

It seems clear to us that any offence against them is an offence against humanity and in turn legitimises punitive as well as preventive action.

Yet the Gulf and the Balkan crises also brought out the ambivalence of the concept. Not that the values have changed,

45

or the morals trimmed. It is the world which has changed, and the West which has succeeded in changing it. The just war theory served a world in which aggressor and injured stood in the arena alone. None of the rest of the world mattered, unless linked to the potential conflict by alliances. There was no world context, no political frame of reference. Neither party needed to consider outsiders or pay heed to their views.

Two successive world wars served to change all that. They gave us the United Nations and a host of other organisations as arbiters. Most importantly, they gave the West options. Wars do not *have* to be fought, unless we are convinced that we want to fight them. How many of them have we avoided over the past half-century? The crises which could have led to war stand out as vividly as those which did: the Berlin airlift, Cuban missiles, the ill-fated U-2 flights. Why did we elect not to fight these but to wage war in Korea, in Vietnam and in the Gulf?

One answer is that the West had to resist communist expansion but could not risk direct confrontation with the Soviet Union or China. Another, less accurate, would be that we could afford to tackle the little guys but not the big bully himself. What is wrong in these questions is not so much the answer as the analysis. In fact, we did fight the bully with all the proper means at our disposal. We recognised that most of those Cold War challenges would have led directly to a nuclear confrontation, and we chose to act responsibly.

No one can say that we chose a less valiant course. The heroism of our pilots flying the air bridge, the unique courage of US presidents over Berlin and Cuba, the firmness and resolve of the NATO alliance attest to that. Yet why did we stand by with nothing but humanitarian aid in the bloodiest of conflicts: Biafra, Uganda, Angola, Ethiopia, Sudan, Rwanda, Cambodia, Laos, Burma, now Chechnya and a still lengthening roll-call of battles and civil wars ignored?

Surely it is because we have learned that there are dramas in which we have no role, which our intervention could only exacerbate. Politically, we have learned to leave well alone; militarily we now know also to leave ill alone. Our role, if any, must be that of attacking the roots of such strife, and to deny the combatants the means of mutual slaughter. As we observe such licensed killing, little by little we are led to question of why the criteria for a just war should be different from those applying in civil life.

Both the moral and the social bases of war are being further eroded as its causes become more sectarian and its locations more remote. A just cause is not necessarily one to fire patriotism. Protection of trade routes lacks the urgency of self-defence. As Oscar Wilde had it: 'A cause is not necessarily right because someone is prepared to die for it.' In future times, people may come to question by what right the command to slaughter – and be slaughtered – can be defended, unless it be solely in self-defence: their lives or ours.

One obvious weakness of assessing a 'just' number of casualties is escalation. How can we predetermine the 'minimum' degree of force and the bloodshed it will bring? The same weapons may, because of their accuracy, minimise civilian casualties, yet produce horrendous carnage when deployed against the enemy's troops. Or they may equally well do the opposite.

In due course it must be asked not whether war is just or unjust, but whether it is a legitimate means at all. In Europe we have already run out of space for anything but restrained peacekeeping. In any superpower conflict we have already recognised that our total armoury is so destructive as to be virtually unusable except to deter. Elsewhere, in the kind of war most likely to face us, we shall find that our weapons have become so highly sophisticated that any traditional conflict becomes largely one-sided. Whatever the provocation, such a war would be unfair and devoid of heroism.

We may thus be at the stage where a just war has ceased to be possible, not because morality has finally disarmed us, but because – as in Bosnia – our weapons have become too powerful to fight with. Whether we are already at that point or not, the only conceivably just war is that of last resort. Before it is ever launched, an extensive chain of other measures must have been applied with timely and maximum coherence.

Preventive Diplomacy

Diplomacy is the first line of both defence and intervention. Diplomacy is dialogue, and – in the words of Thorvald Stoltenberg (then co-chairman of the steering committee of the International

Conference on the former Yugoslavia and former Foreign Minister of Norway) on the lessons of Bosnia: 'We must avoid putting ourselves in a situation where the negotiating process stops and no real dialogue exists.'[1] The skilful use of alliances, coalitions, pressure points and interests at risk can already produce a disposition towards dialogue. From then on, highly developed techniques of conflict prevention can be engaged to continue a dialogue. These may encompass a full range of touch points such as reconciliation between hostile groups and the reciprocal righting of perceived wrongs. Carrot-and-stick techniques will play a substantial role. Identification of cherished interests can provide incentives for yielding on matters in time seen as less important. The wooing of China into the World Trade Organisation (WTO) recently combined both aspects, accompanied by not insignificant concessions from both sides. The important element is to identify the high-value cards to play.

Results of preventive diplomacy have been explored in a series of case histories of human disasters by two UN Secretaries-General, the then President of the International Court of Justice, the Secretary-General of the Organisation of African Unity, Cyrus Vance and David Owen, and a former head of Médecins sans Frontières.[2] Their judgement is that in places like Namibia, Mozambique and El Salvador, among others, actual cures were achieved. Somalia, where no treatment proved effective, was the exception, not the rule. Peace-building efforts have brought partial successes in negotiating precarious ceasefires in Colombia, Liberia, Sierra Leone and Sri Lanka; but the majority of peace agreements have failed to prevent a relapse.

The UN has since developed new techniques which seek to concentrate the efforts of all its relevant departments on specific conflict prevention tasks, grouped under four areas:[3]

- an early-warning system which tries to collate intelligence received by all UN departments and agencies;
- preventive diplomacy which reacts to the danger signals;
- preventive deployment, as in the original securing of the Macedonian border to avoid the overspill of hostilities; and
- preventive disarmament to sweep up small arms and conventional weapons and guard against the outflow of weapons from post-revolution areas.

In addition, the Secretary-General has created a fast-response Virtual Intellectual Resource Group of private persons of insight and judgement who set out their ideas and comments on specific security challenges by e-mail. Intended originally for the Zaïre (now Democratic Republic of the Congo) conflict, it has been used in relation to Afghanistan and the Eritrean war. A task force on humanitarian intervention operates on the same principle.

If problems remain in the UN system, they will be progressively less on the analytical side than on the political and financial. The Security Council shows a continuing reluctance to become seriously engaged in conflict resolution and conflict avoidance, despite the fact that for the UN a strong non-military role is often more effective in promoting peace than the – usually belated – deployment of armed forces. The Council is too easily swayed by rejection of international intervention by the parties to a dispute, and by considerations of sovereignty which could set worrying precedents even for the permanent members. The international community as a whole still lacks a culture of prevention and remains unwilling to sanction the resources.

Yet prevention is patently more cost-effective than conflict suppression. A study of nine recent conflicts has set against the actual costs an estimate of what preventive measures might have cost. It argues that, in every case, 'Conflict prevention cost, or would have cost, the international community much less than the conflicts themselves.'[4] Speculative, ex-post facto examination can reveal not only what international action could have done to prevent the conflict erupting, but the stage at which it would have been effective to do it. Such a guide could be of extreme value to future policy making.

An even finer but more ample calculation has since been made by the Oxford Reasearch Group. In examining 50 successful interventions worldwide it found that in none did the cost of involvement exceed $4 million. In some, the price of averting or ending a conflict came as low as $2,700. By contrast, NATO's aerial action in Serbia cost $4 billion, to say nothing of the further billions needed to rebuild the infrastructure destroyed.[5]

If these benefits are to be seized, there is a clear need for increased investment in the non-military components of security policy. That will necessitate a more coherent approach and closer co-ordination between the military, political and humanitarian communities. It will also call for greater consideration of development policies. Conflict can destroy development gains built up over decades and arrest economic and social progress long after hostilities have ceased. Developing countries are, of course, precisely those most at risk from their own political and economic weaknesses. It is therefore no coincidence that the majority of contemporary conflicts have erupted in the developing world. The World Bank has lately given recognition to this fact and is beginning urgently to address the reform of the security sector in its client countries.[6]

This is an area in which the European Union (EU) also has a particular role to play. Through the five-yearly Lomé Convention from 1975 onwards, it has had a close relationship with over 70 of the world's more vulnerable developing countries in Africa, the Caribbean and the Pacific (ACP). In the last renegotiation leading to the 20-year Cotonou Convention, commencing March 2000, much thought went into the contribution the pact could make to conflict prevention. Thus the new ACP–EU partnership agreement recognises that a range of parties need to contribute to 'peace, security and stability and promote a stable and democratic political environment'. It calls for political dialogue at regional, sub-regional and national levels. The inclusion of conflict issues and of non-state bodies as partners constitutes a ground-breaking achievement for a multinational agreement.

But the EU is also acquiring further substantial responsibilities in the security field through its nascent Common Foreign and Security Policy (CFSP). Its newly created Policy Planning Unit, responsible for developing-country and regional strategies to guide the EU's external policies, will need swiftly to master the analytical and rapid evaluation techniques (as well as the political recognition) essential to the proper discharge of its role. Once more Thorvald Stoltenberg: 'Today, security and stability have become more a matter of political and economic integration. The EU is the only organisation with a mandate wide enough to perform that task.'[7]

Other regional groupings have developed their own procedures, among them the Organisation for Security and Co-operation in Europe (OSCE) and the Organisation of African Unity (OAU). The Association of South-East Asian Nations (ASEAN) has developed into a hub of confidence-building activities and preventive diplomacy. It has adopted negotiating methods derived from traditional Malay governance – *mushawarah* and *mufakat* (consultation and consensus) – which have been taken on also by the Asia–Pacific Economic Council. The method simply accentuates the positive, focusing on common interests from which multilateral co-operation can be developed. Divisive issues such as Myanmar or Cambodia are simply passed over for later resolution – or set aside until they have become irrelevant.

A useful reinforcement for preventive diplomacy would be for all such alliances, including NATO, to begin to analyse and collectively agree their intervention options and possible strategies. Detailed work of this kind would help to build an awareness of what might lie in the future, and an informed opinion to support eventual action.

The Harvard Techniques

Institutional and governmental initiatives are clearly essential to marshal the international community. There are, however, equally effective conflict prevention initiatives in the private, academic and civil society sectors. High among these are conflict management techniques developed at Harvard University, which have lately culminated in a major contribution to the territorial settlement between Peru and Ecuador.

The Harvard technique centres on shifting the emphasis from the static of *solutions* which no one will accept to the dynamic of *process*. The first step of mediation is to gain an understanding of opposing positions; contrasting the perceptions of each side can already reveal clues to areas of flexibility. For mediators to put themselves into each of the parties' positions in turn is part of an essential learning process; they will find their own minds opening to a new range of possibilities. Role-reversal techniques also help to identify a range of underlying interests capable of indicating room for manoeuvre: people's real motivations are often hidden by the rigid positions attributed to them. 'Passengers in a lifeboat may discover that one prefers bread and one prefers cheese, leading to a prompt and amicable division of rations', say the authors of a set of 'tools' for conflict.[8]

If conflict persists, it is clear that the messages sent by one side to the other have been ineffective or provocative. Demands are often seen as threats, and offers obscure for lack of precision. There is a parallel between US objectives in the one-time bombing of North Vietnam and the bombing of Serbia: in both cases the purpose was to influence someone to change course, yet the accompanying messages failed to achieve this or to avert catastrophe. As important as message analysis is an appraisal of the opposing decision-maker's current perceptions and vision of the consequences of changing course. From this it may become possible to deduce the elements of a new choice more palatable to the decision-maker than abandoning the old. 'The easiest way to change the balance is not to add weight to one side or the other but rather to shift the fulcrum.'[9]

The Harvard tools rely on tabulating for each side the current positions and perceptions, the main and subsidiary interests, the perceived content of messages, and the pros and cons of any particular solution or change of stance. This will in the end result in an 'X plan', subjected to the same analysis, which may serve as a basis for negotiations requiring neither side to lose face by retreating from existing positions. The technique has been honed not only by two decades of practice but by being applied analytically to a range of past conflicts like Vietnam, the Syrian–Israeli conflict, Cyprus, the Gulf confrontation, as well as some classic international negotiations. As documents on some of these have been released, it has become clear that in many respects the analysis had been accurate.[10]

Out of these efforts have come some guidelines of general application. A four-quadrant analysis, developed for the 1993 negotiations on a new South African Constitution:[11]

• asks the question 'What is wrong?';
• demands a general diagnosis;
• prompts reflection on general approaches; and
• seeks action ideas.

A more specific diagnosis is then carried out through analysis of seven identified elements of a conflict situation. This constitutes a checklist:

• interests,
• options,

- legitimacy,
- relationships,
- communication,
- commitment, and
- alternatives.

This checklist is used to lay bare the underlying problems. The novelty of the four quadrants is that they combine a political view with an academic approach. This mixing of disciplines needs, of course, to be taken much further for a more complete understanding of a conflict, combining comprehensive academic evidence with a wide pattern of professional views. However, a broad perception of what may be wrong in a conflict should already produce an equally broad view of possible strategies to pursue.

Any resulting proposal must be able to pass a counter-analysis test. Does it do more than just satisfy our wishes and offer the other side an acceptable alternative? And is it accompanied by a plan for an immediate follow-up which can serve to consolidate it? It is then necessary to identify some influential person as the entry point into the decision-making process on each side. Not only need the parties to be convinced, but there has also to be some thought as to the terms in which each would ultimately be able to announce a decision on the proposal. The whole gamut of hurdles at which a proposal might founder must be foreseen.

Now that the Harvard 'tool kit' is reasonably complete and tested, the role of third-party mediator can be more widely practised and supported. To pass on those skills, the Negotiation Project and the Conflict Management Group run workshops both to train and to monitor ongoing processes. International organisations are still short of staff skilled in negotiating and mediation techniques; how much more then are the average parties to disputes – the governments, paramilitaries and even guerrillas. The Harvard courses and workshops have already seeded many countries and institutions with individuals possessing an understanding of these new approaches to coping with conflict.

These training activities have ranged from building up the African Union's (AU) conflict management capacity to instructing grass-roots organisations in Burundi. Some are unexpected, like the seminar on negotiating techniques at the Ecole Nationale d'Administration, the bastion of training French elites; and others, such as the joint training for Chinese and US diplomat negotiators in Beijing, just immensely imaginative. The essential skill they teach is that progress lies not in inventing new solutions but in the patient posing of a series of questions to uncover the hidden areas which can yield progress. 'Better questions are not about who is right and who is wrong, or about one-shot solutions, but about the process for dealing with conflicting views about right and wrong.'[12]

The methods of conflict management had their first test in the 1978 Camp David negotiations, employing the 'one text' formula, where each side is encouraged to produce a draft settlement which can progressively be merged into a single agreed document. Then came work in support of Algerian mediation in the Iran hostage crisis; with Farabundo Martí National Liberation Front (FMLN) guerrillas and the government of El Salvador on their eventual peace accords; with the National Party government of South Africa, the ANC, the Inkhata Freedom Party and others; and with the Greek and Turkish Cypriots to build a constituency for peace. More recently, the Conflict Management Group has worked with constituents of the former Soviet Union: with parties to the Georgia–Ossetia conflict, on the invitation of President Shevardnaze, and through the Hague Initiative, dealing with centre–periphery relations among breakaway regions and their central governments.

Domestically, too, the group has had an impact, for instance through the Urban Peace project, working with youth in Boston to develop their conflict-resolution and negotiating skills; and in helping the city of Springfield, Massachusetts to manage racial tensions and improve police–community relations.

Those techniques have also been helpful in Northern Ireland where the group worked with the Royal Ulster Constabulary (RUC) on the same topic. From exchange visits with the New York Police Department emerged an initial agenda. A unique informal dialogue session was then held to bring together people from both Protestant and Catholic communities, activists and senior RUC officials. Finally, the Harvard techniques were presented at a retreat organised for the RUC team and applied to three defined areas: external awareness, internal awareness and uncertainty about the reform process. The retreat framed ten recommendations which were then presented to the Commission on Policing. This work resulted in the group being asked also to provide training in collaborative decision-making skills for political leaders. These sessions were attended by a number of party leaders directly involved in the Northern Ireland peace talks.

A fully illuminating picture of the anatomy of peace initiatives can be glimpsed where the process has reached a definitive outcome. Resolution of the 170-year old Peru–Ecuador border dispute is one of the more prized. Since the Maranon–Amazon River was imposed as the border between the two countries, successive negotiations – even with the King of Spain and the US as arbitrators – had failed. Hostilities were briefly interrupted by the Rio de Janeiro protocol of 1942 but resumed shortly thereafter. Then, in 1985, the Harvard Group proposed an informal brainstorming session to the former Ecuadorian President and the Peruvian deputy minister of Foreign Affairs. A small group of six people sat down as individuals and began to focus on how relationships could be improved and the dispute resolved. That session was to have a lasting influence on how the two countries came to regard each other.

In 1998 Jamil Mahuad was elected President of Ecuador. In order to fulfil his principal objective of settling the border dispute, he turned to the Harvard negotiating strategies. Although asked to be his emissary to the Peruvian President, the Group decided to act as a neutral third party. Mahuad thus became the first Ecuadorian President directly to respond to President Fujimori's attempts to negotiate. Initially, the two presidents concentrated on their personal relationship; then they turned the formerly adversarial approach to negotiations into a common problem solving one. They rapidly began to understand each other's problems and motivations and maintained direct communication.

As often happens, the greatest obstacle proved to be an apparently unimportant region which nevertheless held compelling emotional significance for both sides. Bilateral negotiations were stalled and it was left to the guarantor countries of the Rio protocol (Brazil, the US, Argentina and Chile) to broker a compromise. With advice from the Harvard Group they proposed a formula under which Peru gained national sovereignty over the area, but with Ecuador also holding it as a private property. This proved acceptable to both countries and finally allowed them to concentrate their efforts and substance on developing their economies. It is not difficult to imagine other historic disputes where such a formula might well be applied.

Peace-Building from Below

Transforming actual or potential violence requires support and action from the people within the conflict area. Dialogue at government level needs to be supported by parallel processes within communities. International Alert,[13] founded in 1985 by, among others, the former head of Amnesty International Martin Ennals, aims to achieve peaceful transformation by addressing root causes. Its activities stem from the assumption that the conflicting parties themselves will need to resolve their problems. Outsiders should provide a 'creative accompaniment', promoting a better understanding of the sources of violence and more favourable responses. Particular efforts have been devoted to Africa's Great Lakes region, to Liberia, Nigeria, Sri Lanka and to the Caucasus and Caspian regions. Efforts are applied to all phases of conflict, but especially during the pre-negotiation phase, since setting the right conditions is a key element of success. When negotiations are about to start, tensions run high and mistrust among communities becomes inflamed. Methods to support these processes range from trust and confidence-building to documentation on ceasefire agreements, liaising between the parties, and encouraging each to take the first step. Techniques centre on building local, national and international constituencies for peace; enhancing the abilities of non-governmental organisations (NGOs) and the political actors involved; and linking parliamentarians with their opposite numbers in troubled areas elsewhere. Establishing communications between hostile groups is particularly urgent in remote locations where isolation has reinforced negative stereotypes and mistrust. Meetings of ex-combatants constitute another vital element.

International Alert also helped to bring NGOs from conflict areas to rally behind the International Action Network on Small Arms, a coalition of foreign-policy think-tanks, development and relief agencies, gun control groups and others.[14] Small arms inflict 20 times more damage in brush-fire wars than heavy weapons and a large constituency is now gathering to control the tide which fuels these conflicts.

The Prince of Wales Business Leaders Forum, the American Council for Economic Priorities[15] and International Alert have also helped to build coalitions of companies within conflict zones to engage business in supporting conflict prevention. This has led them to adopt a more sensitive approach to their operations in areas such as the Caspian, where international oil companies risk being caught up in renewed hostilities. Working with corporations as well as the local populations pre-empts at least some of the causes of friction.

Significantly, the International Alert experience has enabled it to assemble tools to gauge the impact of such actions. Its Peace and Conflict Assessment allows international donors and NGOs to measure the effects of their economic, security and development activities on conflict prevention and peace-building. More importantly, when the Impact Assessment is applied to specific instances of conflict prevention it becomes a powerful tool in planning effective strategies for sustainable peace. Together with Saferworld, that organisation is now helping the EU to subject its development co-operation policies to such an analysis.[16]

Many conflicts arise because of unconcern by national elites, who are mostly the only available partners for international dialogue. Their tenure therefore becomes entrenched through the support of outside agencies. This, and the distance between any national peace processes and local communities, makes the latter a more promising field for grass-roots activists. NGOs are often better placed to pursue peace building at this level. An account of the role of civil society organisations and peace processes in the South – in disturbed areas like Colombia, Guatemala, East Timor and South Africa – shows how tentative and painful such efforts tend to be. Yet the experience gathered offers a valuable guide for the future. 'In Colombia, as elsewhere,' it concludes, 'it is a mistake to assume civil society is a peace-loving force caught between a repressive state and terrorist guerrillas. Civil society is itself often divided. ... Many factors make it difficult to scale up local peace efforts into an effective national peace strategy. ... Local initiatives are unlikely to survive unless they are linked to efforts at other levels.'[17]

One positive example is the Moravia Conflict Resolution Centre in Medellin, founded in 1994 to institutionalise previously disparate activities to deal with local disputes which could otherwise have led to armed violence. A survey found that 96 per cent of those involved believed they had been helped to resolve their conflict.[18] Similar but far from identical strategies proved successful in South Africa and initially in East Timor. Recommendations to Northern governments and NGOs from this experience stress the need to support local peace-building efforts, above all through training in negotiating techniques, and then to link these with national peace processes. In parallel, pressure has to be exerted on governments and other belligerents to comply with peace agreements, sanction the deployment of an international presence and allow on-site verification. Such measures have also been used to good effect, particularly in Guatemala.

The churches, too, can play a crucial role in these strategies. Their well-developed infrastructure and communications networks can deliver clear messages which resonate among their followers. They can easily create linkages between the community and the national and indeed international levels. At the grass roots, they are able to provide essential protection to those who remonstrate against official repression; and they are both monitors and witnesses to whatever takes place there. Their position is potentially so powerful that Douglas Johnston of the International Institute of Strategic Studies (IISS) in Washington has referred to religion as 'the missing dimension in statecraft'. That is, unless they are themselves ultra-nationalists, like the Serb Bishop who warned: 'In the Serb Church we teach people to worship the land, not God.'[19]

This role is notably illustrated by Coventry Cathedral's International Centre for Reconciliation and its satellites.[20] Born out of the carnage of the Second World War blitz, it has for more than half a century striven to take conciliation to all those, of all religions, who need to compose their differences. Immediately after the war, a cross of three medieval nails from the Cathedral ruins was taken to Kiel, Berlin and Dresden. It has since been taken to all five continents to provide assistance and support to those working towards peace and reconciliation within their own communities. The Centre's reconciliation consultations provide a safe and confidential environment for such communities to work through their differences. Dialogue, listening to one another and understanding the other's story, can heal wounds and bring mutual understanding, and thus begin the process of reconciliation.

The International Centre for Reconciliation and its 65 affiliates deliberately seek out those for whom reconciliation is vital. Its workers come face to face with the warlords, especially those within different faiths, and the fundamentalists. In Iraq they are bringing together the three religious communities of Christians, Shias and Sunnis, as well as the Chaldean Church, and have taken their leaders to the UK and USA. In Israel, they have initiated a reconciliation dialogue for Palestinian Christians and Messianic Jews. In Northern Ireland, they deal with conflict within communities, between communities and on the national level.

There is hardly a flashpoint of contention which the Coventry ministry has not visited and subsequently brought into its circle. From Jordan to Germany, Rwanda and Kenya to Uganda and South Africa, from Cambodia to India and the Philippines, from Cyprus to Mozambique, patient effort has borne the slow but satisfying fruit of local communities and civil society taking the reconciliation process onto their own shoulders.

The handful of organisations mentioned here represent only a few of a great and growing number of civil society initiatives. In addition, there is a rich profusion of others which – alone or in international coalitions – are labouring towards the same end. And these are supplemented by the quiet perseverance of a myriad local and often individual initiatives which are securing fragments of a peace to restore their community's tenuous fabric.

Fear-Reduction Measures

Many of the above techniques can be drawn together in an organised set of fear-reduction measures. These seek to link national and international organisations patently regarded as neutral in concerting their actions and influence towards agreed peace-building goals. If successful, this builds a wider coalition in both geographic and political terms. Such a coalition then creates a network primarily for the flow of information from the local to the national and international level. Combined with monitoring of usually local abuses, this engages all available responses to an approaching conflict.

Technological advances have provided the basic tools for such measures. Safe and instant communication through the Internet, and mobile communications independent of the formal telephone network, reassure local communities that help can be swiftly invoked. More far-reaching are the possibilities for monitoring. Microverification methods developed in the arms control context can also be adapted for protection against intercommunal incidents.[21] Camcorders and still cameras with date and time registration should be basic equipment. Smoke canisters with individually analysable smoke can be used to identify those present at an incident and support witness testimony and outside forensic investigations. The smoke stain can even be made traceable from the air to provide more immediately accessible evidence and support.

External support can be activated by the network: first, almost automatically through availability of internal Internet communications and, second, through dispatches by participating NGOs. Press and television can be alerted and the donor community brought, in the last resort, to adjust aid flows and co-ordinate diplomatic pressures and sanctions. The threat of war crimes tribunals, supported by such microverification evidence, is also a potentially potent dissuader, as the capture and trial of war criminals becomes more commonplace. The Coalition should also recognise the importance of a regular flow of information to retain the attention of the international community and establish the channels to relay it.

Paul Schulte, Director, Proliferation and Arms Control in the UK Ministry of Defence, has said that, while different arrangements could evolve to suit each situation, the overall, open and self-evident intent would be constant: 'to prevent, mitigate or end conflicts or persecutions by using systematic, focused, collaborative procedures, coupled with the latest and most appropriate technologies to record, announce, analyse and disseminate events as they unfold'. The possibilities of micro-verification for crisis avoidance and stabilisation will be further enhanced when 'Dragon Eye', a cheap backpack portable miniature plane with video-link to ground stations, enters the list of US army equipment in 2002.[22]

Defence Diplomacy

The use of the armed forces to promote goodwill is well established. Calls at Commonwealth ports by the Royal Navy, disaster relief missions by sappers, even the Farnborough Air Show have traditionally been gestures towards friendly countries. Defence diplomacy, by contrast, is that part of co-operative security directed at formerly hostile states, predominantly in Central and Eastern Europe (CEE). When the US and Soviet defence ministers agreed as long ago as 1988 to open bilateral military exchanges, it heralded an enlarged role of military establishments in support of their government's foreign and security policies.[23] The 1998 UK Strategic Defence Review defined it as providing forces 'to meet the varied activities undertaken by the MoD to dispel hostility, build and maintain trust and assist in the development of democratically accountable armed forces, thereby making a significant contribution to conflict prevention and resolution'.[24] In the USA, 'preventive defence' came to be promoted to the first line of defence, with deterrence second and military conflict as the last resort. Germany, too, highlighted co-operation with former Warsaw Pact countries among the core missions of its armed forces, as have a number of other NATO members as well as France.[25]

Defence diplomacy efforts assist the reform of armed forces, the introduction of structures that place the military under strict civilian control and define their role in a security rather than a narrow defence context, the reorganisation of defence ministries, drawing up of budgets, officer training and military-to-military exchanges. Bilateral programmes are accompanied by NATO's Partnership for Peace (PfP), which since 1994 has sought to bring Central and Eastern European states into co-operative arrangements amounting to an associate membership. This has already led to full membership for Poland, Hungary and the Czech Republic, which all succeeded in meeting NATO criteria – as well as posing no insuperable political problems in the process.

Defence diplomacy is not without cost. NATO's PfP spending is modest, but is dwarfed by the bilateral programmes. The US Cooperative Threat Reduction Program is planning to spend $4.5 billion in 2000–5 on help to Russia in dismantling nuclear warheads, reprocessing nuclear material and reducing its stockpiles. The UK Defence Assistance Fund for CEE's expenditure amounted to $5.5 million in 1999–2000, and even the PfP countries themselves are required to bear a substantial proportion of their own costs. No one will ever be able to prove how sound that investment is – unless despite all the effort things were to go wrong. But the cost of a real conflict in the CEE countries would be incalculable and have potentially unlimited consequences.[26]

Meanwhile it will be important to avoid disenchantment setting in because of the slow – and for many uncertain – pace of enlargement of NATO and the European Union. The effectiveness of the whole action needs to be reinforced with longer-term programmes for deeper force integration, military interoperability and nuclear security. Not only the budgets of defence ministries but those of multilateral institutions and civil society should be brought into play to cement the links at every level. The EU and its detailed European Security and Defence Policy (ESDP), agreed at the European Council meeting in Nice in December 2000, will have a particular role to play in this and needs to consider the balance of effort in relation to that of the USA.[27] But, beyond that, it may also have a role in transferring the same techniques to the many ACP countries that stand in need of them to reduce the risks of military confrontation, and to extend understanding and trust among countries in transition to democratic government.

There are other ways in which military assets may be used for peace-building purposes. When France was asked to mediate in a dispute between Eritrea and Yemen over the Hanish Islands, the negotiations were brought to a swift conclusion with the results of aerial mapping.[28] Aerial and satellite surveillance and reconnaissance techniques enabled high-resolution images of the precise positions of the parties to be tabled, which immediately precluded further argument. This Observation, Orientation, Decision, Action (OODA) complex was also employed in former Yugoslavia for infrared and electromagnetic mapping to support the search for a peace formula.

If All Else Fails

However, when silent diplomacy fails, mobilising public opinion is the next step to intensify pressure. Great care is needed in this, since megaphone diplomacy is often counterproductive: making concessions can then appear as surrender. Such pressure also develops its own dynamic, giving rise to demands for more extreme and overt action than the underlying situation warrants. However, UN Secretary-General Kofi Annan insists: 'As we approach each crisis, we must ensure that the public at large has the firmest possible understanding of what lies before us. Strong, sustained support on their part is absolutely vital.' By this time, be it noted, the strategies are no longer silent and it is time to become more intrusive.

Interdiction: the Physical Means

A potential aggressor has above all to be boxed in. Throughout this book runs a clear distinction between large states, like China, which are potentially able to ignite a major war, and those whose local or internal feuds pose a regional or human rights threat. For the latter, the international community will have to develop a system of quarantine whose grip is so tight that there is no escape other than to yield. For such a system to be effective implies that it begins to be activated at the first sign of aggressive intent, be it towards neighbours or domestic society.

Effective interdiction would therefore demand a series of logical and predetermined steps, progressive in their severity. They should be automatic in their application, which means that they form part of an internationally approved and sanctioned programme for general application – except, by definition, to the five permanent members of the Security Council whose veto cannot be overridden. Such a programme would need explicit doctrines, in the same way as those laid down for military operations. Not only must one stage be the precursor to the next, but the aggressor must be fully aware of the process of escalation that has been set in motion.

An effective interdiction programme might be mapped out as follows. It is worth noting that there are international precedents, indeed UN procedures, for virtually all the steps it includes.

Economic sanctions

These would be applied in two stages:

- The first would place an immediate and total embargo on all exports of military equipment, ammunition, spare parts, strategic materials and any supplies which could be used to fuel a machine for war or repression. It would be logical for these sanctions to be imposed *before* such a capacity has been built up. An international monitoring system as described in Chapter 6 will therefore be an integral part of the programme. Furthermore, a number of countries patently building up a war machine beyond the needs of self-defence may have to be put on the embargo list immediately such a programme is approved. Clearly, such action would be triggered only after a patent intent had been demonstrated by political actions and intimidation perpetrated over a sufficient period to allow the international community to agree on its necessity.
- Stage two of economic sanctions would deny the country concerned all imports other than food and medical supplies. It would equally close its export markets by imposing a boycott on its products, as well as freezing its external assets. Here also, timing is of the essence. Full economic sanctions have in the past been used as punishment for a crime already committed. Small wonder that there is perennial debate about their effectiveness. Once blood has been shed, few have the patience to give sanctions time to work. Meanwhile the aggressors have already achieved their objectives and their defiance will carry them well beyond the point at which they would otherwise submit.

If full economic sanctions are seen as part of a conflict-prevention programme rather than as *post-delicto* punishment, the element of doubt over international reaction – which has given encouragement to so many past aggressors – is removed. With it will go the delays in decision making, as well as the lack of conviction which have left the evidence of past cases apparently so open to debate. Aggressors aim to make their moves when their armouries are full and they feel secure against any measures they judge the international community will impose. It follows that the success of those measures is severely prejudiced once they have acted and been conceded the advantage of surprise. By waiting until after the event, peaceful pressures like sanctions no longer correspond to the requirements for swift relief for the victim and prompt redress for the wrongs committed.

Physical means to enforce the sanctions must clearly be part of the mandate. It would be idle to suppose that all outside states would immediately observe the call for sanctions, even if it carried the force of an international obligation. Some neighbouring countries – Jordan in the case of Iraq – will have reasons to resist. Others will be reluctant to do more than be seen to acquiesce. The ease of sanctions breaking will be a function of the geography, or of the ability to offer high financial rewards, or shared strategic interest or sympathy with one side.

UN action has traditionally been concerned with the behaviour of states. More often than not, sanctions are circumvented by private dealers or consortia. The growth of organised crime, particularly in the area of arms dealing, means that such trade has become stateless. Powers to proceed against individuals under international law must therefore be an integral part of the sanctions mechanism.

While an interdiction programme must comprise the right to enforce observance, the actual powers may need to be reserved. Since enforcement inevitably means proceeding against third countries or their carriers, each case will need to be judged on its particular merits. Machinery for such reviews should be provided under the programme. Recognised procedures should be available, to be activated by the requisite political decisions.

The effectiveness of sanctions has its adherents as well as its critics. The latter tend to be those impatient for other forms of action. Trade and financial sanctions were applied to Iraq on 9 August 1990 in the expectation that they would take between six and 12 months to force Baghdad to negotiate. Yet by 30 October the first President Bush approved the plan for Desert Storm, while the administration gave every sign of impatience and lack of faith in sanctions as a means of avoiding war. Thus sanctions were abandoned well before their effectiveness could be gauged, even though early indications showed that they caused the regime extreme discomfiture. If post-conflict sanctions have been less than effective, it is because Saddam could not afford to declare himself defeated twice; and meanwhile they serve to demonstrate a convenient martyrdom imposed on him and the Iraqi people by the West.[29]

Most other instances are equally ambivalent. Sanctions against South Africa were opposed by several large powers, even if lobbies within them strove to incite consumer boycotts. Against Serbia they were applied too loosely and too late, and again in the face of substantial non-compliance by neighbouring states. Yet the presumption must be that timely action, pressure on the international community to comply, a patient turning of the screw and a willingness to reap the results through negotiation can, in time, bend the will of most recalcitrants.

The lore of sanctions has in any event made progress. If old-style sanctions on Iraq and Serbia have been contentious because of suffering inflicted on their populations rather than their elites, 'smart' sanctions are becoming more sophisticated. Not only can they be targeted to achieve specific aims, but their effectiveness can be enhanced by making them one of a range of co-ordinated policy instruments in a composite regime such as that outlined here.

Political sanctions

These will be equally important. Virtually all countries belong to international organisations and groupings from which they derive an array of benefits. UN specialised agencies such as the Food and Agriculture Organisation (FAO) and the UN Development Programme (UNDP) provide direct assistance. The UN Conference on Trade and Development (UNCTAD), the WTO, the Group of 77 developing countries within the UN General Assembly – all provide political support to their members in multilateral negotiations or the review of grievances. They are the trade unions of the developing world, capable of signalling unfair treatment of their members, collectively or individually.

Developing countries are generally wary of taking positions against one of their number. Their institutions are even more hesitant. Yet there are signs that suspension of the rights of membership could be developed into a recognised mark of censure *en famille*. During the 1990–91 Iraq conflict diplomacy within the UN Security Council broke significant new ground. A majority of its members, including China as one of the Permanent Five, belongs to the group of non-aligned countries. So does Iraq. Yet no fewer than 12 resolutions affecting Iraq were passed by the Security Council, generally with 13 out of 15 votes. Cuba and Yemen predictably formed the opposition. On only one occasion was there an abstention by China.

This was as much a signpost to a new relationship as a feat of joint Coalition and late Soviet diplomacy. Russia's comportment since then has signalled its recognition of a common interest in responsible crisis management; even the Kosovo crisis was finally ended by Russian political intervention with its former Yugoslav ally. If this stance can be maintained, few rational steps for restraint will remain out of reach.

The UN system has been among the most difficult to mobilise for punitive action. It is a glass house inhabited by nearly 200 delegations cringing at the prospect of having to throw the first stone. But since the crises of the 1990s the world will never be quite so diffident again. Secretary-General Kofi Annan himself has shown his determination that the organisation shall henceforth play a dynamic role, and, with the creation of a strategic planning unit and a more focused management structure, he and his predecessor have implemented a series of practical innovations to that end.[30]

Other fora can swing behind political sanctions rather more swiftly. The World Bank Group and the International Monetary Fund (IMF), which provide both a stream of their own resources and a key to bilateral assistance, continuously monitor the behaviour of their client states. Refusal to undertake new lending is by no means unknown. The causes are normally unwillingness by the borrower to implement harsh economic remedies, or failure to reach agreed targets. Military expenditures have already been taken into their prescriptions, since they bite deeply into economic performance – and the ability to service loans. The World Bank has lately begun to develop a more comprehensive approach to security sector reform, and the IMF may follow its example.

Another nettle waiting to be grasped has been that of monitoring human rights. Here the European Union broke new ground with its last Lomé Convention. This effectively made its aid and trade relationships with over 70 developing country signatories subject to suspension in the event of human rights abuses. Others – such as the Organisation of American States, and perhaps the regional development banks for Africa, Asia, Latin America and the Caribbean – might now follow suit. The fact that the potential miscreants are themselves full members of such organisations – as they are of the UN, the World Bank, the IMF and the ACP Convention – should not inhibit such an advance. The European Bank for Reconstruction and Development was born with this silver spoon: its lending is strictly geared to advances in political and economic freedoms.

Most bilateral aid programmes, too, have increasingly been made subject to performance on human rights and 'good governance'. The criteria may vary, particularly in line with the strengths of long-time relationships, but the mechanisms for reducing aid flows, and ultimate banishment from the lists, now exist. Earlier actions on these grounds against Kenya, Nigeria, Indonesia and others have already shown the way. A co-ordinating body of bilateral agencies, NGOs and research institutes, the Conflict Prevention Network, set up in 1997, develops analysis and policy options for the European Commission and the Parliament. It also helps the agencies to plan responses where such offences threaten hostilities.[31]

The EU now requires that development assistance be targeted to address the root causes of violent conflict. That means engaging the full range of instruments available to it, covering trade, investment and diplomatic initiatives. It follows that, where the EU's partners transgress, this panoply of powers can be harnessed to influence the situation.

All these represent potential instruments for the transmission of effective political sanctions. What is still needed is for them to be orchestrated into a programmed whole, a system through which the international community can apply its will to curb anyone transgressing against its norms of behaviour. The prime needs are now to establish a rapid system for formal cognisance of transgressions and for stimulating the will to act.

It had been tacitly assumed that the most likely threat to Western peace and security would come from somewhere within the Third World; the terrorist attacks on the USA on 11 September 2001 proved this correct. This is the area, after all, where the overwhelming majority of the 250 or more conflicts since the Second World War have had their battlegrounds. That is by no means to ignore the real possibilities of further ethnic conflict in Eastern Europe, or unforeseen emergencies such as experienced in Cyprus in 1964 and 1974. Yet the same principles would apply, perhaps with greater effect, since the political and economic pressure points are clearer to us. However, though containment may be easier, cases of ethnic strife are notoriously long-running. They may yield in the end only to dissolving the perceived injustices within some higher authority. Even if stillborn, the proposal by Gibraltar to bypass the contention between the UK and Spain over its status by opting for autonomy within the European Union may come to commend itself to others.

Observer forces

These or preventive deployment would constitute a next step in the interdiction programme. Having applied all available external pressures, it will be necessary to monitor what is happening on the ground. This is a delicate operation if lives are not to be put at risk. In most cases, however, the observer force would be dispatched before local tensions had led to fighting. Its mission would therefore still be preventive, with the local government held fully responsible for their safety.

At this stage it is particularly important to remember that each step is part of a carefully graduated and well-publicised regime. Thus it would be known that the sending of observer forces is the precursor to a further sequence of specific steps of increasing severity. It remains within the offending government's choice at each stage to call a halt both to its aggression and thereby the implementation of those further steps. The determining factor at this stage would be the reports of the observer force and the treatment and co-operation accorded to them.

These forces – the thin blue line – may be mounted directly by the UN or at its behest by other non-controversial organisations within the area. In Bosnia in 1992, the initial direct command by the UN of its Protection Force in Yugoslavia (UNPROFOR) relief operations as well as their protection proved less than successful. It led to the post-Dayton Agreement civil and military co-operation (CIMIC), under which the UN organised humanitarian operations and relied on NATO to assess and provide the necessary air and ground support. The UN already has considerable experience in this field, built upon more than 50 missions as observers, relief operations or acting as buffer between actual and potential combatants. In Somalia it also went beyond the peacekeeping role in 1993 by using assigned troops in an attempt to quell the feuding warlords.

Neither observer nor peacekeeping forces are required to fight; their rules of engagement are limited to self-defence. Their role is not only strictly neutral as between opposing factions, it is to preserve or restore peace. At this stage enforcement is not part of the objective. Nevertheless, their security from attack or hostage-taking will need to be strictly safeguarded, backed by a capacity to repel any assault upon them.

Intrusive action

Such action in support of human rights is the stage at which a degree of enforcement enters into the regime. As in the case of the Kurds and Shias in Iraq, and of Bosnia and Kosovo, Rwanda and Somalia, extreme and massive violations of human rights can no longer pass without international intervention. This is the newest and most sensitive doctrine. Examples are still few of spontaneous intervention without the request – sometimes without willing permission – of the sovereign power. UN Security Council Resolution 688 of 5 April 1991, which called on Iraq to cease atrocities against the Kurds and authorised humanitarian intervention, was the most spectacular innovation. The monitoring of South Africa's dismantling of apartheid, and the return of political exiles there, and of repatriated boat-people in Vietnam, are others. These have been overtaken by resolutions authorising intervention in Bosnia and Somalia, which have now firmly established intrusive procedures.

Resolution 688, as with all those pertaining to Iraq, derived from Article 51 of Chapter VII of the UN Charter, recognising the right to interim action while the Security Council is deliberating: 'Nothing in the present Chapter shall impair the inherent right of individual or collective self-defence if an armed attack occurs against a member of the United Nations, until the Security Council has taken measures necessary to maintain international peace and security.' While actions under Article 51 are not carried out in the name of the UN, they are nevertheless recognised, and therefore legitimised, by the UN. In consequence, Resolution 688 came to be interpreted as providing justification for subsequent military action.

Almost all the world's states are members of the UN. It follows that Article 51 can be applied to any act of aggression. The definition of what constitutes an 'armed attack' is uncertain. Article 51 was invoked on at least two occasions to deal with *internal* events: US aid to the Contras in Nicaragua in the 1980s and the restoration of a friendly regime in Grenada in 1983. Both, of course, involved more or less substantiated fears of external subversion. Yet both were effectively attempts to restore internal order, whose breakdown was considered imminent. More dubiously, the same Article 51 was invoked by the USA in June 1993 to legitimise a punitive air strike on Iraq in retaliation for an alleged conspiracy to assassinate the first President Bush during a visit to Kuwait.

Haiti represented a more felicitous case, largely because there were no Great Power interests opposed to the USA, which nevertheless regarded it as inimical to its security. Both Chapter VII enforcement operations and Chapter VI peacekeeping and peace-building measures were brought into play in 1994. This served as one more advance in the legitimisation of intrusive action.

In spite of the non-intervention provisions of Article 2 (7) of the UN Charter, there is thus an expanding body of case-law to justify intrusive action. In time the conditions under which it may be used will become more clearly codified. It will then be a powerful instrument for automatic defence against major human rights violations. It is also worth noting that, in the case of Kosovo, the NATO Allies did not wait for positive UN Security Council legitimisation before initiating action.

A UN rapid reaction force

This would be the next and final stage of the physical inter-diction programme. It would need to be a well-equipped force deployed to achieve strictly defined military objectives. These would include enforcement missions where hostilities had already been engaged but were still short of full-scale warfare. Its objectives would be various. The most hazardous would be to separate and disarm combatants; another to restore order where specific provocation was driving events towards open and irreversible conflict. A further one would be to proceed against sanctions breakers, to plug gaps through which arms and materials could still pour in defiance of international agreements.

Such a force should preferably be a permanent or standing one; but it need not be. For the time being it will be made up of national units earmarked for the purpose. In that event, the only additional cost to participating member states would be that of regular joint exercises – which events themselves seem intent on providing. In that way, units will be used which also form part of similarly composed rapid reaction forces, such as the Franco-UK forces deployed in Bosnia and Kosovo and, of course, the new European Rapid Reaction Force being created. Experience of multinational training and operations is thus in any event being transplanted from one to the other.

The mobilisation, risk assessment and direction of such a force will require a competent command structure. Up to now this has been assured by the USA and its major allies; but objections to US pressures have frequently been voiced. In the long run the Security Council's Military Staff Committee, created under Chapter VII of the UN Charter and comprising the Chiefs of Staff of the five Permanent Members to advise the Council on military action, appears the only organ politically qualified to assume the supreme responsibilities of launching such operations. While it has an ongoing but marginal existence, it has never yet been used for a major task of this kind. A first step in the planning of a UN rapid reaction force would therefore be to ensure, through training and attachments, that the committee acquires at least a monitoring, analysis and planning capability which might eventually qualify it for operational tasks. Some of the more powerful members have so far resisted this; but the more that Security Council legitimisation is seen to be vital to operations, the more the need for such an independent capacity will be demonstrated.

For the moment this remains a highly contentious area. The USA insists on retaining its forces under its own commanders, though is not usually averse to taking charge of the operation as a whole. The UK is insisting that peace-enforcement operations are endowed with overwhelming force in accordance with its own doctrines; and that these operate under a NATO-style military headquarters rather than the UN's peacekeeping department. The UK seems convinced that in any operation there is a potential space *between* peacekeeping and war and wants the initial UN mandate to allow also for *enforcement* of peace where necessitated by 'mission creep'.

Legitimisation of a physical interdiction programme

Legitimisation will be the first concern. Here, too, one can build upon previous experience. On the one hand, there is the example of the Gulf Coalition; and, on the other, the much less felicitous one of UNPROFOR operations in Bosnia. The significance of invoking Article 51 has already been stressed. Equally important is its context within the UN Charter. Chapter VII, of which it forms part, empowers the Security Council to take and enforce decisions binding on UN members. The latter are thereby obligated to accept and carry them out. It was the use of this provision in 1990 which made the implementation of economic sanctions against Iraq mandatory.

The original UN Charter already envisaged the creation of military units for enforcement purposes. But it anticipated that such forces would come into being through an agreed system of arrangements between the Security Council and the member states. In other words, the Charter expected that the UN would in time have under its command forces dedicated to upholding its aims and purposes. The time appears to be ripe to consider the implementation of these Charter provisions.

Because these provisions have not so far been given effect, the Security Council's resolutions on the use of force against Iraq could not be mandatory, even though they were passed in accordance with Chapter VII. Member states could therefore only be *invited* to take part in measures which were nevertheless *authorised* by the Council.

It is clear that, in these various ways, the legal and practical mechanisms exist – at least potentially – to make the UN fully responsible for all stages of the physical interdiction regime set out above. In most cases it can base itself upon precedents already successfully accomplished. And as to dedicated forces and their command, it is technically a matter of activating the existing provisions of the Charter. A better augury there could not be, as there could hardly be a better moment. The political nettle has rarely been so willing to the touch.

Is the UN a Credible Instrument?

Reliance on the UN to the extent proposed must raise the question of how far it is really capable of implementing these tasks on behalf of the world community. A short – but less than constructive – answer might be that it is the best instrument we have. It alone groups virtually all the nations of the world; and it alone has the authority to legitimise any action which is intrusive and cross-border.

It is true that the UN actions in Somalia and Bosnia were largely without glory. A cumbersome command structure, apparent rivalries with NATO and national commanders, indecision, different agendas between New York and local representatives and, critically, unwillingness among providers of military forces to accept casualties – all these have been heaped upon the standard criticisms of waste, bureaucracy and political pliancy. Some of its contingents also stand accused of arms smuggling, drug peddling and using emergency supplies as a money-making activity.

None of this should cause surprise in an organisation as vast as the UN system. By definition, international organisations are cumbersome. The greater their responsibilities, the longer it takes to activate them; the wider their membership, the heavier the political inertia before their processes can be set in motion. Sadly, loss of speed and sacrifice of efficiency stand in direct ratio to their size. But so does their ability to take decisions which carry the seal of international approval. Once taken, only their implementation can be criticised.

It must also be asked to what extent irritations with the 'failure' of the UN are not symptomatic of the general frustration over problems which have proved unyielding to force or diplomacy. The tensions this has produced within the Atlantic partnership are at least as high as those between its members and the UN. The general malaise is one of excessive expectations followed by despondency as these find themselves disappointed. Let it be said that this cycle of disappointed expectations applies with equal force to US demands on Europe and to European reliance on US leadership; and to their combined faith in superior fire-power as the solution to every crisis.

If the grander problems are inherent both in the mammoth format of the organisation and in the intractable situations with which it has to deal, an answer which is already becoming apparent is for the UN to take the overall political decisions, then to delegate their implementation to smaller, more compact regional bodies. Perhaps unexpectedly, NATO has become the UN's most effective regional implementing organisation. The OSCE, whose terms of reference include the relevant tasks of conflict prevention, safeguarding of human rights, and the monitoring and intervention in disputes, would appear pre-qualified as another, since it clearly has a special standing in the Balkans and Eastern Europe. The Economic Community of West African States (ECOWAS) has played a putative role in conflicts in Liberia, Sierra Leone and elsewhere, lately with Nigeria as a powerful regional force. Most recently, Australia has emerged as the regional leader in calming the East Timor terror.

Another dimension of UN operations is the civilian duties required to return a strife-torn territory to civil administration. These include Disarmament, Demobilisation and Rehabilitation (DDR), policing, instituting democratic processes, monitoring elections, and a host of civil administrative activities. With the help of member states (for example, the reserves of police and administrators which the USA and UK are forming), these are roles for which the UN is supremely qualified.[32]

Hand in hand with entrusting more wide-ranging responsibilities to the UN must go a measure of reform, which has in the past been ferociously resisted. Realistically, there is little chance of reforming the institution as such. But the Secretary-General's structural reforms (see above), notably the establishment of executive committees to focus on five core areas, and a Senior Management Group to include their convenors, are beginning to bear fruit. A small strategic planning unit to analyse global issues and trends will lead to better informed decisions in those core areas of peace and security, economic and social affairs, development co-operation, humanitarian affairs, and human rights. Such a structure ought specifically to avert repetition of the situation when, at the height of the Rwandan massacres in 1995, the Security Council was left in ignorance of the true course of events because available intelligence was not shared by the members with the UN, or by the Secretariat with the Council.

Many models also exist for reform of the Security Council, for dealing with the five permanent members' veto rights and for allowing its mandate to relate more closely to current trends towards intervention on humanitarian grounds or where internal conflict is demonstrably a threat to international peace and security. Whatever the fate of such reforms, it will still remain necessary to set out clear rules and procedures for the implementation of any new responsibilities. It is for the Security Council to accompany its resolutions with such instructions, and to ensure their being applied *ab initio*, well before the organisation's bad habits have a chance to take root.

Pessimists should recall that in 2001 the UN was involved in 35 peacekeeping and observer operations in conflicts across the world. Of its 16 active peacekeeping forces, only two, Bosnia and Somalia, have attracted such bitter criticism on grounds of management or political weaknesses. And these two are the instances where the organisation has been required to break almost completely new ground, without benefit of experience or firm guidelines.

Thanks to the proximity into which instant communications have moved once-distant disputes, and the prevalence of civil wars among them, peacekeeping demands on the UN have become grossly inflated. The Secretary-General and the member states alternate between the theory of limiting involvement and the reality of a gravitational pull towards escalation. While the figure of UN peacekeepers deployed worldwide has risen from

10,000 in 1988 to nearly 30,000 today, some 75,000 peacekeepers are also being deployed on mainly non-UN missions.[33]

Since its establishment in 1945, the UN's diplomatic efforts have also effectively brought about 172 peace settlements that have put an end to regional conflicts – even if a few have become reignited. These have included hastening the end of the Iran–Iraq war and the civil war in El Salvador, and the withdrawal of Soviet troops from Afghanistan. Its diplomatic efforts are also credited with averting more than 80 imminent wars.

It has helped with self-determination and the bringing to independence of more than 100 countries. Its observer missions have enabled people in 50 countries to participate in relatively free and fair elections through the provision of electoral advice and monitoring of results. The more recent include Cambodia, Namibia, El Salvador, Eritrea, Mozambique, Nicaragua, South Africa and East Timor.

Through the International Atomic Energy Agency (IAEA), the UN has an active role in minimising the danger of nuclear proliferation. The IAEA operates a programme of inspection of nuclear reactors throughout 90 countries, to ensure that nuclear materials are not diverted for military purposes. The UN's Human Rights Commission has been equally diligent in the monitoring of abuses and generating international pressures to have them redressed.

All this may not have been carried out with the dispatch and efficiency that characterise some national actions. But there is no other way in which the world community could have attempted to manage the momentous changes which have overtaken the world during the last 50 years. It is a balance sheet worth remembering when we lay blame on the UN for failing to resolve conflicts for which none of us is able to find an answer. Who, in the last resort, is the UN if it is not ourselves? And much of our support for it is half-hearted: aside from the most obvious case, it seems that UN officials were recently unable to find a single one of the 188 members which had paid all its current and past dues.

The deeper question is whether peacekeeping – let alone peace enforcement – mandates given to the UN offer a realistic means of dealing with disputes at all. There are those who protest that intrusive intervention merely favours the weaker contestant; it buys time to regroup and achieve an advantage not otherwise available. Others claim that humanitarian aid feeds not the victims but the winning side which is strong enough to mis-appropriate it. The danger is that UN involvement may un-wittingly serve to prolong the conflict.

That suspicion can be removed only by ensuring the effective-ness of UN actions. Where political instructions are incongruous and self-contradictory, failure and prolonged misery are bound to result. The confused dual mandate for protection of both aid convoys and safe areas in Bosnia should stand as a salutary lesson. It proved fair neither to the UN nor to its commanders in the field – and fatal to those it was to shield. If protection means the use of armed and lethal force, the UN's personnel are immediately put into an inferior and untenable position. Only if member states were prepared to change their protective equipment and rewrite the rules of engagement accordingly could we expect the UN to intervene effectively in conflict field operations.

Bending Resistance Without a Fight

This chapter has surveyed the panoply of techniques available to forestall conflict erupting or developing into a vicious cycle of repetitive violence. Only a small number of the increasing cast of practitioners in this field has been used to illuminate them. The non-governmental actors addressing conflict management are legion; more and more are forming themselves into inter-national coalitions with a widening outreach.

An attempt has been made to demonstrate how it is possible today for skilled bodies and individuals to dominate the full process from conflict prevention to conflict management and post-conflict reconciliation; from integration of armed forces with former enemies to the taming of those who remain recalcitrant. The sum is a comprehensive programme for countering the manifestation of violence and aggression without resort to all-out war. An important part relies on conventional means, authorised and where possible exercised by the United Nations. The other part is through the refinement of negotiating and psychological techniques already in existence and tested. Neither set of measures contains anything whose efficacy has not been adequately proved. Above all, neither puts lives at risk.

Now that such powerful tools exist, the challenge is to order them into a coherent programme of actions, designed to meet the demands peculiar to each emergency. The new multiplicity of practitioners will make it possible to mount initiatives simultaneously: launching the Harvard techniques at the same time as NGOs practise peace-building from below at the community level, fear-reduction measures to link the two levels, and reconciliation techniques to consolidate the peace. Yet each should be given space to develop its effectiveness. In the last resort, these initiatives will give the signal when more severe action is required, and the forum best adapted to project it. The imperative must be to maintain control over the situation and not to forfeit to the other side the decision to use force.

Wherever violence is practised, armed force and combat must remain the ultimate restraint. That in itself is a powerful suasion in the conflict management process. But the real objective must be to avoid those battles having to be fought at all.

Notes

1. Thorvald Stoltenberg, *The Management of Intractable Conflicts: Bosnia Hercegovina*, The Wyndham Place Trust, 1995.
2. Kevin M. Cahill (ed.), *Preventive Diplomacy: Stopping Wars before They Start*, The Center for International Health and Cooperation, Basic Books, New York, 1997.
3. Speech by Sir Kieran Prendergast, UN Under-Secretary-General for Political Affairs, at the House of Commons on 'The Role of the UN in Conflict Prevention', 2 May 2000.
4. Michael E. Brown and Richard N. Rosencrance (eds), *The Costs of Conflict: Prevention and Cure in the Global Arena*, Carnegie Commission on Preventing Deadly Conflict, Washington, DC, 1999.
5. Dylan Mathews, *War Prevention Works: 50 Stories of People Resolving Conflict*, Oxford Research Group, Oxford, 2001.
6. 'The World Bank and Security Sector Reform', *Conflict, Security and Development Bulletin*, King's College, London, March–April 2000.
7. Stoltenberg, *Management of Intractable Conflicts*.
8. Roger Fisher, *Beyond Machiavelli: Tools for Coping with Conflict*, Harvard University Press, Cambridge, MA, 1994.

9. Ibid.
10. Ibid.
11. Ibid.
12. For more information see, *End Notes: Peace by Piece*, quarterly bulletin of the Conflict Management Group, Roger Fisher House, 9 Waterhouse Street, Cambridge, MA 02138, USA.
13. International Alert, 1 Glyn Street, London SE11 5HT (www.international-alert.org)
14. International Action Network on Small Arms (IANSA), launched at the Hague Appeal for Peace Conference in May 1999 (www.IANSA.org).
15. Prince of Wales Business Leaders Forum, 15 Cornwall Terrace, London NW1 4QP; American Council for Economic Priorities, 30 Irving Place, New York, NY 10003, USA.
16. Saferworld, established in 1989, is an independent research group working for practical solutions to armed conflict; 46 Grosvenor Gardens, London SW1W 0EB.
17. Stephen Baranyi, *The People's Peace: Civil Society Organisations and Peace Processes in the South*, CIIR, London, 1998.
18. See ibid.
19. As related by Sheikh Dr M.A. Zaki Badawi of the Muslim College in London to a Wyndham Place Trust conference on 'Resolving Conflict: Are Religions a Help or a Hindrance?', London, April 1999.
20. International Centre for Reconciliation, Coventry Cathedral, Coventry CV1 5ES.
21. See Paul Schulte, 'Proposals for Confidence-Building Measures', prepared for VERTIC (Verification Research, Training and Information Centre), 1997.
22. Ibid.
23. IISS, *Strategic Survey 1999/2000*, IISS/Oxford University Press, London, 2000, p. 39.
24. *The Strategic Defence Review Presented to Parliament by the Secretary of State for Defence*, HMSO, London, July 1998.
25. IISS, *Strategic Survey 1999/2000*.
26. See ibid.
27. Presidency Conclusions on the European Security and Defence Policy, European Council, Nice, December 2000, Council of the European Union, Brussels 2000.
28. Henri Labrousse, 'Le règlement du conflit des Iles Hanish', Défense Nationale, Paris, February 1999.
29. See James M. Murphy, 'Sanctions in Transition', David Davies Memorial Institute of International Studies, Occasional Paper No.12, London, June 2000; see also Roger Williamson (ed.), *Some Corner of a Foreign Field: Intervention and World Order*, for the Council on Christian Approaches to Defence and Disarmament, Macmillan, London, 1998, p. 97.

30. 'Renewing the United Nations: A Programme for Reform', Report of the Secretary-General to the General Assembly, 16 July 1997, UN HQ New York.
31. The Conflict Prevention Network (Chaussée de Vleurgat 159, B-1050 Brussels) is a network of research institutes, NGOs and individual experts providing the EU's Analysis and Evaluation Centre with confidential policy advice.
32. Presidency Conclusions on the Common European Policy on Security and Defence, European Council, Helsinki, December 1999, Council of the European Union, Brussels, 1999.
33. IISS, 2000 Chart of Armed Conflict, *The Military Balance 2000/2001*, IISS/Oxford University Press, London, 2001.

4 Sieg ohne Krieg

'Since war begins in the minds of men,
it is in the minds of men that the
defences of peace must be constructed.'
UNESCO Constitution, 1946

Psywar

All threats are fundamentally psychological; they become military
only if unchecked – or actively or unwittingly condoned. Whether
war is an option or not, threats to stability need therefore to be
countered with psychological means.

Psychological warfare ('psywar') is a term which gained
currency in the two world wars. The advent of total war meant
the involvement of more than opposing armies. Civilian populations became an inextricable part of the drama, through bombing,
occupation or the need to work in factories or on the land to produce the materials to sustain the war. Their will and bearing
became as important as that of the fighting soldiers.

Traditionally, psywar has seen service on three fronts: at home,
for the morale of civilians and the military; within the enemy
camp, to bend the will to resist of the forces and the people
behind them; and for the disorientation of the opposing generals
and politicians. A fourth dimension, that of courting the neutral
countries, became more pronounced in the First and Second
World Wars, in particular when persuading the US leadership
and people to join the war in support of the Allied cause.

The rules of psywar have developed pragmatically; there is a
substantial body of experience and documentation, but as yet no
manual of procedures. Its origins stretch back into history, as far

82

as when a human being picked up the first stone to slay an adversary. The Old Testament and the Greek legends are rich in examples of people's realisation that muscle and skill on the battle-field are one thing, the ability to outwit and dominate the mind of an enemy quite another. They range from sophisticated essays like Egyptian spells to the terror induced ahead of advancing troops in brutally fought campaigns like the Thirty Years War in seventeenth-century Europe.

These remained isolated stratagems; psywar came into its own only once the behaviour of populations not exposed to the fighting became a crucial element of total warfare. By then, new tools had become available for reaching out to them. Mass-circulation newspapers were capable of carrying photographs from the combat zones; vivid posters could be printed to hurl messages; the telegraph, and soon the telephone and radio, brought an immediacy to reporting. These – and today's tele-vision reports – became the tools of psywar.

Charles Roetter's *Psychological Warfare* [1] provides a detailed glossary of the development of psywar instruments throughout two world wars. From the execution of Nurse Cavell in August 1915 to surrenders provoked by meticulously researched misin-formation broadcast to German forces, it chronicles the successes and failures of Allied psyops. Despite the prevalence of the former, it concludes: 'No battle, no campaign in the two world wars, has been won by propaganda alone. Propaganda is no substitute for military victory.'

Clausewitz developed a standard rule: 'War is an act of force, designed to bend the adversary to submit to our will ... Force is therefore the means; the enemy's submission to our will is the purpose. To achieve this purpose, we need to render him defence-less; and that is patently the real aim of the act of war.'[2] However, others have questioned this rule. Topitsch[3] argues that there is such a thing as 'war in peacetime', corresponding completely to Clausewitz's definition, yet not with force but with psychology as the means. He in turn cites the analysis of Hitler's psycho-logical offensive against the French in Wilhelm von Schramm's *Speak of Peace if You Want War.*[4]

Not only did Joseph Goebbels invent the modern propaganda weapon, but Hitler appears as the father of twentieth-century psychological warfare. In his own words, 'There is a wider strategy, war by means of the mind. What is the main objective in war? That the enemy capitulates ... Why do I have to demoralise him by military force, if I can do it more cheaply and effectively by other means?'[5]

This thesis found its apotheosis in the Cold War, when the deterrent clearly placed a massive constraint upon open warfare by the classic means of force. Nuclear weapons have therefore put a premium on precisely these 'peaceful' means of waging war and meeting the challenge of adversaries. Indeed, to the extent that they are capable of producing palpable fears – reinforced by the mass psychoses of occasional nuclear leaks and accidents – they have themselves acquired the character of psyweapons. The real nuclear war was fought in the rallies of nuclear disarmers and their political lobbies. They provided an ideal field for the Soviet dialectic of alternating hope with disillusion.

Glasnost and *perestroika* began to provide an insight into the importance placed on these methods by the former Soviet Union. The 1986 reforms of the psywar system introduced by Mikhail Gorbachev also revealed much of its previous structure. The International Department (MO) consisted of at least 200 officials and experts in subversion and so-called active measures; while the Propaganda Department (OP) had a staff estimated at more than 1,000. In addition, the ubiquitous KGB served as the executive arm for a variety of subversive and intelligence functions.[6]

The outcome of the Cold War may well be seen as full vindication for deterrence. In fact, it has hidden some of its shortcomings, which were already beginning to be seriously questioned. The frightfulness of nuclear weapons mesmerised so much attention that little notice was taken of the non-nuclear, non-military war being waged against the West in their shadow. Indeed, the tide of revulsion against weapons of mass destruction provided not only a mask but a powerful instrument for the pursuit of that war. The Falklands campaign, the Gulf War and the Balkans were subsequently also to prove the limitations of conventional deterrence in the face of nationalist or paranoid illusions.

Soviet propaganda was aimed as much at domestic opinion as at the conduct of the Cold War. To both, its signals sought to stress the Soviet Union's desire for peace, and in equal measure the West's resistance to it. The carefully engineered spy episodes, the campaign against Star Wars, were all part of a cleverly improvised game of chess which placed – or found – a succession of pawns to serve a specific purpose at the appropriate moment. These would be used to engage or disrupt negotiations or initiatives, in the well-rehearsed cycle of Pavlovian techniques. Playing upon the Western public's desire for peace and *détente*, continuous demonstrations were orchestrated of smiling Soviet offers and their rejection by dour US generals, of giving hope and then dashing it with the unmasking of the latest 'spy'.

That for so many decades the Soviet effort proved effective must not overshadow the fact that, in the end, it was the West that survived the contest; and that victory was achieved without the need to go to war. Now that the archives have become accessible on both sides, a major effort must be mounted to learn how it was done, to codify the techniques, and to build up a coherent system for the effective deployment of the psywar weapon.

Meanwhile the Gulf War gave rise to new forms of psyops linked to technological progress in electronic weaponry. A new concept, Command and Control Warfare (C2W), has been accepted by both the Pentagon and the UK's defence establishment. The latter defined it as 'the integrated use of all military capabilities, including destruction, electronic warfare, psychological warfare operations and operations security to deny information, to exploit, influence, degrade, confuse or destroy a command and control capability and to protect friendly C2, intelligence and communications and information systems against such actions'.[7] Once again, psyops are seen as part of counter-force, yet no longer as ancillary but as a fully integrated part of a modern response system.

Psyops must also be integrated in other ways. According to Colonel Frank L. Goldstein, 'The psyops weapon system, if employed properly, must precede, accompany and follow all military force employments while being closely co-ordinated with all agencies of government and while being integrated with US national security policy and objectives throughout the spectrum of conflict and in peacetime.'[8] Curiously, Saddam Hussein's suspicious domestic divide-and-rule policies, which meant distributing responsibility for propaganda, achieved precisely that co-ordination and made it a potent persuader among his own people and in the Arab world.

Political and Psychological Weapons

By now highly developed, psychological warfare is based essentially on orientation and disorientation. Orientation is the passive part, ensuring that one knows – and is eventually able to influence – the adversary's mind. Monitoring, the breaking of cyphers and codes and similar forms of reaching into the enemy's mind, thoughts, decision-making and command processes, form an essential part of this. Disorientation constitutes the active part of using this knowledge to obtain specific advantages. The application of these techniques to prevention and interdiction of hostilities – in other words in a peacetime setting – will be examined below.

Passive measures

Passive measures are in part mechanical, in part communicative.

Mechanical measures
The mechanical are those involved with interception techniques, intelligence gathering, access to the adversary's electronic and other traffic, and the monitoring of dispositions. These provide a basis for observation and the formulation of more active intervention.

Communicative measures
These govern the extent and effectiveness of dialogue arising from the monitoring, or preparatory to any action. At the lowest level they concern the clarity of communications. Much has been written on this subject, both for civilian and for military use. Any communication must have a highly specific aim. Its formulation will determine the extent to which it succeeds. Of prime importance is that the communicator should be clear on the essential part of the message. It must then be framed in words and terminology which convey that precise meaning to the receiver.

The search for exact equivalents to convey the information and emotive charge of the original is one of the skills to be mastered.

Even where the message is delivered and received in English, it still needs to be 'translated' into the English usage current for the recipient. The training of diplomats and others in these clarification techniques is still rudimentary. Indeed, the more important a message is deemed to be, the more its text is likely to be rehearsed in diplomatically coded form. It may be delivered with precision according to the spokesperson's precise intentions; sadly, what the recipient hears can well be fundamentally different. A long-serving foreign minister might be schooled in the code, the president almost certainly not.

US Ambassador April Glaspie's misinterpretation of Saddam Hussein's intentions on the eve of the Iraqi invasion of Kuwait has made her perhaps the most celebrated victim of this phenomenon in recent times; but she is only one in a distinguished line which includes many eminent political leaders. Whatever her instructions on that fateful day in Baghdad, she will have been at pains to make the US position clear. But since that position contained sub-clauses to still fears about more general US involvement in relations between Arab states, Saddam Hussein heard what he wanted to hear and ignored the rest. Most of the time conciseness is all.

Fashioning messages to the mental receptiveness and attention span of the recipient is another vital dimension of passive psychology. People of action, more especially autocrats, are known to be short on both. Their thoughts continually seek to translate information into action. Their minds become disinclined to take in and sift side issues. This branch of psychology is a science worth cultivating for dealing precisely with those likely to be among the aggressors.

The substance of messages is of equal importance. From the time of the Crusades Christians in the West have tried to convince Muslims of the error of their ways. They have expounded to Muslims their Christian morality, explained to them – often with great patience – their transgressions in terms of Christian ethics. Time and again Muslims have been branded as treacherous and uncomprehending, people who profess to live by honour and religion but fail shamefully in both. Their puzzlement is instructively set out in the story of the four centuries of Crusades as written by contemporary Arab historians.[9]

The same dialogue of the deaf is still prevalent in the Middle East today. The Christian (or Judaic) ethic is used to tell others how they should behave. Like their forebears facing the Crusaders, they find it difficult to comprehend what all the fuss is about. Often they have even greater difficulty in understanding why Westerners should take the role of the injured party. What, they enquire, are Western interests doing there anyway? 'Nationalism is 90 per cent of the religion of 90 per cent of the people', said Arnold Toynbee, in a rare self-observation for a European. If their religion is different, so is their nationalism. But both are vigorous.

Much of Western diplomacy fails because it is based on the assumption that humanity shares a common morality. We exhort other races to observe the principles of Western religious-based ethic, ignoring the fact that they, too, live by age-old traditions. There may well be ethical similarities between the major religions, but inevitably the language and priorities they occupy are different. The whole world knows an atrocity when it sees it, but to censure it in biblical terms will not prove helpful. An international policy based upon preaching and moralising is bound to be counter-productive, creating resentment rather than fostering compliance and co-operation.

None of this is an apologia for an aggregation of Arab peoples who have inflicted as much cruelty on the world as any one, but have also given it as much civilisation. If the West wishes to avoid more bitter conflict with these people in future, our effort will be more profitably applied to understanding their minds, impulses and temperaments. This will yield double dividends at the moment when we decide that any potential hostilities should first be averted by non-combative but equally effective psychological means.

It is then that we need a full understanding of their psychology and its processes, of its pressure points and anxieties, of which stimuli will produce which kind of reaction. 'The supreme achievement is to bend the resistance of the enemy without fighting him', stated Sun Tzu.[10] For that you need to look into the enemy's mind and map the levers which control behaviour. The scientific techniques for doing so lie at hand. To use them is not softness. On the contrary, it is to have the wisdom to win this battle and the next – whether born from defeat or stalemate. That is what this chapter is about.

Active measures

Active measures build upon information gathering and psychological mapping. They take us into the realm of manipulation, applied by a variety of means. Having established the adversary's orientation, the first objective to deflect the adversary from a belligerent course becomes disorientation. Confusion, not about our firmness or purposes, but about our precise intentions, produces self-doubt. It also allows activities and defences begun in one place to be shifted elsewhere, then to be moved again almost at will. These tactics were employed by the Coalition with almost elegant effect during Operation Desert Storm. They are now being used against the West by Iraq and North Korea in nuclear and missile hide-and-seek.

One of the major instruments, as became swiftly clear to those watching the daily Gulf briefings, was disinformation. The truth about operations became distinctly partial. One could imagine observers on the other side straining to glean snippets of intelligence about the strength of units, their locations, and the Coalition commanders' intentions and battle plan. One reason why the game was played out in this manner was the fact that early raids had denied the Iraqis effective ground-to-air communications, and with them the ability to carry out aerial reconnaissance.

Those conditions simulate more precisely a peacetime application of disinformation. In the absence of war, everything is shadow-boxing. Decoys and feints form part of the technique, in peace as in war. They allow implementation of an important element of psychological operations, that is to divert the adversary's energies from independent action to controllable reaction. In the end that becomes the same as denying the capability for offensive action, by keeping the adversary wholly occupied with reacting to such feints.

Certain intrusive operations can, of course, accelerate this development. Special Air Service (SAS) raids on specific targets, carried out with well-oiled discretion and difficult to trace or attribute, can enhance the effects of disorientation. Co-operation with internal resistance groups can achieve the same. Training in civil disobedience, and the techniques of *satyagraha* (nonviolent civil disobedience), can help to achieve such objectives while avoiding incitement to violence and casualties. Careful planning of targets can make the extent of opposition and sabotage appear many times its real strength. Such intrusive measures can, of course, be used only with some degree of international authority. They will therefore be meshed into the relevant stages of the physical interdiction programme.

In psychological terms, the cumulative effect of these measures can be to provoke a state of trauma. This manifests itself in a diminished will to act, since every action becomes associated with an unconnected reaction. The condition is characterised by confusion, self-doubt and withdrawal. In military terms, the result will be indecision, and an inability for logical planning and risk analysis. If expertly carried out over a sufficient period, the adversary can come close to being immobilised.

Yet, as the end of the Gulf campaign sadly demonstrated, we must be equally clear about our own objectives and the limits to which we are willing to pursue them. The strategies that helped the Coalition to win the war failed to be pressed to secure the peace.

The Psytools

Psyweapons are those which provoke a self-reinforcing reaction. The armoury of psywar is by now so varied and plentiful that it has earned the more embracing names of political communication or information operations. This at once makes it an instrument in its own right, rather than an auxiliary or precursor to military operations. To appreciate what an array of power it represents, it is useful to analyse its main constituents.

Propaganda

In one form or another propaganda is the principal component of psyops. It is the active dissemination of information which has been made to conform to a chosen objective. All news, all comment, all pronouncements are filtered as it were through a special lens which is trained upon that objective. While it can be fine-tuned to particular policy turns, its main value is that it remains constant, continuous and unremitting. Propaganda becomes effective over a period because its relentless repetition eventually wears down even the sceptic. It is the political equivalent of the artillery barrage.

Propaganda is concerned with presentation, not the truth. Its foremost modern practitioner, Hitler's information chief Joseph Goebbels, held that the bigger the lie, the more likely it was to be believed – provided it was repeated often enough. Examples that can never be forgotten are the hate campaigns against Jews and other 'enemies of the Reich', whose targets steadily increased as time went on. Used in this immoral sense, propaganda bears the seeds of its own destruction, for lies will need to be heaped upon lies to maintain the fundamental fiction. Unless the manipulators themselves remain objective, they will also court the risk of becoming the victims of their own distorted reality.

In more honest hands, it can be freer of these dangers. What counts is the honesty of purpose and its logic. The BBC inevitably became a powerful channel for propaganda during the Second World War. Some of those functions remained to serve the Cold War. The wartime programme 'The Two Nazis' continued to be broadcast to East Germany as 'The Two Communists'. During the 1950s, the then Information Research Department of the Foreign and Commonwealth Office (FCO) ensured that clandestine intercepts of Eastern communications became material for the BBC's Berlin correspondents.[11]

Most other countries by now have their 'information services' whose task it is to screen news and release it to achieve the best effect. In the West, these services operate under parliamentary scrutiny which monitors at one and the same time their methods and their efficacy. The evidence taken by successive committees of enquiry has consistently endorsed the effectiveness of propaganda, even if it defies numerical measurement. Nevertheless, it is useful to recall Martin Wight's distinction between diplomacy and propaganda: 'Diplomacy is the attempt to adjust conflicting interests by negotiation and compromise; propaganda is the attempt to sway the opinion that underlies and sustains the interests. Conversion therefore undercuts the task of compromise.'[12]

Agents of influence

These represent an ad hoc and short-term form of propaganda. They are used to boost a particular policy objective and achieve a specific effect. As with all information activities, they may be fictitious, embroidered or have a strict basis in fact. An early but potent example of the last type was the mailing list of US opinion formers compiled in 1914 by Britain's 'publicity' department at Wellington House in its efforts to constitute a network for disseminating comment and information helpful to encouraging the USA to join the war.[13] As in that case, delivery is often personal.

In peacetime and in war, particular stories have continued to be planted since then. They project a rendering of real events which are capable of influencing decisions at sensitive moments. Soviet accusations against the Moscow correspondent of 'US News and World Report', Nicholas Daniloff, were released in order to influence the Reagan–Gorbachev summit in 1986. The Mitrokhin archive, smuggled out of Russia by the former KGB archivist,[14] reveals the seriousness of Soviet political warfare activities, especially its promotion of 'conspiracy theories': President Kennedy's assassination was the work of the CIA, while Martin Luther King was alleged to be in the pay of the administration. Real or manufactured, the plant has become an effective modifier in international relations.

The poison drip

The poison drip is a more structured and longer-term version of the plant. A series of stories and descriptions of events is disseminated regularly, aimed at people occupying strategic functions to undermine their resolve. Though often based on misinformation, in these cases it is important that messages contain a few verifiable facts which are able to lend credence to the whole message. In the Second World War, these whispers (or sibs) assumed a role of their own which proved to have potent consequences over the longer term.

A famous example was the BBC's 'black' station 'Soldatensender Calais', which, from 1943 onwards, broadcast to German troops on the Western front. Its messages were deliberately ambivalent, to leave a lingering doubt whether this could really be an enemy station. The Nazi leadership was not attacked directly, but the tenor aimed to correspond to the unspoken feelings of jaded infantry soldiers increasingly homesick and critical of the

92

generals who were imposing this fate upon them. To enhance the mental uncertainty, comment about Churchill and other British leaders was often as uncomplimentary as that aimed at German cadres. At the same time as maintaining doubts over the origin of the programme, this evenhandedness served also to demonstrate that there were parts of the world where free speech was possible.

Roetter relates that 'every story, however slanted, was carefully built up on a foundation of accurate information supplied by intelligence or German prisoners of war'.[15] Minor faults detected in German fighter planes, snippets of gossip from captured staff officers, information about U-boat movements, all served as crumbs of truth which appeared to authenticate stories about sabotage in German aircraft factories, divisions within the High Command and infiltration of naval communications. Such stories, interspersed with the latest in American dance music, made compulsive listening. At the same time, by playing on the German soldiers' sympathies, they undermined their faith in their political leadership which – here and there – was to facilitate eventual surrender. They served similarly during the Panama operation for the capture of General Noriega.

During the Gulf crisis, the Pentagon is said to have drawn up plans for hijacking Iraqi air waves to broadcast propaganda against Saddam Hussein. US operations during the conflict made use of a wide range of airborne systems which included the Air National Guard's Volant Solo radio and television-broadcast aircraft. All these came to be used to good effect in exhorting Iraqi soldiers to surrender.

Bluff and deception

Bluff and deception have been in use through the ages. The Trojan Horse is a fine early example. Even earlier, Sun Tzu declared: 'All warfare is based on deception. When many, you should appear to be few. When near, you should appear to be far.'[16] During the American Civil War, Lieutenant General Stonewall Jackson was to say: 'Always mystify, mislead and surprise the enemy, if possible.' In wartime as in peace, the advantages to be gained by throwing one's adversary off the scent, sowing confusion and false trails, are obvious.

The most extravagant example of modern times might well have been 'Star Wars' (the Strategic Defense Initiative), the elusive shield in space against multiple ballistic missiles. The Pentagon decided to confuse the Soviets with a series of false reports and half-truths containing real information wrapped up with improbable detail. One such concerned the accuracy of interceptor missiles: despite their hit-and-miss record, US space scientists fitted them with an electronic signalling device which registered only the hits. Unfortunately this convinced not only the Soviets, but also totally misled the US Congress about the progress of the project, causing it to vote even more money for its pursuit.

Less costly but more spectacular in scale were the various feints and deceptions surrounding the Second World War D-Day landings promoted by Operation Fortitude. The initial objective was to mislead the Germans both over the point of embarkation and the site of the landings. The illusion of the assembly of a vast army in Kent was linked to increased air reconnaissance over the Pas-de-Calais. It was reinforced with large numbers of dummy vehicles, armour and aircraft, as well as fictitious communications traffic; and completed by a couple of raids on the coast around Boulogne.

Once the real assault had taken place, Operation Titanic managed to convey the impression of two airborne divisions having landed around Le Havre and Isigny behind the Normandy beaches. In reality, the effect – and the large-scale diversion of German forces it produced – was created by two lightly armed detachments each of five men from the SAS. Their drop was accompanied by 500 dummy parachutists, primed to explode on landing – and gramophones playing recorded bursts of small-arms fire and soldiers talking as in battle. More macabre, even in name, was Operation Mincemeat: a dead man was dropped off the coast of Spain, dressed as a British officer and equipped with documents evidencing an Allied deception that landings were planned in Sardinia and Southern Greece, rather than the real site in Sicily.[17]

The Gulf conflict brought new opportunities for deception campaigns, in particular one which convinced the Iraqis to concentrate their forces along the Kuwaiti foreshore in the expectation of a seaborne Coalition invasion of Kuwait. Such operations have since become codified as 'perception manipulation', presenting the enemy with plausible but wholly incorrect information.

The use of psychology

The psychological approach has been adapted both by the fighting forces and for civilian political purposes. In both areas it has become a sophisticated tool. *War on the Mind* by Peter Watson[18] documents its modern uses: how skills and abilities are recognised, how appropriate operatives are selected, how to define the psychology of leadership and promotion, behaviour under stress, and the psychology of counter-insurgency.

The role of psychology in psywar and psyops is examined in detail. This includes techniques for the selection of psywarriors, the identification and exploitation of psychological weak points in target countries, and the psychological analysis of guerrilla groups. It forms a textbook for the application of psychology and the lessons that have emerged from its use.

Mental judo

Albert L. Weeks used the term 'mental judo' to describe effective deception – 'a set of techniques for handling an opponent by lending just a little extra strength to *his own tendencies*. Hence, the most fundamental operational requirement for deception is knowledge of the target's prejudice – what does he want to believe? what is he disposed to accept? and who in the target's camp is disposed to accept what? Impressions conveyed to a complex body politic must be intended to strengthen lobbies for a particular point of view within that body politic. Clearly, knowledge of the target's predispositions is even more important than knowledge of the target's reactions.'[19]

The same point is made by Murray Dyer in *The Weapon on the Wall*: 'Any response by the target ... must be one that can be made with dignity. It follows that [the target's] way of life ... must enter into our considerations ... we must understand its cultural, social, political and psychological character. Furthermore, it is essential that we be prepared to take as well as give. Communication is a two-way process, not a monologue.'[20]

Exploiting the will to believe is an essential part of this mental judo. In its extreme form this will to believe has been focused on fear of nuclear weapons: relief from the threat of imminent annihilation was worth looking for. For this reason alone, the whole of the Cold War developed the character of a protracted psywar judo match.

Psyops are also often circular. People become persuaded by their own propaganda, as did the German leadership in 1944 with the invincibility of their Atlantic Wall.[21] The publicity given to these coastal defences was so overwhelming that it induced a totally false sense of security. This, too, relied on the latent desire for reassurance and a temporary relief from the anxieties of war.

Is it Ethical?

Although psychological warfare has traditionally served as an auxiliary to conventional warfare, psychological operations are no longer that. It may not even be correct to apply to them the name of political warfare, for war is precisely what they are here intended to avoid. The utility of war and armed intervention has become more and more limited, and the balance of usefulness has begun to swing in favour of non-belligerent means. Psyops are hostile only to the same extent as when civilian trans-gressors need to be restrained, and in such a way that they also are prevented from using force.

Lest we should feel driven to consider psyops methods demeaning and underhand, especially in the light of some of their most vile past practitioners, it may be useful to recall the extent to which they have already invaded our own lives. Various forms of all these techniques are employed for secular and personal objectives. Spin-doctors fine-tune the utterances of politicians and supervise the strategies for vilifying their opponents. Public relations (PR) consultants shape and tend the image of their clients, be they corporations or individuals, to groom their market share or ratings. Perhaps it is no coincidence that many of the people who began to develop PR as a distinct discipline for British companies during the 1950s were Special Operations Executive (SOE) colonels who built upon their wartime experiences for civilian purposes. Since then, the techniques of marketing and the manipulation of human psychology have continued to go hand in hand.

In addition, real psyops are often directed just as much at ourselves as at the adversary. Domestic opinion needs to be moulded to foreign-policy objectives, for example by bringing the Iraq factor into play during US election years. Once embarked on a campaign, there is then also a continuing need to maintain support for the war effort. Only days after an opinion poll revealed the reluctance of Americans to go to war solely to protect access to Middle East oil, but confirmed that they would support a military effort to prevent Iraq from getting the bomb, the then President Bush began to suggest that Iraq was within months of making nuclear weapons.[22] Ministry of Defence briefings during the bombing of Serbia served a similar purpose; lack of such hyperbole among continental allies clearly accounted for the progressive waning of the support of their publics.

Manipulation of public opinion is part of the standard equipment of dictators. Their apparatus is highly developed and becomes a primary tool in the conduct of policy. It is less often recognised that, although with a free press the difficulties are more formidable, the Western public is frequently exposed to not dissimilar news management. Carefully selected releases by the US military during the Gulf War aimed to convince the public that it was a 'clean' war, in which precision bombing and surgical air strikes excised enemy positions with an accuracy which created little or no collateral damage. There was a similar ambiguity about civilian casualties in Serbia and Afghanistan. Such control becomes the more potent as reactions to news coverage showing the horrors of war have been found to be ambivalent. A study conducted by the Institute of Communications Studies at Leeds University, cited by Christopher C. French,[23] showed that if people accept that a war is 'just' they will also accept the inevitable death and suffering which is its consequence. Only 'once the justification is already under question, then scenes of destruction and death will reinforce anti-war sentiment, but not before'. Between the Vietnam War – when the latter caveat began to operate – and the Gulf War, the techniques of military releases became considerably more professional, and hence manipulative.

The primacy of domestic policy, whether ours or theirs, must never be forgotten. The late speaker of the US Senate, Tip O'Neill, held that 'All politics is local politics.'[24] Many conflicts are born of the need to divert attention from domestic short-comings and to focus it on an external threat. Rational calculations will have little scope where leaders have reached this point. Janice Gross Stein cites the classic case of Egyptian decision making in 1967 and concludes that its choice of poorly conceived military action was probably determined by the ability of policymakers 'to foresee and visualise domestic disasters more vividly than foreign ones'. At the same time, 'Egypt's calculations were so flawed [by wishful thinking] that they defeated [Israeli] deterrence.'[25]

This encapsulates both the limits of objective external analysis and the absolute necessity for psyops as an accompaniment to the deterrence of force. If there is nothing between declamatory deterrence and its actual use, poor judgement, wishful thinking and domestic pressures can make such adventures potentially disastrous for both sides. Psychological counter-pressures on both policymakers and populations offer the only sane remedy. Political and psychological solutions, though protracted, have more frequently proved successful, while military intervention – in Suez, Vietnam, Lebanon, Somalia – often has not. In many cases the threat of force has proved effective, but only as a psychological means of exacting political results. Indeed, General Richard Stilwell maintains that in Vietnam 'the Communists' political and psychological campaigns were decisive – on the international scene, within the US body politic, and in the country'.[26]

Yet there are sensitivities, especially in France, over the role of psyops. Such sensitivities reflect a conflict between information activities forming an essential part of democratic debate and the darker side of propaganda wars and violation of consciences – possibly in reaction to their own experiences during the struggles in Algeria. In particular, the French are doubtful about the UK definition of 'the use of information, ideas, doctrines or the recourse to special means of dissemination to influence opinions, emotions, the attitudes or behaviour of a specific group with the object of benefiting the sender either directly or indirectly'.[27]

As against those scruples, one must bear in mind that those who disturb the peace are not always rational human beings. Nothing can be achieved without the realisation that paranoia, dissimulation and the loss of a grip on reality tend to be the distinguishing marks of tyrants and dictators. While game theory has guided us more or less successfully through the perils of the Cold War, it has little to say about those whose reason is impaired, or whose major impulses remain hidden from us. At the same time, such dictatorships tend to have a countervailing advantage: supreme authority and all decisions rest with a single individual. Despite the necessity to undermine that individual's support, within the individual's coterie and public, in the end psyops have a single target.

At the same time, effective psyops seek to reverse the depersonalisation of the individual imposed by the group to which the individual belongs. It is the group which constitutes the adversary, and the group depends on that partial depersonalisation, for instance to maintain the discipline and loyalty of its recruits. Human beings have a dual nature, capable of being altruistic as well as aggressive, co-operative as well as mean. Loosening the grip of the group can make them revert to their more gentle qualities.

The ethical question is one which needs to be judged against the over-arching need to avoid collisions or, where this is no longer possible, to ensure that they break out at the moment of best advantage. In practice, the question tends to resolve itself through a judgement as to the greater evil. Experience shows that situations of potential conflict are of two types: those which appear to promise swift resolution through a short, sharp military campaign, and those where superior risks counsel prudence. The former has usually led to military intervention, the latter to patient diplomacy. Sadly, however, in neither category are outcomes predictable. Unless we wish to repeat the errors of a Vietnam or a Somalia, we now need to give preference *ab initio* to the tools of diplomacy and psyops.

A final consideration of ethics is that war distorts our own societies. An ample literature on the psychology of the causes and propagation of war has demonstrated also the protracted effects on both combatants and victims. They have wrought fundamental changes in individuals and their societies. We will do better by ourselves to use all available tools to prevent that.

Elements of a Psyops Campaign

Successful psyops will always depend on tailoring a campaign closely to the specific and most personal characteristics of its target. Correct analysis of the situation is therefore of cardinal importance. Conflicts typically rest on a wide range of incompatibilities of 'national interest', cultural and religious traditions, political systems, ideologies and a myriad of other propensities and characteristics. Political and military analysis is therefore insufficient. Even social analysis will not reveal the deeply ingrained images which determine people's attitudes to their chosen foes.

Analysis

Psychological analysis
Psychological analysis of the parties to impending conflict is therefore an essential preliminary. Its results will be of equal importance in designing a successful psyops programme and in an ultimate resolution of the conflict. For it is precisely those psychologically determined images and attitudes which will need eventually to be modified to arrive at a lasting peace. This is an aspect so fundamental that it cannot be over-emphasised. Where, as in the Balkans, intervention is based on sketchy and mainly material perceptions of the impulses which drive the combatants, those who are aiming to help are as guilty of fencing with vague stereotypes as are the parties fighting these images. Rigorous and wide-ranging analysis, not only of the situation itself but of the factors that have produced it, is the first requirement for effective intervention.

Intelligence
At the core of any psyops campaign must clearly be accurate intelligence. In addition to the psychological analysis, it is essential to know all facets of the parties' objectives and plans, their preparations for action, where and when this is intended to take place, disposition and identity of units as well as their ethnic composition, arms and their provenance, and all matters which affect their material ability to pursue any threatened

action. Equally important will be to know the command and decision-making structure, and the identity and background of those in the chain.

Intelligence monitoring

Intelligence monitoring is an indispensable complementary element. Any psyop needs of necessity a means of assessing its impact. A network of agents has to be in place to provide regular reports on reactions to broadcasts, diplomatic initiatives and other elements of the campaign, among the elites as well as the population. In this way the content can eventually be fine-tuned to maximum effect. A typical structure for this might be the UK's Defence Intelligence Staff, whose highly capable analysts routinely evaluate technical, military and political data from worldwide sources. Both intelligence gathering and monitoring are nowadays helped by the ability of the press and others to move relatively freely around the areas of tension.

Analysis must, however, be a continuous process, with the flexibility to update its conclusions. One should never forget the plaintive words of the US Secretary of Defense, William Perry: 'We know from long experience that the first assessment of what happened is almost always wrong.'[28]

Data

In order to devise the most telling messages, a great deal of historical data must be assembled. The detail must be sufficient to reveal the ethnic, cultural and emotional diversity of the population and any potential lines of fissure. Similarly detailed insights are required into the political background and beliefs of individual members of the ruling faction, so as to delineate possible divisions to be exploited. Historical enmities and political rivalries offer the tools for undermining a united will to act.

Most feuds with neighbours or domestic populations have a historical background. It is vital to know what represents the emotional fuel for the conflict and, equally, what atavistic longings and objectives are to be requited through the threatened course of action. All these are additional instruments upon which psyops will need to play.

Psyops programme

This background intelligence will illuminate the scene and provide the basic data for a programme to direct the target's actions
into non-aggressive channels. The next step will be to devise the
psyops programme itself and its detailed constituents. These
will consist in part of finely graded diplomatic initiatives – both
soft and hard – to test the temper of responses and reactions.
The intelligence data will at the same time have been analysed
to reveal the pressure points to which the operation is to be most
usefully directed. The overall programme will consist of a model
incorporating evolutionary features, able to recognise its own
successes or failures and adapt itself accordingly.

The message
Intelligence analysis will also have defined the parameters of the
message. In the first instance this clearly needs to be constructed
in such a way as to indicate how the target's objectives may be
attained without conflict. To the extent that those are atavistic
rather than rational, the next message should contain the
reasoned consequences. Even if that, too, is likely to remain
ineffective, neither will be wasted. Much of the essence of subsequent propaganda will be to say: 'We warned you, but your rulers
did not let you listen.'

The wedges
Next will come the wedges. However melodramatic it may sound,
plants, slants and poison drips are the tools to exploit and widen
divisions and suspicions among the ruling elites and to sow
doubts among the population. This chapter has outlined the
forms which were developed successfully in earlier conflicts.
Once the personalities have been researched, and the force lines
laid bare, these stories can be devised almost in the same way
as the plot of a novel.

Delivery
Modern conflicts provide unparalleled opportunities for open
means of delivery. The press corps in Baghdad was able to send
up-to-the-minute reports on the fighting and to make the world
witness the effects of the bombing. Few will forget the live

pictures of a Cruise missile rounding the corner of a hotel; or the real-time flares of Belgrade power stations. The CNN network brings us any war it chooses, live, delivered hourly direct to our hearth. In pre-conflict situations, before censorship is applied, it is capable of doing the same for all sides. Careful briefings will be able to reach their target by the same channels.

Covert operations

Progressively, these simple actions will need to be backed up by more covert means. These will be an interaction between the directing agency and the network of agents in the field. They will clearly be devised in such a way as to reinforce the psychological pressures already built up by means of intelligence and communications. They may range from assistance to local opposition groups, to guiding agents on specific missions, and to simulating larger-scale interventions and operations. Such operations need not be military or hostile in character; their targets may equally well be administrative or financial systems.

Disorientation

Finally will come the programme of feints and disorientation. This may involve a combination of diplomatic moves, international pressures, troop movements, simulated mobilisations and other signs of escalating severity. The objective of such late-stage manoeuvres should be to engender maximum confusion. They should no longer appear part of a logical and progressive plan to increase pressures upon the transgressor. They should confound all predictability and deliberately veer in different directions, both geographically and practically, as well as rapidly alternating peaceful and bellicose messages. By sowing confusion and removing the framework of reason, adversaries can be brought to the point where they lose the horizons which enable them to take rational and effective action themselves.

C2W is designed precisely for this task. In the case of Iraq, US Army Colonel David Tanksley described its processes as 'paralysing the leadership'.[29] He defined C2W operations as having three goals: slowing an enemy's speed of operations, disrupting planning and decision making, and degrading the ability to implement what decisions can still be reached. With some justification, General Colin Powell called this 'the weird stuff'.[30]

Throughout these operations we must remain prepared to respect any genuine change in the posture of the adversary. Psyops are not warfare with unconditional surrender as their aim. They are a process of redressing the intentions of transgressors, actual or potential, until their behaviour ceases to threaten the community. We need therefore to be alive at every stage that we are engaged in a *two-way process* which will demand adaptation from us as soon as the other side shows evidence of positive movement. Indeed, it must be an integral part of our message that such movement is to be rewarded.

Truth

One last prescription, which may sit oddly with what has been described above, is the importance of truth. Clearly, truth in this and any other context of hostility cannot be absolute but only relative. What has to be safeguarded, however, is the respect of those whom we serve as well as of those we oppose. We cannot afford to undermine perceptions of our own system by showing it as underhand, subversive and devoid of fundamental values; otherwise we fail to offer oppressed people a viable choice. It follows that any action we take must be capable of being recognised as deviating from that truth only through the very necessity it is aiming to express.

A further requirement for all such action is that our basic facts must be correct. Agents of influence, stories to discredit personalities, all the paraphernalia above described must have a basis in fact and truth. If they fail this test, they may achieve their limited purpose but lead to the failure of the overall operation and its long-term objectives. Economy with the truth may be excusable to protect those engaged in an otherwise honest endeavour, especially where lives may well be at stake. To descend into untruth and expediency will change the nature of our fight – and of ourselves.

Many of these tasks are traditionally carried out by the secret services. Their activities, however, are often regarded as peripheral and intentionally separate from the 'real' action. An effective psyops campaign, on the other hand, must invest each of these elements with the same importance given to logistics in a military operation. As with the latter, meticulous preparation, anticipation and execution are vital. Psyops require the same total commitment and coherence, but with far greater demands for patience, flexibility of response, adaptation and control. They must also be able to rely on close co-ordination of policy among numerous allied states.

Technology and the Means of Delivery

Today's military relies crucially on information technology, that is the ability to collect vast amounts of data using optical and electronic sensors, terrestrially or on satellites and aircraft, and to exploit it. Technologies exploiting the latest Command, Control, Communications and Intelligence (C3I) vector are based on advances in commercial information technologies – communications, computers, software and the like. C3I is therefore one of the most powerful elements in information gathering. Its components have transformed the extent of data collection and its analysis for psyops design. Modern imaging and listening devices are of unparalleled sensitivity and definition.

Electronics and the computer age have also vastly enhanced the means of delivery and intervention. Much can be achieved today merely by sitting at a computer. Power and influence can be projected from an armchair. Broadcasting, the Internet, capturing the airwaves and a host of subsidiary applications enable information to be passed even through the most impervious barrier. Much of the technology is obvious, but essential parts – and especially their combinations – remain classified. So do the techniques employed in framing messages and mind games. Here and there, however, one can catch a glimpse of one of the delivery vehicles and is vouchsafed a more awesome illustration.

One such is the US Air Force's EC 130 Commando Solo, a flying broadcasting station dedicated entirely to psychological operations. Its hold contains a sophisticated radio and television studio served by five operators. Some of its equipment clearly owes its design and objective to the USA's 'black programs'. With the super-powerful emission equipment on board, it is able to block broadcasts, itself transmit prerecorded programmes, relay programmes transmitted from earth in real time or at intervals, or itself broadcast live programmes presented by linguists on board. The six Commando Solos are backed by 14 EC 130 Compass Calls, a version of the C 130 adapted for electronic warfare. Its principal function is to block an adversary's military communications, but it can equally support psychological operations directed at opposing forces by intrusion into their communication systems with transmissions and messages, and even entertain a dialogue with its own multilingual board personnel. Such aircraft are fitted with advanced avionics and ground contour radar which allow them to operate at low altitude as well as at night.

Under the US Air Force Special Operations Command they have seen service in most areas of more recent US military involvement. In Grenada and Haiti they served to condition the local population to the arrival of US troops; in Bosnia to counter the Serb media campaign emanating from Pale. But the aircraft also have a place in civilian operations, such as information to guide distressed populations and their rescuers in the wake of a natural disaster. The potential for interaction with events on the ground is now persuading European forces to equip themselves with similar materiel, while the USA is already planning a more advanced generation with greatly enhanced coverage.

A more detailed account of the 'strategic information operations' (SIO) in Haiti and Serbia is provided by three specialists in the field in *Munitions of the Mind*. But, significantly for current actions against terrorism, they also shed light on the SIO stratagem used to lead to the arrest in Pakistan of the original World Trade Center bomber in 1994. From that and other evidence it is clear that substantial advances are also being made on the soft part of such operations, in the design of messages and the modalities of their delivery. For obvious reasons, not much of that is in the public domain: effective persuasion relies on retaining its face value, without visibility of the means. It is the privilege of the historian to be able to chart those – and to debate the fairness of seeking to influence minds in the context of the time and its pressing needs.[31]

And Then the Peace

As in war, so in the operations to prevent it: we need a clear statement of aims and objectives. Most wars are seen as actions to gain victory, to humble the enemy. Too often little thought is given to detailed war aims, let alone the kind of peace to be constructed. If military operations are materially destructive, leaving behind a carnage that is itself inimical to peace, psyops work on the social, political and psychological fabric which is crucially important in building a stable condition or peace – even where it has been successful in averting war.

The levers used in psyops are delicate and may themselves produce long-lasting effects inappropriate to times of peace. It is sobering to think how much twenty-first-century Balkan conflicts owe to the malevolent incitement of the same divisions between Croat and Serb by Italy and the Great Powers to serve their own ends during and after the First World War. Precisely those enmities and murderous urges which have today again found free play were put at the service of Italian aspirations in Slovenia and Dalmatia, German and Austro-Hungarian aims to cement conquest, and those of the victors to attain a stability characterised only by the absence of war.

Peace and stability can be harvested only if the settlement is 'organic'. It must not be a bargain solely to suit outside powers, as in former times the Concert of Vienna, the Congress of Berlin or the division of spoils at Versailles. Such 'solutions' imply the long-term presence of the dominating powers to police a peace negotiated among themselves. They make no allowance for the recrudescence of hostilities once the exhaustion of defeat is over. Instead of being imposed from outside, an agreement must be broadly acceptable to the country pacified, and to its population. That means it must correspond to some of their own objectives, moods and attitudes, insofar as it has not proved possible to modify these during the operation itself.

Peace must not contain the seeds of its own destruction. The psychological dimension is essential to identify what these are and to avoid laying them into the new cradle. The same analysis as is made to underpin an effective psyops programme will itself yield the parameters of an acceptable and enduring peace. Such a peace represents the ultimate victory, irrespective of whether it is preceded by combat in the field or in the people's minds.

Can Psyops Really Work?

The Commander of the Joint Task Force Noble Anvil during the Kosovo operation Allied Force, Admiral James O. Ellis, US Navy, has given an unequivocal answer: 'Information Operations have incredible potential. They must become our asymmetric "point of main effort". But they are not yet understood by war fighters and remain classified beyond their access. Properly executed, Information Operations could have *halved* the length of the campaign.'[32] The adversary had been better at public information than NATO: the Serbs killed innocents by the thousand, but witnesses were discouraged; NATO accidentally killed a small number and the world watched it on the evening news. 'Public Information is a much underutilised instrument of national and Alliance power. Ignore it at your peril.'

Psychological operations, he concludes, are more important than ever. 'Psyop is at once an art, a science and a *force multiplier*.'

Notes

1. Charles Roetter, *Psychological Warfare*, B.T. Beresford, London, 1974.
2. Carl von Clausewitz, *On War*, Book I, Ch.1, W. Hahlweg, Bonn, 1952.
3. Ernst Topitsch, 'Psychologische Kriegsführung – einst und heute', ASMZ 7.8.86.
4. W. von Schramm, *Sprich von Frieden wenn du den Krieg willst*, Hase & Koehler, Mainz, 1973.
5. H. Rauschning, *Gespräche mit Hitler*, Europa-Verlag, Zurich, 1940.
6. Albert L. Weeks, 'Psy-War – Persuading the West to Lose', *Journal of Defense and Diplomacy*, Vol. 4, No.12, December 1986.
7. Ministry of Defence Command and Control (C2W) working group, cited by Martin Streetly, 'The Weird Stuff', *Flight International*, 3–9 August 1994.
8. Frank L. Goldstein *et al.*, *Psychological Operations: Principles and Case Studies*, Air University Press, Maxwell Air Force Base, AL, 1996.
9. Francesco Gabrielli (ed.), *Storici Arabi delle Crociate*, Einaudi, Turin, 1957.
10. *Sun Tzu on the Art of War: The Oldest Military Treatise in the World*, trans. Lionel Giles, British Museum, London, 1910.
11. See Michael Nelson, *War of the Black Heavens*, Brassey's, London, 1997.

12. Cited in Hedley Bull and Carsten Holbraad (eds), *Power Politics*, Leicester University Press, Leicester, 1978, p. 89.
13. See Roetter, *Psychological Warfare,* p. 64.
14. See 'The KGB's Masterplan – Documents that Trace 50 years of Sabotage', *Observer*, 12 September 1999.
15. Roetter, *Psychological Warfare*, p. 177.
16. *Sun Tzu on the Art of War*, Ch. I.
17. See, for Operation Titanic, M.R.D. Foot, 'Project Titanic', *The Times D-Day Supplement*, 6 June 1994; and, for Operation Mincemeat, letter to *The Times* by John Julius Norwich, 9 March 1998.
18. Paul Watson, *War on the Mind: The Military Uses and Abuses of Psychology*, Hutchinson, London, 1978.
19. Albert L. Weeks, 'Psy-War: Persuading the West to Lose', *Journal of Defense and Diplomacy*, 4 (12), December 1986.
20. Murray Dyer, *The Weapon on the Wall*, Johns Hopkins University Press, Baltimore, MD, 1959.
21. See M. R. D. Foot, 'The Myth of the Wall', *The Times D-Day Supplement*, 6 June 1994.
22. D. Albright and M. Hibbs, 'Hyping the Iraqi Bomb', *Bulletin of the Atomic Scientists*, 47 (2), 1991.
23. Christopher C. French, *Psychological Aspects of the Gulf War*, SANA, London, 1992.
24. Tip O'Neill, *All Politics Is Local Politics and Other Rules of the Game*, Times Books/Random House, New York, 1992.
25. Janice Gross Stein, *Psychology and Deterrence*, Johns Hopkins University Press, Baltimore, MD, 1985.
26. Col. Frank L. Goldstein *et al.*, *Psychological Operations: Principles and Case Studies*, Air University Press, Maxwell Air Force Base, AL, 1996, p. 325.
27. Comité d'études de défense nationale, *Défense Nationale*, February 2000.
28. As quoted by Nik Gowing, BBC.
29. See Streetley, 'The Weird Stuff', p. 35.
30. Ibid., pp. 35–6.
31. Robert D'Amico, Dennis Lynn and Eric S. Wexler, 'Strategic Information Operations', *Strategic Review*, Winter, 2001.
32. Admiral James O. Ellis USN, 'A View from the Top', briefing notes, 1999.

5 A Strategy for Co-Operation

'Traveller, there are no roads. Roads are made by walking.'
Spanish proverb

How Can it Begin?

More advanced tools and devices to influence behaviour and intentions also lie to hand. Some of these are harmless, if noxious; others involve substances or processes which fall under the Chemical Weapons Convention agreed in 1989. This chapter will, however, concern itself with one instrument which is ethically uncontestable. Moreover, enough empirical evidence exists to give the West the confidence to use it in order eventually to promote more willing compliance with its objectives.

We have already examined some of the tools with which adversaries can be held at bay or even disarmed, so as to avoid conflict on *their* terms and preserve peace on *ours*. We have seen how some of these have proved effective and how an armoury of non-belligerent weapons can be expanded in the areas of diplomacy, psychological operations and physical restraint. What we still lack is a grand strategy to employ all of these tools with confidence and to certain effect.

The starting-point of such a strategy must be positive and not reactive. It serves us little if we employ psychological weapons without knowing the objective towards which we wish to manoeuvre their target; or non-lethal weapons merely to arrest an adversary or stop a single act. Instead of acting blindly, we must have before us a concept of what we wish our relationship to look like when all the confrontations and hostilities are over.

Such a concept used to be called war aims. However self-evident, it was rarely applied. Involvement in a life-and-death struggle is not conducive to reflections on how to fashion the peace. The immediate purpose is clear and sufficient: victory, survival and an end to the fighting. In essence, the most desired state is a return to the *status quo ante*. Only after the Second World War did leaders achieve a better ordered post-war world, having set out during its final stages to construct the United Nations. That became an important peace aim, but still left the war aim simply as unconditional surrender. There was at that time no picture of a humbled and disarmed Germany – let alone Japan – being rehabilitated to join the new family of nations.

Once we begin to use intelligent and deliberative weapons, however, we are able to surmount that limited vision and required to think further ahead. We may then see beyond a foreground peopled by enemies and recognise that it serves little to bend adversaries to one's will, only to leave them smarting for revenge as soon as they have regrouped their forces. The final state must be not a rigid stand-off but a positive and durable peace, made fruitful and secure through a relationship of effective dialogue and co-operation.

Co-operation is a product of experience and expectation. The experience of history must eventually bring its lessons even to the most bellicose. Centuries of feuding with neighbours will in time lead to an assessment of net gains. Reckoned in casualties and territory they are likely to be slight. More important, both gains and losses will, in all probability, be found to approximate those of the other side. In the end what will be seen to matter is the political gain of survival.

Among the immediate incitements to be overcome are the glories of past triumphs, upon which by now will rest the ethos of one's people, and the urge to retaliate against the enemy's last move. Few more salutary illustrations of this exist than the railway station in Metz. At its inauguration in 1908, its grand clock tower was invested with the statue of a Roland, the traditional symbol of the Germanic sovereign's protection. His shield bore the imperial eagle, his head the features of Field Marshal von Haeseler, one of the architects of the Prussian victory and commander of XVI Army Corps stationed in Metz.

In 1919 the eagle gave way to the Cross of Lorraine and the head changed to one bearing a likeness of Maréchal Foch. By 1942 the head had been once more replaced with that of von Haeseler and a shield displaying the colours of Metz. Finally, in 1944 the liberation of Metz caused the knight to lose his head one more time. The arms of Metz were to remain on the shield but, as an early sign of French readiness for reconciliation, its head is now again that of Roland, who rode for Christendom, often with but never against the Germans.

Today, both sides commemorate their dead rather than their victories over each other. The escalation of losses and the transitoriness of the gains added up to a no-win on both sides. Tactfully, the great glories have been reassessed and neither Napoleon nor Blücher has remained a folk hero. In this case, the element of vendetta was also relatively easy to overcome. The Allied victory, the terms of the peace, and the revulsion of Germans themselves against the acts perpetrated in their name, in the end proved enough to rule out a further round of retaliation.

In a historical perspective, the Franco-German estrangement was a relatively short one. Not much more than a century before, Frederick the Great had espoused all things French, to the extent of frequently refusing to speak his own language. Only the French Revolution and its Napoleonic aftermath put an end to that earlier entente.

Further to the east, the feuding proved far less tractable. For an entire millennium Slavs, Poles, Balts, Teutons and Turks launched wave upon wave of aggression and revenge across the Vistula, the Balkans and the Russian steppes. The hostility of a multiplicity of different races, faiths, empires and nations within their bondage produced a vast arena over which feuds and vendettas were endlessly rekindled. One after another, civilisations were razed, religions and aspirations suppressed. Peoples in between were trodden underfoot, pillaged and converted to an alien faith, first by one side, then the other.

Poland may finally feel secure within its 1945 borders, no longer challenged by its neighbours. For Serbs and Croats, Bosnians and Montenegrans, the hour has still to come. So have the realignments within the Commonwealth of Independent

States (CIS). Their outcomes may well differ spectacularly in time and intensity.

Is it possible for these diverse examples of history to teach us anything about the promotion of co-operation? Can we identify a common thread which could illuminate the future outcome where fighting still rages today?

In the Franco-German case we may note that reconciliation, followed by co-operation, began with the realisation that their enmity had led to two world wars, as well as a series of continental-scale feuds. In other words, once the problem had been identified as a largely bilateral one, rather than in terms of Germany against the rest, the remedy lay close at hand. A focus for co-operation had been posited.

The same principle may lie behind the ending of the Cold War. The pre-war Soviet Union had felt itself threatened by anti-communists on all sides. Its post-war coalescence into a single bloc, paralleled by that of the Atlantic nations within NATO, produced a similarly simplified bipolarity. Already in the 1960s, probings by both sides began to test the possibilities of limited co-operation. Even though their scope was minimal and any act of bad faith severely countered, they clearly announced the mutual desire for reciprocal co-operation. Indeed, this proved so strong that it was able to progress quite substantially in limited areas, despite a succession of belligerent acts in many more fields elsewhere. Neither the Soviet invasion of Afghanistan, nor Angola, nor KGB activity and defections, were able to arrest its progress towards the ultimate achievement of arms reduction treaties, *glasnost* and *perestroika*.

Simplification of the hostile horizon is therefore the first criterion for spontaneous co-operation between old enemies. Once the real focus has been found, it becomes relatively easy for co-operation to be tested and reciprocated. Note that old-fashioned alliances, entered into with a multiplicity of partners for ill-defined ends, always proved counter-productive. Instead of producing stability they sowed mistrust and uncertainty. By widening the simple focus of hostility, they built up unrequitable pressures which finally led not to campaigns but to world wars. By contrast, the much-feared principle of opposing blocs offered a far more stable framework for co-operation in time to become established.

Stability may indeed be taken as the second criterion. Even where two systems continue to exploit any weakness which either of them shows, open hostilities have first to give way to a truce, however uneasy. In the former Yugoslavia, that bipolarity principle was manifest in the policy of matching Croat against Serb; but it had still to be fully consolidated. Not even tentative co-operation could be engaged without the relative stability of a voluntary or independently supervised ceasefire.

A further criterion to allow co-operation to develop is proximity. It was lack of proximity which led Germany to calculate in both world wars that the USA would have no interest in becoming involved. Yet already in its earliest days, the Barbary pirates had persuaded America that its frontiers lay where freedom was threatened. Since then the speed of communications – and of potential destruction with the advent of inter-continental ballistic missiles – has dramatically reduced political distances. For today's world powers, there are few areas so remote as to present no political or economic incentive to test and promote some form of co-operation.

A similar perception of proximity must, however, exist also in the other partner. If that partner fails to believe that there are common interests, or threats, with a nation on the other side of the globe, there will be little will or opportunity to co-operate. Indonesia's annexation of East Timor springs to mind. Such a perception can be considerably improved by frequency of contact. The UK had proximity with China through Hong Kong; the USA has had to create and maintain it through diplomatic *démarches*, both in Beijing and in the Security Council.

The conditions which allow co-operation to begin to grow spontaneously are therefore:

- recognition of a focused and simplified antagonism, usually by way of bipolarity;
- some relative stability and predictability within that antagonistic relationship;
- the stimulus of proximity;
- frequency of contact.

Wherever these are present, or can be developed, the opportunities for co-operation become greatly enhanced – so long as the situation can be controlled so that one side does not at any point see an easy option in military attack.

Co-operation is capable of beginning spontaneously even in the most primitive and unpromising context. That it did so in the most bitter days of the Cold War demonstrates that it does not require trust. Reciprocating a probe is sufficient response; and a cold shoulder implies no loss of face or position. Nor does rudimentary co-operation require enforcement by some independent authority: it is self-policing as long as the response is sufficiently visible and not too long delayed. Verification will ultimately help to reinforce the process, especially when it reaches a more complex contractual stage where trust will become a factor. But it is vital to remember that co-operation can be generated and gain a hold without any more sophisticated responses or mechanisms than the curiosity of the first one astute enough to make the attempt.

The Growth of Authority

Once co-operation has begun to be a conscious policy on both sides, an element of organisation will need to be introduced. From simple essay and response, some of its elements will move onto a contractual level. Limitation of arms production and deployment, withdrawal of aggressively positioned units, a network of reciprocal policies for confidence building, all these will then require a binding treaty basis to elicit compliance and acquiescence for verification.

Still at the height of the Cold War, the 1975 Helsinki Agreements on Human Rights, leading to the Conference and now the Organisation for Security and Co-operation in Europe (OSCE), became the first such mechanism. Soon the dynamic of co-operation provoked by it became multiplied, as human rights groups found in it both focus and legitimisation. Much later came the treaties for the limitation of conventional armed forces in Europe, short-range nuclear weapons and finally strategic arms. By then, the Helsinki process had done its work. Meanwhile the dissolution of the Soviet Union gathered pace, so that new accords on implementation had also to involve several of its successor republics; while NATO's powerfully demonstrated capacity for surveillance and verification provided a form of interim guarantee.[1]

On the Western side of the Iron Curtain the history of co-operation took a different, no less momentous turn. The NATO Alliance, the Brussels Treaty of 1948, the first step towards recognising the Federal Republic of Germany anew as a member of the comity of nations, and its repository, the Western European Union (WEU), established the institutions for a common Atlantic defence. But much more was happening internally in Western Europe. If Franco-German reconciliation was the cornerstone of the new *pax europea*, it also powered the revival of the centuries-old dream of a united Europe. This time neither revolution, nor the ambitions of Napoleon or fascism to impose it by force, was able to arrest its advance.

The whole of the European Union's impressive architecture stands as a classic example of second-stage regulation between former adversaries. The Schuman Plan of 1950 called for the merger of the coal and steel resources of France and Germany so that neither country had command of the industries basic to a war machine. Two years later, like-minded countries joined in to found the European Coal and Steel Community, the first of the three European communities. The other two, for atomic energy (Euratom) and the Economic Community itself, were to follow by 1957. Successive enlargements of an eventually single union have by now associated virtually the whole of Western Europe in an enterprise without parallel in history.

Nor is the process yet complete. Almost simultaneously with the steps towards full economic and more than partial political union, association agreements have been progressively reached with the countries of Eastern Europe. These are the precursor to eventual full membership, whose ultimate confines are still hard to estimate. To a significant extent they will be dependent on the durability of Russia and the CIS, but also on the will and wisdom of the EU's member states.

Not only the EU but also NATO has acted as a magnet to attract potential new members from the East. After the demise of the Warsaw Pact and the disintegration of the heartland of the Soviet empire itself, there is an understandable desire for security and protection. Even the colossus of the Russian Federation has given preliminary notice of its intent to explore

NATO membership. This has been anticipated by the Partnership for Peace (see above), a prelude to membership for most other Central and Eastern European countries. Even if Russia is still contesting the partial advance of NATO almost to its borders, it is difficult to conceive of a more dramatic reversal of enmity through the patient pursuit of co-operation.

Significantly, though Russia was deeply hostile to NATO's bombing of Serbia, its behaviour brought about the latest example of the bipolarity principle. When it finally overcame its hostility to the NATO action against a one-time ally, and the slight of not being given a role in resolving the crisis, Russia made it clear to the Serbs that they could not expect further support. By effectively making common cause with the international community on the issue, the conditions for Serb withdrawal from Kosovo had been created.

An immediate question is whether such a pursuit is capable of offering the same results elsewhere. Certainly, each situation will demand its own individual approach. The basic elements will vary significantly according to whether it is the Middle East, Korea or perhaps even Myanmar. So will the remedies and the choice of potential instruments. What is important is to enquire whether the underlying principles of the search for co-operation can amount to the ingredients for a more widely applicable strategy.

Co-operation and the Middle East

The one area of tension in which preventive diplomacy has helped not only to keep a relative peace but once made substantial, if measured progress towards durable stability is the Middle East. Its early successes (and subsequent reverses) were due to certain characteristics which are highly pertinent to the development of co-operation strategy and need therefore to be examined. Principal among these is that none of the major powers is any longer seeking to gain a significant advantage over the others, and all are determined to avoid conflict among the litigants, let alone to become involved in hostilities. It is therefore an exemplar for the strategies we wish to test.

117

How then would a strategy of co-operation as described measure up to the problems of the Middle East? Is it likely that conditions did, or can exist in which cautious attempts at co-operation may arise spontaneously even in so deeply riven an area? To assess the extent to which the progress already achieved – however halting and protracted – is in line with the criteria established above, let us measure them by this last.

The Middle East exhibits problems not totally dissimilar from those of the Balkans. The inheritors of the Ottoman Empire were a series of drawing-board states which perfectly suited the divide-and-rule principles of international order espoused by Britain and France. The yearnings of pan-Arabism were thwarted once more, but remain the more acute for being frustrated. Yet they are still not strong enough to overcome the great dissimilarity of political systems and objectives which guide individual countries. Nor are pan-Arab ambitions likely to survive a recognition of the practical impact they would have on individual societies, especially if their achievement were to be fuelled by fundamentalist doctrines.

Factors for unity are theoretically potent: suspicion of the European powers, anti-Americanism and – so far the greatest cement of all – enmity towards Israel, the foreign body in their midst. Arab language and culture are the outward and natural symbols, the latter regarded as an intimate and living expression of Islam. The more the first set of factors is recognised as negative and increasingly sterile, the greater becomes the impulse to build upon the positive. Islamic 'fundamentalism' must be seen in this light, as a symbol of Arabness and an attempt to invest it with an ancient spiritual strength. In this quasi-political sense, today's fundamentalism corresponds in some degree to the Reformation in sixteenth-century Europe. Yet one of the greatest ironies is that Islam's Martin Luther, Ayatollah Khomeini, turned out to be an Iranian, and therefore a non-Arab.

Nor is that the only sense in which Arabism and Islam so irritatingly refuse to correspond. The Arab world has been unevenly cursed with the riches of oil. The poverty of some and the wealth of others fly in the face of the teachings of the Prophet; the more so as the rich are few and the poor many. And here, too, the blessing has been indiscriminately showered upon Arab and non-Arab. Both factors, the politico-religious and the economic endowment, contribute heavily to the tensions of the Gulf.

The schisms within the Arab world are plain and manifold. Politically, economically and psychologically, they fuel the frustrations of a once proud and progressive collectivity of peoples, a society advanced in learning and discovery, and the one-time leader of the civilised world. Under the yoke of that frustration, not the progressive corruption by men of the teachings of Islam, but the advent of the Crusaders is now seen as having caused its decline.

The contradiction of being the cradle of sublime religious revelations and of dark hatreds and suspicions, the counterpoint of arabesques and asses' dung, of poetry and death, are symbols of the deep divisions within the Arab soul. But they also spell out the many facets of longings and aspirations, pride and fatalistic submission which colour the political problems of the region.

It is through this web of passions that one must try to discern the milestones of the nascent peace process. Arguably the first is the slow march towards the emergence of bipolarity from the original maelstrom of conflicting forces. Once Iraq, Jordan, Lebanon and Syria had been effectively neutralised in successive conflicts, Egypt and Israel remained as the two fundamental contestants. During their trials of strength from 1967 onwards, they progressively came to re-enact the Franco-German paradigm. Though compressed into a far shorter time-frame, their hostilities ended as soon as their contests had drawn enough blood – a process diligently monitored and guided from outside. In time, relations between Egypt and Israel were to advance so far that it became possible to apply the bipolarity principle to the Palestinians directly.[2]

The second criterion was the creation of a frame of stability within which co-operation could begin. Astute forbearance by Israel and the outside negotiators from exploiting Egyptian military and political weaknesses revealed during the fighting and its aftermath, but rather to build upon them, led to the conclusion of treaties capable of creating a constructive basis. This recognition already included one of the cardinal tenets of psychological conflict management, the proffering of both deterrence and reassurance. The military victories had achieved the former; economic support provided the latter. Within such an enlightened framework, economic and – eventually – political and even military co-operation was not slow to grow.

For Israel the third factor, the incentive of proximity, had been present throughout, implicit in the role played by the outside powers. Despite its restraining role in the 1956 Suez adventure, US support was axiomatic, as demonstrated not only by its active involvement but by its seemingly endless tolerance. The proximity was brought closer through the US role in NATO, whose bases have formed an omnipresent guard-rail around the northern and eastern Mediterranean. What became of increasing relevance was the US interest not just in stability but also directly in Egypt. As internal political changes caused Soviet influence to recede, the sense of proximity between Egypt and the USA grew markedly.

Both factors also served to increase the fourth element, the frequency of contacts at all levels, as well as their intimacy. As the famous Middle East shuttle diplomacy gathered pace, so all four of these factors were brought to bear on other hostile Arab parties. Care was taken for negotiators to probe those parties in turn on every round. This gave all of them status, but also allowed the order for substantive negotiations to emerge. First with the Palestinians, then with Jordan, with Lebanon and increasingly with Syria, the process began to bear fruit. The technique was effectively that set out here: in each case the clearing of the field to allow the focus of bipolarity to be sharpened; the negotiation of a frame of stability which took into account the interests of each, and those that were mutual; and the promotion of practical co-operation and frequency of direct contact between the parties bilaterally.

In consequence more and more problems came to be regarded as common. The *intifada*, fundamentalist attacks in Egypt, Hamas-inspired revolts by Palestinians, violent demonstrations of Israeli settlers, even Syrian obduracy all became equally disturbing to both sides. The will to find solutions and use them to expand the peace process seemed to have taken root.

For the moment, the growing strength of Hamas and Hezbollah has added a pernicious wild card to the bipolarity process. One must wait until those movemente have gained sufficient self-confidence to link themselves to one of the existing factions. To the extent that Hezbollah is a proxy for Iran, it has unbalanced the bipolarity by introducing a further actor. If the European Union is looking for a constructive role in the Middle East process, it could well look in this direction. The EU's insistence on maintaining a 'critical dialogue' with Iran against earlier US opposition will have endowed it with the better qualifications.

Bipolarity needs now to be restored. This can be achieved as soon as Arabs and Israelis recognize that both are being brutalised by an outside force which incites and feeds on their hostility, and that they have a common and urgent cause in restoring peace. It is now clear that the most violent of recent attacks have been against the peace process itself, and to frustrate any new initiative. Both the principal litigants should learn to create a common front against those who seek to perpetuate their feud.

Another route to re-establishing the bipolarity principle was the 'two-basket' approach proposed by King Abdullah of Jordan, subsequently formalised by Crown Prince Abdullah of Saudi Arabia. This would give the entire Arab world the responsibility of guaranteeing Israel's security, in return for Israel's agreement to the setting up of an independent Palestinian state. The proposal appeared to enjoy the support of all the major actors, yet the violence which overtook it once more demonstrated the potency of the forces ranged against the peace process.[3]

Many things can still go wrong. The picture remains complex, confusing and fraught with perils. Meanwhile, even if civil strife has consistently obscured the real achievement of keeping war at bay for decades, the Middle East has become a textbook – if protracted – illustration for the application of non-belligerent techniques of peacemaking and co-operation strategy. Reconciliation requires time; but, provided there is a determination to stay the hounds of all-out war, there is still enough of that before demographic growth and depletion of water supplies threaten once again to alter the equation.

It Pays to Be Nice

Co-operation theory

Cold War sparring and the imbroglios in Korea and Vietnam began to prompt social scientists and psychologists to attempt to chart the interaction of responses made by opposing sides. They established certain behavioural patterns which are now seen to have application in fields as diverse as diplomacy and bacteriology, computer games and natural selection. From its beginnings in the 1960s, their work has been codified into what has become known as co-operation theory.

Robert Axelrod describes how a series of computer tournaments based on a situation game called 'The Prisoner's Dilemma' helped to formulate the general principles.[4] The game has two players (recalling the bipolarity principle demonstrated above), each of whom has a simple choice either to co-operate or to defect – that is to behave badly. Unilateral defection brings higher rewards, but the dilemma lies in the fact that, if both defect, their score is lower than if both had co-operated. The game is devised in such a way that, while the best score for each player individually can be obtained by defecting, if both pursue their self-interest simultaneously, they will each achieve a lower score than they could have gained with mutual co-operation.

The novel and unpredicted element in the outcome of successive tournaments was the pre-eminent performance of a 'nice' strategy named Tit-for-Tat. As its name implies, it is never the first to defect, but will then follow precisely what its opponent does. It therefore invites co-operation, will reply to provocation in kind but then immediately forgive, and continue to make it clear that it wishes to co-operate. Not only did it achieve the best ranking; it also triumphed over a series of 'mean' and highly cunning strategies pitted against it.

Further work has shown that it is also capable of converting most of those with whom it comes in contact. It can therefore establish a strongly co-operative population and, what is more, prevent them from being invaded or corrupted by meaner strategies. Axelrod has since expanded these concepts to examine not only their biological implications but also to derive an understanding of the conditions that can foster co-operation among individuals, organisations and nations. By teaching the method of reciprocity to others, he believes that it may be possible to achieve a measure of self-policing within any community.

His results are supported by similar experimental procedures conducted and described by Morton Deutsch.[5] Here the tournaments were essentially between three strategies: Turn the Other

Cheek, the Non-Punitive Deterrent and the Punitive Deterrent. In this case also, the rules encouraged the players to maximise their personal gain. As it turned out, however, this could best be achieved with a co-operative stance which enabled *both* parties to score the greatest number of points.

Notable in this series, as related by Deutsch, was the fact that, despite the emphasis on individual gain, the points earned by those attempting to exploit the Turn the Other Cheek strategy could not compare with those achieved with the Non-Punitive Deterrent strategy. In contrast to the Axelrod tests, the Deutsch tournaments were played by pairs of whom one was an 'accomplice' fully versed in the game and intent on provoking certain responses from the opponent. The 'accomplice' tried in all cases to nudge the other player into a realisation that co-operation would earn the best score. All three strategies were designed to leave the field clear for reaping the high points, which only co-operation could secure. Each of them, however, was based on provoking different reactions.

From the point of view of game theory, the most important result was that the Non-Punitive Deterrent proved far and away the most rewarding strategy for both players throughout a succession of tournaments. This strategy happens to resemble closely Axelrod's Tit-for-Tat which achieved similarly uniform and striking results.

The wider implications are explored by Deutsch in a later contribution to *Psychology and the Prevention of Nuclear War*. His prescription for the development of a co-operative framework is to change one's conception of the adversary from enemy to fellow contestant, recognising that both parties are bound together by their common interest in preventing a real conflict. This tie has then to be strengthened by enlarging the field for co-operative action, in particular through the 'provision of repeated and varied opportunities for mutually beneficial interactions'.[6] To aim at co-operation is not to be confused with appeasement. A productive stance is one that combines firmness of purpose with the willingness to co-operate for mutual benefit.

The success of co-operative strategies discovered by both Axelrod and Deutsch is found to be due to the principle that their aim is not to beat but to elicit from the other player behaviour which allows both to do well. Unlike most games, serious or playful, what matters here is not to do better than one's opponent but to aim at the best results for both.

What has been lacking in our strategic armoury is a unified theory of confrontation for war and peace. Co-operation theory may have gone some way towards supplying it. However, it still leaves a need for a working procedure for dealing with chaos and the apparently unpredictable; and with people who do not behave in accordance with our rules and react in seemingly random and unpredictable ways.

Evolutionary theory

Such refinements have more recently become possible through the development of evolutionary theory. This bases itself on a rejection of the conceptual framework of traditional science – that is of mechanical equilibrium systems – in the exploration of possible futures. Instead, it believes non-equilibrium phenomena to be greatly more significant for the understanding of the natural emergence of systems with many interacting individual elements – such as human actions and reactions over a variety of fields. Its great conceptual advance is that it takes account of 'evolutionary' factors, that is the changing of attitudes, behaviour and objectives by the participants in the system as it develops over time.

Most concepts of human behaviour recognise the initial complexity but for purposes of extrapolation are forced to rely on ever more sketchy macro-processes. Mathematical simulations have helped to overcome some of these inherent limitations by advancing the reach of micro-detail. They have broken through at least the first barrier between mechanistic functioning and the intricate processes of self-transformation, that is of evolution. They have enabled us to trace a kind of dialogue between average or normal behaviour and the non-average by amplifying the latter and observing the structural changes it induces in the system as a whole.

The advance lies in the creation of a 'possibility space' representing the characteristics and potential behaviours of individuals in this non-linear world, how they interact and modify each other through successive 'generations'. By exploration of this possibility space, certain fresh characteristics will become

124

manifest, new populations will evolve, and their differential success can be followed. The method thus provides an understanding of the central aspects of the increasing – rather than decreasing – complexities of change.

Peter Allen, the foremost exponent of evolutionary theory and its application to human activity, holds that in most human situations there is no 'problem' to be solved, nor does there exist a simple 'answer'. 'The world is just not made for simple, extreme explanations. Shades of grey, subjective judgements, post-rationalisations, multiple misunderstandings and biological motivations are what characterise the real world.' For two millennia science has sought to eliminate uncertainty; instead, the new thinking accepts uncertainty as inevitable. If this were not the case, it would mean that things were preordained. 'But', he concludes, 'creativity really exists; it is the motor of change, and the hidden dynamic that underlies the rise and fall of civilisations, peoples and regions, and evolution both encourages and feeds on invention.'[7]

Our Cartesian instincts lead us to regard the world in terms of problems to be solved. Most of the time there are no 'problems' in the simple sense, and there are many which have no 'solution'. The solutions we predict are perverted along the way by unpredictable and evolutionary interactions. Once again, the moral is that the difficulty we have in capturing enough of these variables for an accurate prediction of outcomes makes it hazardous to embark on a course of action which is irreversible – such as warfare. This is not to deny that the taking of risks, for creative and 'entrepreneurial' courses of action, is essential to progress and survival. But risk and creativity must be contained within a frame of reference which fully allows for adaptation to their own success. Diplomacy and the other measures discussed here provide such a system. Warfare does not.

Most classical theories are insufficient because they induce the belief that an adversary's behaviour will accord with their predictions. Even co-operation theory has developed its own laws of probability for predicting reactions, though it already goes further than most by following these into the realms of modified behaviour. Indeed, it shows that behaviour *can* be modified, in part through reason and in good measure through conditioning reflexes. Its game scores have done an inestimable service to both diplomacy and deterrence: they have provided a factual, rather than a solely moral framework for believing that 'it pays to be nice'. Evolutionary theory now enables us to extrapolate those mechanistic results into a more distant future, to confirm the extent to which the potential behaviours are likely to remain unperverted by evolutionary effects, and ensure more perfectly that the nice actually do inherit the earth.

Deterrence Revisited

Both theories demonstrate that a transgressor must be deterred by the belief that some punishment will be meted out. Deterrence is therefore the first line of defence. The existence of a superior force, and the clear determination to launch it, is an essential part of such a system. The principles of deterrence, which underpinned the stalemate that was the Cold War and eventually led to its resolution, could well be applied not only among superpowers but also to contests of will between unequals. It is therefore useful to look at what general rules can be derived from its earlier practice.

Undoubtedly the great achievement of deterrence has been the absence of major war. Despite lurching from challenge to challenge – from Berlin to Cuba to Hungary and Czechoslovakia – the peace held and the missiles returned to their silos. The balance of terror was maintained with sufficient skill and conviction to contain the level of all such transgressions without invoking the ultimate response.

A further achievement, barely realised until they had done their work, were the economic effects of the arms marathon. The cost of sustaining the technological leapfrogging, of maintaining a standing army of some 4 million men, of garrisoning the buffer states, assumed such a weight as ultimately to ruin the economy on which they had to feed. Not the use of arms, but the price imposed upon the Soviet Union by the Western policy of deterrence became the major instrument of its destruction. That included the future price of the intensification of the contest into areas of ever higher technology.

An important distinction needs to be made here between 'deterrence' and the 'deterrent'. As we have seen, the general principles of deterrence have a limited validity. Containment demarcates the territory we intend to protect, announces our intent to do so against all comers, and conditions our responses to any challenge. The deterrent, on the other hand, represents one of the potential means which we may use to defend ourselves; it is the final instrument, not a policy. Yet its presence and the threat of its use were implicit in every action throughout the period.

Deterrence was not, in fact, confined to direct confrontation with the Soviet Union. It was applied in many other theatres and in response to a large gamut of challenges. It delivered notable successes, for instance in Taiwan and South Korea, once the West's interest in both areas had been made manifest. Both could easily have fallen prey to their ruthless neighbours. In such cases, however, it is significant that the West had first to become involved in resisting their challenge; only once the area of interest had been defined could deterrence become operative.

The Korean conflict might well have been avoided had the application of deterrence to the area been made clear earlier. As with the Falklands in 1982 or Iraq in 1990, the ambiguity of signals contributed heavily to encouraging opportunism. US withdrawal from South Korea in 1949–50 may easily have encouraged a belief among North Koreans that it had been ceded to their sphere of influence. Thirty years later, the announcement of the withdrawal of HMS *Invincible* from the Falklands patrol was to have a similar effect on the Argentine junta.

This demonstrates again that the effectiveness of deterrence is heavily dependent on the adversary's comprehension, which in turn depends on the coherence of our own foreign-policy objectives and the clarity with which they are stated. Yet, in practice, even that has not invariably guaranteed respect for the Western position. If deterrence theory is to guide us in the future, and in very different circumstances, it is necessary to analyse the extent to which deterrence itself was responsible for these achievements. There is some evidence that they may indeed have served to hide a number of deficiencies.

One such was clearly the 1962 Cuban missile episode. The signals from Washington could not have been clearer. Yet Khrushchev was not deterred from his attempt to outwit US intelligence and introduce ballistic missiles onto the USA's doorstep. Deterrence theory is about deterrence; if people refuse to be deterred, it has no answer. In the end, Kennedy diplomacy and the uncontestable naval force which sealed the US blockade had to retrieve a situation gravely out of hand.

This was the most spectacular example of bluff during the years of deterrence. It was preceded and followed by many others. Some, certainly, were challenges to test the boundaries of deterrence; a by no means negligible number was of an irrational and uncalculated kind which might easily have led to war had deterrence theory been rigorously applied. The whole Middle Eastern theatre presented a succession of such rash challenges from 1967 onwards, despite the knowledge that both superpowers were intimately involved with one or more of the protagonists, of whom Egypt and Israel were only the most obvious.

It is the apparent inability of deterrence to tame this foolhardy element which raises doubts about the theory itself. In postulating a rational pattern of response and behaviour it has failed to take account of variations from the assumed universal behavioural norms and left us unprepared for them. In basing itself on a bipolar interaction of communications and perceptions it made no allowance for the urgency of alternative stimuli. Political action is rarely determined by foreign policy, or foreign policy alone. Add to that the difficulties of making one's key messages understood, and the extremely tenuous bases and applicability of the theory become exposed.

Without deterrence we might never have survived the communist challenge to our world. By trusting in it as our compass we probably sailed closer than anyone knew to the rocks which could have shattered us all.

Nevertheless, some lessons can well be restated, even where the final option of our nuclear deterrent does not apply. The level of tolerance must be defined for each situation – and widely advertised. Time was when such clarity might have been regarded as a threat or intimidation. Today's world is more likely to repay frankness with respect. Stability is born not only from the enjoyment of the status quo but from knowing the cost of disturbing it. Sovereign governments must be left legitimate latitude for action but, like any other member of society, they must know its boundaries. Failure to delimit these is not only to invite adventurism; it is tantamount to denying this latitude.

A tenable theory is that deterrence will result in an escalation of enmities and thereby lead to an eventual confrontation which would not otherwise have occurred. Deterrence can be seen as containment, and containment produces physical and psychological pressures which will one day need to be requited. This theory equates deterrence with hegemony. The stronger will seek to intimidate the weaker in an attempt to freeze the status quo and pursue interests elsewhere. The weaker is therefore required to give up all pretensions to active participation in determining the political environment and neighbourhood. As a result the weaker has no choice but to resist coercion and develop increasingly belligerent objectives. That is bad enough when the 'injured' party is a state with which parleys can take place. It has now become clear that similar reactions also affect individuals and groups; they lie at the root of terrorism, with which there is little possibility of communication or negotiation.

The problem becomes aggravated if, at the same time, the country feels itself enfeebled in relation to its neighbours. Regional rivalries have themselves been the flashpoints for repeated and protracted hostilities. These have in the past been distorted by superpower intervention. It sufficed for India to become friendly with the USSR to turn Pakistan into a US arsenal. The Middle East abounds with similar examples. To make matters worse, such problems almost by definition affect arch enemies. If countries feel themselves impotent to resist such pressures, their resentment will become compounded.

The result among the larger and more resourceful will then be to strive for the ultimate weapon and develop a nuclear capacity. The number of putative nuclear powers has already grown alarmingly. The examples of Iraq and South Africa have shown how readily such countries can gain access to advanced technology and fissile materials. Not only has China been a traditional supplier of these goods but there is now evidence of new trade routes through Eastern and Southern Europe. Narcotics for plutonium may become the latest form of countertrade.

Nuclear weapons do not have to be sophisticated to be effective. Nor do they need costly delivery systems; with more development, the Iraqi Scud missiles aimed so indiscriminately at Israeli

129

and Saudi centres of habitation could have carried a small nuclear device. In any event, the main purpose is not destruction, which at close range could reap its own revenge, but blackmail. Most ambitions could be achieved, most non-nuclear neighbours brought to heel, once such a weapon is brandished. That, at least, is how it seems to the nuclear aspirant.

Reality, as always, takes a different turn. Exercising blackmail means declaring one's hand. That will expose one to opprobrium and sanctions if not retribution, and entrain the fear of potential search and destroy missions against one's installations. Whether real or imaginary, such fears form part of the process of entering the big game at the nuclear table. Unfortunately, these feelings of isolation are inseparable from the act, and can too easily lead to a spiral of delinquency. That in itself is a dangerous psychological state in the possessor of a nuclear device.

One clear result of this analysis is that nations will strive to answer deterrence with deterrence, even where the initial relationship is wholly unequal. We have discussed above the shortcomings of deterrence theory; we now need to add to them this fresh danger and paradox. As in Newton's third law, so in politics: action and reaction are equal and opposite. Where a force makes itself felt, inevitably a reaction to it will grow, and continue to expand until it has reached equality. That is the process which the West itself went through when originally confronted with the Soviet challenge. It is the process which the Soviet Union followed when it witnessed the awesome spectacle of US nuclear might. It is, in effect, the process which resulted in Mutual Assured Destruction, or deterrence.

We have seen that deterrence theory is at best two-dimensional; it lacks the ability to respond, particularly to the fruits of its own success. It therefore assumes a permanent state of hostility. We have also seen how it actively contributes to keeping that hostility alive and festering. At best it drives the ambition for parity. The result must be a continuous leapfrogging of responses to challenges engendered by the policy itself.

On the other hand, there is no denying the successes it has had, most notably in shielding us from the greatest conflagration the world would have seen, and possibly the last. That very success requires from us not only an acknowledgement but also to draw from it the lessons which will enable us to use the experience to our future advantage:

1. Deterrence is vital in certain circumstances. It must, however, be more clearly formulated than has been the case. Staged objectives should be built in by which one can recognise and measure its effectiveness and outcome. An indefinite winter of armed confrontation is an insufficient objective for a civilised nation; more appropriate aims should be ready to be adopted in response to these measurements. The real aims should be foreseen and defined from the start, and policy made sufficiently pliable to accommodate them.

2. Deterrence should be regarded as an interim policy. The fort must first be sealed and held, forces marshalled and defences strengthened. The adversary must be left in no doubt about one's determination and the consequences of any transgression. But then should come stocktaking and a more subtle approach. As in evolutionary theory, the adversary's objectives and reactions must be assessed and kept under review. Military objectives should once more become subordinated to political scrutiny and control.

3. From all we have seen it is evident that deterrence needs to be accompanied by a variety of flanking policies. These will not deflect from the iron purpose of adequate defence; on the contrary, they will be aimed at making it more cost-effective, at gaining more with less. But, as in judo, they will seek to take advantage of new dynamics created by any movement on the opponent's part.

4. Deterrence is an instrument first to position oneself, then to buy time. Unless one wishes to engage in an indefinite stand-off like the Cold War, that time must be limited and used to good purpose. The ultimate aim must be the return to a stable, friendly and co-operative partnership. However venomous the initial confrontation, that final objective must never be lost from sight. Other kinds of regime seek to thrive on perpetual enmity; democracies do not.

5. As with Deutsch's Non-Punitive Deterrent, the final outcome of deterrence must therefore be not stalemate but partnership. Only that can bring a return to permanent peace and stability. But that, too, must be made a conscious policy, however remote the prospect may seem at the outset. Time and

131

again we have seen huge efforts mounted to win a contest. Then the cost in blood and specie has been squandered because, with everything concentrated on winning, no one had sought to set out constructive peace aims.

6. Peace aims can themselves become an instrument for overcoming the confrontation. There is no shortage of instances where hostilities have been accompanied by concurrent negotiations. In the case of deterrence – that is, no war – negotiations are the only way forward. It will be vital progressively to give them more substance. It will not be sufficient to 'Wait and see how you behave in future'. The rewards for good behaviour must be made visible and attainable. We must not forget that the hand of friendship regained will also be the moment of victory for us, and the vindication of all our policies – the judicious use of deterrence included.

Notes

1. The 1990 Treaty on Conventional Armed Forces in Europe (CFE) regulates the size of armed forces of 30 states in Europe. The Strategic Arms Reduction Treaty (START I) between the USA and USSR entered into force in December 1994, and START II was signed in January 1993 (see also p. 27 above).
2. Hostility towards Israel's establishment as a separate state reached a climax in the Six-Day War of 1967, launched in reaction to Arab support for guerrilla raids on Israeli territory from neighbouring states, and leading to Israel's swift occupation of the West Bank, the Old City of Jerusalem, the Gaza Strip and the Syrian Golan Heights. Resentment became further inflamed until Egyptian and Syrian forces made a surprise attack to start the Yom Kippur War of October 1973. Although much of the ground they captured was recouped by Israel, it resulted in the visit to Jerusalem by President Sadat of Egypt and the first peace talks. Peace with Egypt and several others of its neighbours did not restrain either the Palestinian guerrillas, or prevent Israel's 1982 invasion of Lebanon to attack their bases. Israel occupied southern Lebanon and created a new enemy, the Shia guerrillas; the frontier with Lebanon continues to be a war zone, despite Israel's eventual withdrawal from Lebanon. Meanwhile, sporadic insurrections in the Palestinian-controlled areas, the *intifada*, and suicide attacks inside Israel, continue with ever sharper Israeli reprisals.
3. King Abdullah of Jordan speaking to *The Times*, 10 November 2001.

4. Robert Axelrod, *The Evolution of Cooperation*, Basic Books/ HarperCollins, New York, 1984.
5. Morton Deutsch, *The Resolution of Conflict: Constructive and Destructive Processes*, Yale University Press, New Haven, CT, 1973.
6. Deutsch in Ralph K. White (ed.), *The Malignant (Spiral) Process of Hostile Interaction: Contributions to Psychology and the Prevention of Nuclear War*, New York University Press, 1986.
7. Peter M. Allen, 'Evolutionary Theory, Policy Making and Planning', *Journal of Scientific and Industrial Research*, 51, August– September, 1992.

6 Arms Control and its Technology

'The military tend to concentrate on capability.
Politicians should concentrate on intentions.'
Lord Healey CH

Superman and Supergun

Man's age-old quest has been for bigger and better weapons to
smite his enemies. Most recently, the Cold War made it imperative to maintain a potent, inventive and highly protected defence
industry. Under the threat of total war, NATO capability had
always to be at least one step ahead. The imbalance of ground
forces made this all the more vital if it were not to lead to premature use of nuclear arms. Guarding the secrecy of scientific
and technical advances was as important as the developments
themselves. All this meant an exclusive relationship between
defence ministries and establishments, contractors and intelligence services.

In the UK in peacetime, the machinery technically exists for
parliamentary and fiscal scrutiny of most aspects of this relationship. Defence expenditure, individual defence contracts, the
development of specific weapons can all be questioned and investi-
gated by the Select Committee on Defence and the Auditor-
General. The UK government now publishes explicit annual
reports on the operation of arms export controls (Annual Report
on Strategic Export Controls). Even the secret services have been
brought within the purview of Parliament. Yet detailed scrutiny
is still inhibited by rules dating back to 1939. Difficult, too, to
penetrate a fellowship, customs and loyalties which developed

over the half century of world and cold wars. The Great Game remains to outwit the questioners and to shroud the battlefield in fog.

Nowhere have the opportunities for connivance which this system offers been better illustrated than during the Scott Inquiry on exports to Iraq. Even without hint of malfeasance, the nod and the wink, the 'given to understand', the tightlipped silence and the refuge of 'national interest' (export earnings) and 'security' (we know best) can maintain a set of policies firmly hidden from casual enquiry.

The results are not only that, as once with Iraq and Indonesia, we risk continuing to arm future enemies or other innocent people until they train our guns upon us or on those whom we ultimately seek to shield. A protected system of this kind will also in time become inefficient. The result will only partly be the secret development of new weapons; it will also serve to continue the production of arms which fail to correspond to future needs. Without the stimulus of open discussion, generals and captains of industry will tend to produce equipment for never to be fought battles. The risk is that, shielded from debate, a combination of conventional thinking and commercial exigencies will carry us along an expensive and increasingly less effective path.

There are also extreme dangers to ourselves. Lack of transparency does not allow us to judge with clarity whether our defence policy is driven by perceived threats, contingencies or capability. Is it determined by the weapons available or is weapons procurement the outcome of clearly defined policy?

Perhaps budgetary stringency is coming to our aid. When budgets were trimmed and the Treasury had to insist on greater cost-effectiveness, the approach began to change. But escalations, in both cost and sophistication, are still the natural tendency. Nor are accountants qualified to judge the strategic or tactical context of new weapons systems. Yet both are too serious to be left entirely to the generals.

Research and development in the defence industry is such a long-haul business that new weapons often do not see the light of day until they are close to obsolescence. The more complex weapons become, the more common are severe time overruns in their development and production. A consequence is that we continue to produce near-surplus weaponry at the very moment when the world is already awash with the offerings of former Warsaw Pact countries and the products of new world-scale manufacturers like Brazil. In addition there are the arsenals regularly being recycled by post-conflict countries. It is therefore time to take a fresh look at how this flood of fuel for new conflicts can be controlled. In doing so, it may emerge that there is as much scope for scientific ingenuity, exports, jobs and commercial profit in producing the controls as in making the weapons themselves.

Where Are We Technically?

Even small wars provide a shop-window for the latest in modern weaponry. The Gulf War was short, but far from small. In most dramatic form it offered the world a showcase of technological progress in the artefacts of war. The bombings of Serbia and Afghanistan exhibited the strides made since then in the accuracy of delivery, at any rate by the US Air Force.

Unbeknown to most of us, the defence industry is trading its ingenuity for ever more costly development contracts. Advances leapfrog each other. Secrets rarely remain so for long, as customers become producers and 'the other side' catches up. The logic of scientific development means that, most of the time, all sides are working independently towards a similar goal. If a little espionage can accelerate matters, so much the better.

The great race is to make weapons smarter. The further from the target pilots can release their bombs, the more deliberate the manoeuvre and the greater their potential accuracy. Personnel and machine, each representing a huge and precious investment, are correspondingly safer. The further to the rear the guidance system, the better for all concerned. What goes for bombs applies equally to guns, missiles and any launching mechanism.

The greatest advance has indeed been in perfecting long-range guidance systems. Already for years past, space programmes have enabled us to witness the most astonishing feats of control across vast distances. From the moment a rocket is launched, the myriad instructions to it and its payload are totally remote. From regulating space motors, to trimming angles of flight, to activating cameras, commands from earth are faithfully executed, whether in terrestrial orbit or in circling Venus.

Nor is this a one-way traffic. The spacecraft carries out its programmed tasks, then reports back to us the results. It does so in code which we can unravel to reveal information about the environment it is researching, conditions on board, or pictures of the space views it is capturing. We can interrogate it on virtually any subject connected with its mission. It has become an intelligent, communicative and responsive robot.

We can communicate similarly with missiles. They, too, can not only be told how to behave, but also to gather information as they cruise towards their target. This they will loyally relay, and do so in a way which cannot be intercepted or read by an enemy. Missile systems with multiple warheads have the ability to transmit visual information, and soon possibly even the capacity to return to base as their hit-and-tell mission is completed.

Of much longer standing is the venerable system of the nuclear lock and key. During the more glacial years of the Cold War, we saw doomsday pictures of the US president accompanied by the black box which held that key, with all the permutations which alone would allow it to be used. Although it made the flesh creep, we felt safer for knowing that no Dr Strangelove was able to usurp the awesome finality of that power.

Where then are we when it comes to the purely technical problems involved in any attempt to control the movement and sale of arms? Given that this is likely to be by far the simplest part of such an attempt, let us begin with that question.

What we see is a complete technology for the guidance and control of weapons systems, even across unimaginable distances. We also see an uninterrupted development of systems which are ever more responsive to such guidance. To complete the control which the makers can have over their product, there is the nuclear quadruple lock which has for decades made the use of the most lethal of our weapons subject to exclusive political control.

To be sure, the smartness of the West's modern weapons systems has as its object their safer, more accurate and effective delivery. Yet precisely the same technology could be used to interdict their use by someone else. Without going into new Star Wars technology, without launching a Patriot missile after the event, a weapon can today be immobilised by a long-range command acting upon its guidance system. If as yet we are unable to gain access to the systems built outside the West, we can certainly control any guided missiles constructed within it, even if in the hands of others. As for ballistic missiles, the USA already possesses an alert system capable of sensing in less than two minutes a firing in any risk area it chooses to keep under surveillance, with the missile still in the booster zone.

What goes for sophisticated weapons can surely be adapted to the more mundane ones with which the majority of wars are fought. Even those not subject to electronic activation or guidance contain parts which are lockable. In essence, any moveable part can now be made to incorporate a locking device subject to remote control. If we can jam an enemy's radar, a little ingenuity can make us capable of jamming the breeches of that enemy's guns if illegally used. Similar technology has already arrived on our roads for civilian purposes. The humble Tracker allows police to locate a stolen car, then to override its accelerator to slow it to a crawl while its thieves are apprehended.

In the wake of the 'Star Wars' initiative, more than 50 per cent of scientific research and development in British universities and institutes of higher education was related to military ends. In the USA, half a million scientists depend on military budgets. Among all of those it should not prove too difficult to find that ingenuity.

A little ingenuity, that is, and a lot of political effort to reach an accord among the manufacturing nations. The switch to remote-instruction weaponry must clearly be near-total to be effective. Let us weigh the chances of reaching such an agreement.

Where Are We Politically?

Politically, too, we may be more advanced than we realise. For a start, under the impact of having Saddam Hussein train our own weapons and technology against us, some vigorous and multi-lateral controls have come into force. Arms control and non-proliferation are now seriously acknowledged and covered by a series of conventions applying to most forms of weapons other than, at present, small arms. Conferences on virtually all aspects of the problem are held the year round to push forward new control regimes. The UN has established a register of conventional arms imported and exported by its members, applying to most forms of weapons, even, if haltingly, small arms. And even China, the world's largest and least scrupulous supplier of fissile materials, is now a signatory to the Nuclear Non-Proliferation Treaty (NPT).

A political stocktaking reveals still more promising facts. Precisely because we all realised that a nuclear war could not be allowed to happen, we began to devise international controls to prevent it. There are the much-heralded but effective bilateral treaties for mutual reduction of nuclear arsenals and delivery capability, START II and the Anti-Ballistic Missile (ABM) Treaty. Then came the global reach of the NPT, which served as a major signpost, though the original absence of China and of France denied it some credibility. Other nuclear aspirants hesitated to sign up, at least until they were safely under the fence. Nor have all signatories chosen to respect their undertakings, as Iraq and North Korea have glaringly confirmed. And modernisation by the UK, while honouring the numerical limits, could easily flout those on capacity. Finally, to reinforce the NPT's provisions, came the Comprehensive Test Ban Treaty (CTBT). Ratified by Russia but not the USA, it nevertheless consolidates the sway of the international community over its deadliest enemy.

The latest review conference of the NPT has shown its determination that the extended treaty should now be more strictly enforced; it also declared with unprecedented firmness the intent – though undated – to destroy the nuclear powers' stockpiles of weapons. UN action invoked to deny Iraq the means to manufacture a nuclear device was already more than a signal. US and EU negotiations with North Korea have meanwhile established new avenues of diplomatic intervention. For the time being at least, the age of superpower client states is over, and international accord should be achievable to legitimise action against those who threaten to become nuclear blackmailers. Meanwhile the number of nuclear pretenders has risen to at least 14, of which up to half may already possess a rudimentary device. That shows how difficult the negotiations will be. Yet it is a pointer also to the urgency and firmness with which they will have to be undertaken.

Fortunately, our moral attitudes have advanced in line with the new hope of effective action. No longer do we need to look primarily to our own position relative to a Soviet threat, or make bizarre calculations about the price of any accommodation with the Russians. The NPT review conference showed a clear determination that the nuclear genie has to be forced back towards its bottle and access to it barred to others who will never have the life-and-death justification that the West once had.

This treaty-based consensus should be sufficient to achieve positive results. Painstaking, at times painful, they will be – for we shall be breaking yet more new ground in international law and behaviour. We shall also be compressing further the absolutism of sovereignty, making new case-law and subordinating it to the right of our neighbours and the world to live in peace and without fear of wilful destruction. Yet there is little doubt that we shall eventually succeed.

If this is possible for weapons of potential mass destruction, why not for those which are actually being used to wreak a horrendous human toll? Are those which take only hundreds of lives at a time, but do so day and night at dozens of insurrections throughout the world, in some way more legitimate? There are parallels with the debate about drugs, and the legitimising of 'soft' ones because in themselves they are less harmful. Yet it is fairly clear that, like drugs, conventional weapons are addictive to most of those who use them, and even more lethal to those at whom they are aimed.

Addictive also has been the use of arms transfers by governments as an instrument of power and influence. US arms sales rocketed after the demonstrations of the Gulf War, especially to the Middle East where Saudi Arabian purchases alone accounted for $14 billion in its immediate aftermath.[1] The UK also prides itself on the vigour of its arms sellers, who over the last decade enabled it to attain close to one-fifth of total world arms sales.[2] Russia too is embarked on a new sales drive.

All these, of course, are the arguments of human liberty, even the liberty to destroy oneself. The far more potent consideration is whether any state should have the freedom to wage war upon its neighbours – let alone to exterminate parts of its own population. More than half a century ago, the UN Charter already gave a categorical 'No'. The international community will have to decide whether the possession of offensive weapons is in itself a transgression. This will need some sensitive definitions if we are not at the same time to deny legitimate holders the means of defending themselves. The West will equally need to decide whether it wishes to continue to run the risk of becoming embroiled in local conflicts which could more easily and economically have been aborted by denying the aggressor the weapons.

Politically, then, we stand at the threshold of a world in which we need to change from a system of autonomous self-defence to one of the rule of law. The gun-carrying wild west is being tamed to respect the law of the sheriff. Maybe guns will not be outlawed, but some system of international control and licensing will need to be introduced. Individual countries such as Germany are already applying such controls on their own industries which once delivered strategic materials, equipment and technology to Iraq and Libya.[3] Coupled with the original boycott by the UK, Scandinavia and others of arms sales to both sides in the Iran–Iraq war, it is evident that some of the political foundations for an effective international system are already in place. Yet time and again we are presented with the well-worn argument that, if we do not satisfy the demand for arms, someone else will; and that it is better for us in the end to have to counter our own exported systems rather than those of China or North Korea, whose technology we do not know. This is the classic argument used wherever law enforcement is struggling to keep up, be it with arms, drugs or prostitution.

Precisely in this ambiguous area, the EU code of conduct on arms exports has posited an original building block for regulating international behaviour.[4] Based on the pioneering work of Saferworld, it stipulates that any country wishing to pick up business after another has refused an export licence must consult that country. This has put a stop to undercutting, especially in relation to countries which misuse arms, and to other undesirable practices. Given that the EU has full legal recourse, countries find themselves deterred from breaching the code. Its reach has already gone beyond EU members: discussions are in train with a view to the USA adopting similar machinery.

A further significant building block is the convention banning the use and export of landmines. Even if it has still to be signed by a number of key countries, it has already halted much of this lethal trade. The UN has now followed this up with an initiative on small arms.[5] Patently, the international climate favours global agreements to curb the 'merchants of death'. In the meantime, straight from the devil's kitchen, the new emphasis on 'interoperability' – that is the standardisation of allied systems – serves to prepare the way also for easier implementation and reduction of the variety of systems that need to be controlled.

The Policeman Will Get You

International agreements involving perceived sacrifices of the magnitude of arms control can, however, be effective only with mechanisms to enforce compliance. They require an authority which is recognised and cannot be challenged. That may be of one of two kinds: a world body with the prestige of the UN; or a more compact regional security organisation capable of exercising political sway over its members.

A world authority

Early proposals for UN intervention in arms control have invariably foundered on the need for a UN police force. If countries are to be disadvantaged in relation to the local bully who, despite all controls, amasses a formidable armoury to use against them, someone needs to protect them. If the UN is the authority to exercise that protection, the argument runs, it must have the means to underwrite the insurance. Given the ephemeral support for the UN in the past, it is not surprising that few of its members were prepared to fund such a force.

All the same it is notable that, even in the Cold War days, UN blue berets were fielded on 46 occasions, frequently for protracted periods. Such firefighting will no doubt continue to be necessary in order to separate combatants who are not hurling large armies against each other. But these are special operations, designed to prevent or defuse wars rather than to fight them. In the twenty-first century as in the last, there is little prospect of the UN becoming endowed with its own permanent fighting forces. The best we can hope for is that, as a result of Bosnia, Kosovo and other UN missions, there is a greater willingness to keep national units in reserve for UN attachments.

No matter, for, as we have seen, technology has helped to erode some of the basis of this debate. In certain circumstances it should now be possible to consider wholly technical means of interdiction, without risking lives by sending forces into an area of conflict. But there will be increasing demands made by – and to – the international community to send observers, as in Southern Lebanon, to assess a situation, recommend appropriate action, and separate the troublemakers. There will also be an abiding need to mount more forceful peacekeeping operations. That cannot be done without much preliminary monitoring to show what kind of intervention is necessary, where it needs to be projected, and what should be its precise tasks. Without clarity on such essentials, lives on all sides would be recklessly put at risk.

There are obvious parallels between the capabilities needed for peacekeeping and arms control operations. Both must rely in the first instance on an effective and comprehensive apparatus for intelligence, monitoring and analysis. Ideally, this would be placed under the control of the UN Security Council, which would establish precise guidelines for its use. In this way it could be made to operate almost autonomously, without prior Great Power debates or bargaining. It could become operative without delay, before a situation had become seriously inflamed and large-scale violence erupted. The mechanism for all this already exists in the Military Staff Committee. As has been argued in Chapter 4, all that is needed is for it to be activated. On the other hand, the intelligence function is the one most jealously guarded by each of the Permanent Five. Even if they gave their support for a UN capability, they would still resist sharing with it their own intelligence.

For the time being, the Secretary-General's new strategic planning unit might begin to show how effectively something akin to a UN analysis capacity can be made to operate and be brought to bear on issues of arms control. It may not be entrusted with military intelligence, but it does possess two quite potent intelligence networks of its own: the IAEA for combating nuclear proliferation, and the hundreds of NGOs which loyally report to it and seek its intervention all over the world against other transgressions.

A satisfactory set of guidelines and doctrines for peacekeeping operations has yet to evolve. It is predictable that this will happen sooner rather than later, now that it is recognised that – in the absence of superpower provocation – the world's security risks *can* remain localised. The most common occurrences – ethnic rivalries, local aggrandisement, and the attempt to acquire nuclear devices – *are* now containable and *can* mostly be dealt with without the fear of escalation. The fact that crisis management has become politically possible means that it is also closer to becoming a physical probability.

Regional authority

Policing and peacekeeping actions should not, however, be confined to the UN system. The 1990 Paris Charter already gave the Organisation for Security and Co-operation in Europe (OSCE) a role in mediation and prevention of conflict. The need for these at the European level is well recognised. The break-up of Yugoslavia in the unrest which simmered in post-totalitarian Eastern Europe has shown the paucity of our existing instruments. That the OSCE is destined progressively to have further peacekeeping responsibilities thrust upon it is confirmed by its 1999 Charter for European Security which provides for the strengthening of its operational capacities in conflict prevention, crisis management, peacekeeping and post-conflict rehabilitation.

The actual enforcement part may be delegated to NATO or the UN, but the OSCE will not for long escape the need to make the political decisions. Whether the actual forces come from NATO or the EU's new rapid reaction force, the overall political command must in the shortest possible time be confided to an organisation in which East and West have an equal voice. The necessity for this was demonstrated when OSCE monitors in Kosovo had to be withdrawn, with tragic consequences, to enable the bombing of Serbia to begin. In any event, the so-called Platform for Co-operative Security appended to the 1999 Charter specifically sets out arrangements for closer ties between OSCE and other international institutions such as NATO, the EU and the UN.

The OSCE formula may in time become the pattern for other regional security organisations. The single most important criterion for such bodies is that everyone within the region should belong to them. Only in that way can they be regarded as even-handed collaborative enterprises, aimed not at those who remain outside but at the common security. The fact that every country in Europe, including all those of the former Soviet Union, and those of North America which have clear power roles in Europe, belong to the OSCE endows it with a political uniqueness. East European membership may also have lent it a more realistic appreciation of what lies within its capabilities.

The long-defunct defence organisations for the Near East, South-East Asia and the Pacific were once thought to be the pillars on which regional security would rest.[6] But their very nature – exclusive, adversarial and limited to those intent on ensuring their defence rather than their common security – made them decay long before the threat which had given rise to them. Clearly, the membership of regional security organisations must be of broadly like-minded states. Yet – as in ASEAN – it is better that a potential rogue should be in rather than out, and subject to the pressures of fellow members. Ignoring this simple truth proved the downfall of the old League of Nations.

The problems of conflict resolution through such bodies remain formidable. Their ability to persuade and influence is limited: politically, because of inhibitions (not always logical) regarding territorial integrity and, economically, because the resources are lacking to offer *post-bellum* aid and investment. On human rights issues they face a further paradox: countries which already have a democratic system offer safeguards to their minorities; those that do not, are being asked to provide them with privileges which are denied to the majority. Solutions for the latter will take much longer than for the former, so that expectations must be lowered and objectives made more realistic.

Naturally, the world harbours bad people as well as good, individuals subject neither to reason nor moral suasion. After all, it is they who make such protective groupings necessary. Yet they usually have few scruples about subscribing to the principles of membership, even if cynically determined to flout them. If such a signature seems of little practical value, it nevertheless legitimises subsequent sanctions against them. And, with the perennial suspicions between the rich and the poor world, it exposes them to peer pressures more effective than those from Western capitals.

We may thus envisage a system of global and regional security organisations guided, inspired and legitimised by the UN system. Though inevitably chequered in quality and performance, within them will grow up the practice and case-law of international policing. Each case will, of course, be different and require a different response. Nevertheless, there will develop a codex to govern the routines of monitoring and surveillance, the forms of intervention, the practical systems of implementation, and the doctrines according to which such actions are pursued. The world will not necessarily be a more perfect place but, as with the bobby on the beat, we shall all be able to sleep rather more soundly.

My Brother's Keeper

Given that both the technical and the political means exist for making weapons not only smarter but more obedient, how should we now proceed?

First, the technical means have to be perfected. With smart weapons there is little problem. They are in any event subject to guidance, and hence control, by remotely activated electronic commands. Whether such commands are 'Do' or 'Don't', whether they originate from the launcher or elsewhere, is of relatively little consequence. If today's traffic police can track and immobilise stolen vehicles from some distance (see Chapter 7), and the USA is able to monitor ballistic missile launches thousands of miles away, the relative technology is no longer over the horizon.

More demanding will be to make presently unguided weapons equally responsive to such commands. Electronics are, of course, playing an ever-increasing role in both ground and naval artillery, in torpedo and missile launchers, tanks and armoured vehicles, in short in anything but the crudest hand-held weapons. But more is clearly needed to make them truly obedient.

In particular we shall need three things. One is a mechanism to locate the piece throughout its active life, so that the progress of weapons across frontiers can be accurately monitored. A major problem currently bedevilling arms control is that of re-export from a legitimate buyer to an unauthorised user. No control system which ignores this problem can be complete. However, it must also be able to spot the dispositions, and in particular new concentrations of such heavy armaments.

We live in an age where the science of precision locating has advanced dramatically. Whether we need to track an aberrant space vehicle over 5,000 miles with laser technology, or monitor a released felon with electronic tagging, our instruments are equal and ready for the task. Across space, we can even listen to the consequences of the original cosmic Big Bang, to sounds emitted 10 billion years ago. What chance does a little artillery piece on an African border have of escaping our detection, if properly designed?

The second mechanism we need is one which will not only reveal its location but be receptive to command. In the event of its falling into unauthorised hands, or of its illegitimate use, we must be able to find it *and* immobilise it. That suggests a 'black box' which is an integral part of the weapon and cannot be over-ridden or dismantled without incapacitating it for good. At the simplest level, we all know what happens when our power steering fails or the gearbox gives up – and that despite the best automotive practice to avoid our being stranded.

A track-and-immobilise technology will be basic to future arms control. We know better than to rely simply upon human nature and observance of international agreements. Even the legitimate arms trade has a huge volume and yields extraordinarily high profits. But, as with drugs, the shadier the customer, the greater the margin. It would be against all reason and experience to suggest that such traffic could be signed out of existence.

The third requirement is a psychological conversion. Objections will be raised that making arms subject to detection, location and immobilisation will entail enormous risks also to our own weaponry. This kinship with the arguments of the US gun lobby shows that we are still at an early stage of recognising the need for a global agreement on arms control. But it also underlines the same need progressively to institute such controls.

Moreover, the export of defence equipment forms a vital part of the trade balance of the major industrialised countries. Non-traditional suppliers like Brazil and South Africa, for years already China and the Czech Republic, have been sharing the feast. To these have now been added the huge surpluses of the former Warsaw Pact arsenals, driven by the desperate need to earn foreign currency. Governments know that their balance of payments would plummet, their own expenditure rise steeply without foreign buyers sharing the cost, and a potent foreign-policy instrument be lost. Since the demise of the Cold War, defence budgets have been trimmed drastically, and industries and the employment they provide are in any event coming under strain.

Policies are not made on moral grounds but on political. Morality may well provide the stimulus for change, and its lobbyists some political motivation. But employment and economic imperatives will first need to be requited. While job security continues to be equated with national security, few politicians or governments will grasp the nettle. Morality will be better served in pressing a functional approach, a bargain to satisfy the major political interests as much as its own followers.

Yet there are signs that the parameters for the UK would be far short of disastrous. The International Institute for Strategic Studies (IISS) has calculated that the £5 billion of UK arms exports in 1998 in fact represented no more than 0.6 per cent of GDP.[7] Other studies conclude that a reduction of one-third in those exports would be equivalent to a maximum of 40,000 jobs. This might be the negative, but hardly dramatic result of a truly ethical foreign policy which denies weapons to customers such as Indonesia, Pakistan and Zimbabwe. On the positive side, the same studies calculate possible savings of £76 million on export credit guarantees, buyers' incentives and the officialdom involved. And the EU's KONVER programme, created in 1993 to help regions across the EU dependent on the defence sector, would help manufacturers with the costs of converting their factories to civilian production. Even without that aid, an estimated 40,000 job losses should be seen on the scale of the 22,000 new jobs created by the Airbus super-jumbo, the A-3XX.

Can we then find such an arms control bargain internationally, at the same time as reducing for ourselves the risks to which continued warfare exposes us? Can we banish major offensive warfare from much of the globe as effectively as we have done in most of Europe – and without bankrupting ourselves in the process? Most crucially, can we strike that bargain not only domestically but so as to bind to it all other major arms exporters?

The answer should be a resounding 'Yes'. There is no immediate reason to cease the manufacture of arms; indeed, there is a pressing need for a greater research and development effort to devise foolproof track-and-immobilise devices and techniques. There is still a large-scale demand for arms for legitimate uses around the world. In due course, the type of weapons produced will adapt itself to their new uses. Less will be offensive, more of them adapted to policing tasks. But both manufacture and exports can continue.

The main prerequisites for combining economic needs with a safer world will be that all weapons beyond a certain threshold carry an integrally built-in 'black box', and that an enforceable international agreement binds all manufacturers to ensure this.

What are the prospects of achieving such a bargain? Technically, as we have seen, few obstacles remain. Perhaps the most serious is to ensure that the black box cannot be dismantled or bypassed. Here technology has already shown the way with a missile which sends signals back to its manufacturer if anyone tampers with the warhead. Politically, too, we have seen that the climate is as propitious as it has ever been. Given a good basis for ensuring the support of the economic interests, a political accord could be negotiated and ratified. As with the treaties on nuclear non-proliferation and landmines, not all producer countries – and certainly not all consumer countries – might initially join. But experience shows that the existence of such a pact will in time generate pressures for more and more of them to do so.

A crucial factor to make the prospect of negotiations sufficiently realistic is the question of enforcement and the enforcer. Who will agree the standards to be imposed on manufacturers? Who will ensure that manufacturers observe their obligations? What sanctions will the authority have to compel compliance? Who will be my brother's keeper? The halting progress of efforts even to make US handguns safer and obedient only to the owner's hand-print shows how protracted such innovation on the international level will be. Yet there is enough political consensus, and enough relevant technological advance, to set the process in motion.

The faults and weaknesses of the UN system, and its ability to carry additional burdens, have already been discussed. It is nevertheless self-evident that all these authorities will need to reside in the UN Security Council, as the highest instance in today's relations between states. It may be debatable through which organs it may most effectively carry out these new duties. The non-proliferation treaty relies to a large extent on the technical capacity of the IAEA. A similarly qualified mechanism will be essential for monitoring purposes, and the spotting and proving of transgressions; but any such mechanism needs to be given sharper teeth from the outset.

The effectiveness of arms control agreements depends heavily upon the quality of intelligence and verification capable of being applied at each level, from manufacturers to dealers to arms users in the field. Modern surveillance and monitoring techniques are already of a sensitivity and penetration wholly equal to the task. Satellite technology and imagery provide visibility to objects a few metres square, both on and below the surface. The intelligence network being built to combat organised crime in all its emanations is equally penetrating. All these systems rely on intelligence-gathering techniques beyond the reach of most malfeasants. They are reinforced by the power of the Internet in monitoring and verification of arms control breaches, especially in remote areas. Perhaps the only vagary lies in interpreting the data and in making the political decision whether to use or ignore it – and whether those with ownership of the intelligence are prepared to share it.

A second set of responsibilities – perhaps even more crucial – must therefore centre on the surveillance of arms movements and the use of the immobilisation key in the event of illegitimate use. Both functions must be vested in an organisation of un-challengeable standing and authority. Here again, the UN Security Council is the only practical candidate, even if it subcontracts some of these functions to regional security bodies as suggested earlier. Moreover, having built up a technical capacity for monitoring treaty observance, it will be logical to use the same mechanism for enforcement of its aims. The combination of political functions – seeking rectification through persuasion and mediation – with the technical ability for undisputed monitoring and enforcement is a typical UN task.

Nor should an international compact be confined to heavy weapons. Small arms today account for 90 per cent of victims of conflict worldwide.[8] The UN, in association with governments and dedicated NGOs, has already gone a long way towards defining the problem and the elements of possible solutions. Here also, the apparent improbability of ever being able to outlaw or control the trade and possession of weapons should not lead to despair making us impotent to take the obvious first steps.

Some important ones have indeed already been taken. Building upon the success of stilling the Tuareg rebellion in Mali, peaceably and with the agreed destruction of thousands of light weapons, the Economic Community of West African States (ECOWAS) established a three-year moratorium on the import, export and manufacture of small arms in the region.[9] Even if limited in time and the capacity to monitor, this is a brave step for an area plagued by recurring civil wars in Liberia, Sierra Leone and unrest elsewhere. Another beacon was the Southern Africa Action Programme to tackle illicit arms trafficking, strengthen controls on legally held arms, and remove arms from society. This was followed by the launch of the International Action Network on Small Arms, a campaigning network similar to the operation which succeeded in outlawing landmines.[10]

Similar initiatives have been taken in Eastern Africa and the Horn, an area equally threatened by the proliferation of small arms. Governments and NGOs are now co-operating on a programme agreed by the 2001 UN International Conference on Small Arms.

Once formalised, the carrying out of the actual arms control tasks should involve activating the Security Council's Military Staff Committee. Although there was discussion of making it operational during the Gulf War and again for the Bosnian operations, it has never met other than informally. Despite resistance to giving it a true commanding role, it remains a potential which might well be given authority for overseeing enforcement operations under an arms control treaty. Its convocation as well as its powers and remit in action would need to be strictly defined as part of such a treaty.

All this is technically, politically and even economically feasible in the twenty-first century. Yet we would do wrong to rely wholly on such means to the exclusion of all forms of direct action. As discussed in previous chapters, there are more potent and immediate ways in which we must ensure our security and self-protection, and curb the power of putative foes to embroil us in damaging military action. Yet at the same time we cannot delay the bid for international consensus to eliminate their weapons capability.

Sending the Wrong Signals

In building up any international system it is vital to establish that it is in everyone's interest. Failure to do so will lead to lack of co-operation and future defections.

It is clearly the developing world which would automatically feel itself to be the loser in a new arms control arrangement. Countries here can also count the number of potential aggressors left in the world, and be legitimately concerned about their own security. Many of them are also today's best arms customers. Of elementary importance therefore is to avoid sending the wrong signals to them.

Here, too, there is scope for a grand bargain. A UNDP Human Development Report estimated that Third World countries could save US$50 billion annually and double their spending on human priority areas with no extra aid.[11] Most of that could come from cuts in military spending, which absorbs more than their combined expenditures on basic education, primary healthcare, rural water supply, family planning, nutrition and social security. All the latter are keys not just to human welfare but to economic growth as such. No doubt the Middle East until recently could afford to spend 10 per cent of its GDP on arms, even if it represented three times the volume of World Bank lending over the same period. But the generality of developing countries is too impoverished for such luxuriant waste.

Yet this perverse order of priorities has long been reflected in the make-up of the world's aid programmes. Until recent times, they have been top-heavy with military aid and ambitious industrial and infrastructure projects. Basic human needs limped behind with a mere 8 per cent. It is tempting to indulge in 'if only' arithmetic, but it stands to reason that even a modest cut in the former category would produce a quite disproportionate multiplier effect in the second. Since then, increasing emphasis on poverty reduction, civil society and good governance (a euphemism for eliminating the corruption often associated with military contracts) has brought about a wholesome shift. Belated World Bank attention to the security environment is consolidating the correction.

The UNDP has effectively outlined the essence of the grand bargain: aid programmes to individual countries should be tied to cuts in military spending, as well as to positive changes in the social and political environment. Yet military aid continues to be a way of bestowing special favours and supporting regimes considered as providing 'stability'. The fact that those most hungry for weaponry are those most prone to collapse from the worms of corruption is generally recognised only after natural justice has done its slow but devastating work.

A significant portion of aid receipts is either in the form of arms or diverted to buy them. In the industrial countries this creates useful export revenues, industrial activity, national income and the ability to continue the aid flows. The recipient government can use the arms to build up a military elite, consolidate its own position, extend its domination over recalcitrant populations, and in the end to devastate its own country or its neighbours. Often the result is famine, which causes more aid to flow, and thus more money to be recycled in this immoral but inextricable symbiosis with the world of the rich. The government of Sudan, through an arbitrary exchange rate applied to emergency relief, succeeded in syphoning off one-third of voluntary humanitarian aid for its own purposes, including the prosecution of a civil war which was at the root of the emergency.

Happily, the abandonment of authoritarian doctrines and moves to political pluralism in much of the Third World, especially in Africa, have created a new climate of co-operation with the West. They have also loosened the grip of leaders who needed well-equipped armed forces to consolidate their power base. The moment is therefore historically favourable for initiating discussions on even so sensitive a subject as mutual respect for arms control.

If it now seems feasible to introduce an effective and progressively global arms control system, then the practical bases exist also for the grand bargain with the developing world. Greater security can be guaranteed even to the weakest through Security Council monitoring and enforcement procedures. This will allow some part of military aid to be switched to human priorities and compliant governments to be appropriately rewarded. For that trust to be created, however, it may be necessary to demonstrate that the large powers are not selective in their prosecution of human rights violations. They will need to vote the UN the means to intervene in a Rwanda as vigorously as in a Kosovo. Not only the donors themselves, but also the World Bank, the IMF, UNDP and others intimately involved in monitoring the economies of developing countries must become identified with this switch of priorities.

In part such a bargain has already been tested. At the same time as the cancelling of the debts of the world's poorest countries was announced by the Chancellor (11 January 2000), the UK announced a ban on export credits to 63 countries for 'unproductive' projects that do not help their development. This was explicitly to ensure that countries spend their debt relief on economic and social development rather than arms.

Politically, industrial countries can continue their special relationships. Indeed, they will be able to give greater substance to them, for the extending of protection in a more secure world can allow concentration on economic rather than military support, thus helping to remove some root causes of conflict. Alliances for progress will become possible in a true sense, not as an elegant circumlocution for client states. As a mark of trust – perhaps the New Partnership for African Development (NEPAD) – military assistance can still occupy an honourable place within these.

Thus the acceptance of a truly international arms control regime can at last bring us to a North–South relationship for mutual progress rather than mutual impoverishment.

Or Doing What We've Always Done

An anonymous sage once cautioned: 'If you do what you've always done, you get what you've always gotten.' Whether that is war or the means of war through proliferation, his homely words express a profound truth. If, for instance, the West pursues the Cold War formula of incremental arms development, it may well succeed this time in laying waste its own economies as it once did the economy of the Soviet Union. This risk is amply demonstrated by the new doctrines of counter-proliferation, to which belongs the proposed US national missile defence.

Counter-proliferation is the fielding of systems to counteract the growth of weapons of mass destruction (WMDs) elsewhere. This requires ground-based passive systems good at forward listening and surveillance as well as capable of launching interceptor vehicles at a moment's notice. The costs of the last generation of these can be read from US attempts to equip the Gulf Co-operation Council countries with a regional missile defence shield. Including all their auxiliaries such as instantaneous read-out ground stations to receive data transmitted from US intelligence sources, their procurement cost is estimated conservatively at $13 billion.[12] The final cost could be much higher, if training, maintenance and other operating expenditures are counted. And all this is additional to conventional equipment, none of which it substitutes.

Over the past five years the USA itself has already devoted $17 billion to development of a ballistic missile defence and is adding a further $7.8 billion a year in 2002 and 2003.[13] Clearly the hope is that some of these costs can be recouped either from sales or from contributions by countries benefiting from the protection of systems installed by the USA. However, even the once oil-rich Gulf states, which have habitually spent huge sums on arms, have declined to co-operate. The moral is that the costs have outstripped the capacity of even the traditional buyers of sophisticated defence systems. The ratchet effect of being tied – as NATO is too – to the best that US laboratories can produce means that the bills are escalating all the time. In addition, the interoperability requirement means that one simply has to keep up with Uncle Sam and bear not only the initial costs but those of periodic upgrading or renewal.

If the USA's friends and customers are wise, they will look to cheaper means to counter proliferation of WMDs and conventional weapons, such as those which arms control and all the other initiatives outlined here can offer. This does not mean leaving themselves defenceless in the meantime. Many of the systems offered and debated by Americans do not yet exist, other than in basic or experimental form. Certainly the enormously complex technology on which a national missile defence would be based has still to prove itself. For many, the same applies to the USA's basic and little-shared assessment of the threat itself. If arms control agreements need time, so too will missile defence.

In sum, arms control is desirable not purely on moral and pious grounds. Its technology is simpler and at least as advanced as that of ultra-modern defence systems and its costs incomparably less. Lastly, the existing array of multilateral and global treaties has already pioneered the political processes. All that is now required is for us to recognise where our self-interest lies, and how close at hand it can be grasped. By breaking out of the mould, we can avoid getting what we've always gotten.

Today we have global regimes for arms control like the Chemical Warfare Convention, the Biological Weapons Convention, the Missile Technology Control Regime, the Nuclear Non-Proliferation Treaty, the Comprehensive Test Ban Treaty, the Landmines Convention and the UN Action Programme on Small Arms; we have semi-voluntary arrangements like the UN Register of Conventional Arms Transfers; we have regional initiatives such as the EU Code and the wider Wassenaar agreement by 33 supplier countries for disclosure of completed arms deliveries, transfers of dual-use goods and technologies and of licences denied; and we have the Nuclear Free Zone Treaty for South-East Asia, as well as voluntary agreements like the initiatives on light weapons in West and Southern Africa. Some of these are binding international treaty commitments, others – like the latest 80-nation Ballistic Missile Code of Conduct – as yet voluntary expressions of intent. The permanent UN Conference on Disarmament is so busy on these and a host of others that it is almost log-jammed. Why should all this not fill us with the confidence to go even further? Real security lies not in untried and permeable defence systems but ultimately in arms control, negotiation and conflict prevention.

Notes

1. Michael T. Klare, 'Lessons of the Gulf', *The Nation*, Vol. 252, 1991.
2. IISS, *The Military Balance 2000/2001*, IISS/Oxford University Press, London, 2000.
3. The Wassenaar Agreement on Export Controls for Conventional

Arms and Dual-Use Technologies and Munitions List, Vienna, 1996.

4. The European Code of Conduct on the Arms Trade 1998 provides detailed export criteria to guide EU member states on the granting of export licences. European Union, Brussels, 1998.

5. Protocols on Prohibitions or Restrictions on the use of Mines, Booby-Traps and other Devices, adopted in Geneva on 3 May 1996 by the States Parties to the Convention on Prohibitions or Restrictions on the Use of Certain Conventional Weapons which may be deemed to be Excessively Injurious or to have Indiscriminate Effects, concluded on 10 October 1980. This was followed up by the July 2001 Conference on the Illicit Trade in Small Arms and Light Weapons in All its Aspects.

6. The 1955 Baghdad Pact between Iraq, Turkey, Britain, Pakistan and Iran was crippled by the coup in Iraq in 1958; the 1954 South East Asia Treaty Organisation (SEATO), linking the US, France, Britain, Australia, New Zealand, Thailand, Pakistan and the Philippines, became defunct after the end of the Vietnam War in 1975; and the 1951 ANZUS Treaty for defence security between Australia, New Zealand and the USA, which still subsists with symbolic significance.

7. Rupert Cornwell, 'A Farewell To Arms Exports Would Actually Save Us Money', *Independent on Sunday*, 23 January 2000.

8. *Saferworld Update*, Summer 1999, p. 4.

9. *Saferworld Update*, Winter 1999, p. 7, 'West Africa Acts to Tackle Arms Flows'.

10. 'Towards Implementation of the Southern Africa Regional Action Programme on Light Arms and Illicit Trafficking', *Saferworld ISS*, London, September 1999. 'Action to Tackle Small Arms in the Horn of Africa', Andrew McLean, *Saferworld Focus*, London, July 2000. 'Small Arms Conference concludes with consensus adoption of Action Programme', UN Press Release DC/2795, 21 July 2001.

11. UNDP, *Human Development Report*, UNDP, New York, 1991.

12. James R. Holmes and Toshi Yoshihara, 'The Puzzling Failure of America's Counter-Proliferation Policy in the Middle East', *Strategic Review*, Fall 1999, p. 42.

13. Ibid., p. 43.

7 War Without Death

'We need weapons to handle what is in effect a giant hostage crisis.'
British electronics expert on operations in Bosnia[1]

The Dilemma of Force

The need to intervene in essentially civil wars has posed a dilemma which is at once moral, political and excruciatingly practical. Natural instinct and long tradition argue that force must be met with force. Yet force against whom? Civil conflict lacks the clarity of friend and foe. In the Balkans, Peter Scholl-Latour summed it up in the words: 'There are no good guys and bad guys, only the strong and the weak. Lord have mercy on the weak.'[2]

In any event, our aim in operations other than war is only rarely to help one side achieve victory over the other. It is to restore peace and put an end to bloodshed and brutality. The question 'Am I my brother's keeper?' is being answered in the affirmative in more and more distant places. The reach of communications and television cameras is inexorably extending the world of suffering which makes its mute appeal for our aid. Mercifully, that appeal still finds an immediate response, even where the suffering is clearly self-induced. Suddenly there is a wide consensus that 'something must be done'.

But what? Often the real problem is neither lack of Western resolve, nor of blinding anger, but the absence of appropriate means of response. Even the West's light and mobile rapid reaction forces are equipped with weapons to be deployed against a hostile front line. They are too cumbersome, destructive and inaccurate to deal with 'enemy' pockets within a civilian population. To fight in conditions of civil disorder, the only answer would be hand-to-hand combat.

What *is* the West's real objective? Neither to roll back a front line, nor to bomb hostile populations into submission: it is simple pacification, without taking sides. For that it needs means of immobilising peacebreakers in hundreds of small locations, wherever they dare violate a ceasefire. Destructive weapons will not do: the need is for weapons with superior power which are non-lethal. Yet much of the West's armoury consists of scaled-down relics of Cold War doctrines of maximum destruction. As usual, the West is girded to fight the last war, if not the one before.

Bosnia and Somalia showed that peacekeepers make easy hostages, to be humiliated, killed as a warning against the use of superior force, or as instruments for political blackmail. Such personnel need to protect themselves with tools which are more effective than the firepower ranged against them. Not only must those tools avoid their becoming combatants; for the most urgent and practical reasons they must also be superior to those of the attackers.

Intervention for non-aggressive purposes requires a whole new generation of *disabling* technologies, to interdict and arrest, but not to kill or maim. Research on these was barely taken seriously until the early 1990s. Unless it is, Western politicians and commanders will continue to contemplate the new breed of conflict without adequate and appropriate resources. Such research may be costly, but its results will be infinitely more cost-effective – politically, militarily and most especially in terms of lives.

The real dilemma is that the most heavily armed and secure nations, the most powerful alliance the world has ever seen, often stands helpless before a few thousand raging and pillaging brigands. Few as yet seem prepared to face the truth that all the developed world's costly and sophisticated materiel is of no avail and that currently it stands naked before such acts. The very armoury which was to protect the West from its own bitter enemies has lulled it into a false sense of security. Real power will continue to be elusive until the West humbles its sights and exchanges its superguns for the tools of crowd control.

The New Tasks

Bosnia, Kosovo and Macedonia – let alone terrorism – were not and are not the Gulf. There was no front line, such as the Kuwaiti border. Until a later stage, there were no strategic targets, open and accessible to low-level precision bombing. In a civil war there is mostly no room for missiles fired from offshore vessels. Worst of all, there is no identifiable 'enemy', except whoever lobs the latest shell from a mountain emplacement.

The 28-nation armada assembled to humble Iraq lies in the past. Early in Bosnia and again over Kosovo, the West shook with fury on the brink, not knowing what action to take. In Bosnia, air strikes became valid only after a front line had been created through the sudden Croat breakout from the Krajina hinterland. In Kosovo, air strikes were effective against Serb armour only after the Kosova Liberation Army (KLA) had launched its major offensive and forced the Serbs to uncover and mass their armour and mechanised forces. Meanwhile, with all the fearsome might of the USA and the rest of NATO, the frustration and indecision gnawed at the vitals of the alliance as much as at our consciences.

The truth is that, aside from a handful of special forces, the West has few effective means of dealing with 'the enemy within'. All its arsenals are designed to counter an assault and roll back a front line. The one-time 'flexible response' was a nice gradation whose very gentlest level would still be enough to flatten most of the Balkans within 24 hours. Its successor doctrine, rapid reaction, will soon involve a super-commando operation of up to 60,000 personnel to quell breaches of the peace. Had a rapid reaction force been deployed in time in Kuwait, it might have served to prevent the Iraqi invasion. Despite the valour of its serving soldiers, its actual role today remains ambiguous.

The bitter fact is that barely a single weapon the West has is appropriate to the tasks in Bosnia and Kosovo and in similar civil conflicts. All of them are designed to kill and, lacking an extensive battlefield, overkill. Part of the West's frustration is that it wants to strike out at murder and treachery; but it also knows that the moment it kills it becomes itself part of the conflict. By then it will have exchanged the status of international arbiter for that of combatant. Worse, it forfeits the option either to withdraw or pursue its goals by more rational means as the political background inevitably changes. The West can no longer take advantage of evolutionary developments in the conflict.

In any event, there is now extreme reluctance to commit ground forces to peace enforcement missions. It follows that most uses of offensive force are giving way to post hoc peacekeeping missions. This circumstance led directly to the dubious decision to launch the air strikes on Serbia rather than immediately to intervene where the atrocities were being committed.

The West's real objective is not vengeance but pacification. For that it does not need to kill, any more than the British army did in Northern Ireland or, come to that, during the bloodiest battles in Brixton or the miners' strike. The weapons for that have to be non-lethal, yet restraining or temporarily disabling. As tear-gas is to the riot squad, so a new generation of longer-range, longer-lasting disabling devices must in future be available to the peacekeepers.

Current research on such devices, mainly in the USA and to some extent in the UK and Russia, is still concentrated on countering heavy and sophisticated enemy equipment: laser guns to destroy a tank's optical equipment or dazzle pilots of low-flying aircraft, microwave projectiles to disrupt sophisticated military communications, and similar mechanisms are aimed at putting adversaries and their equipment out of action, albeit *before* they have time to use it.

Closer to the needs of operations in proximity of civilian populations is the development of ways to harness sound, either as acoustic 'bullets' or at low frequencies to cause nausea and disorientation among snipers or hostile pockets, or a variety of basically simple substances to immobilise materiel or disable people.

Some of these devices are already available for current actions. Several have seen service in Vietnam, Somalia and probably Northern Ireland. The carbon-fibre bomb was used to great applause to halt Serbian generating capacity without destroying it. Time will, however, be required to develop the rest, if only because commanders will be wary to rely on them without adequate field testing and training of personnel in both their use and counter-measures should they be captured. What is necessary now is the recognition that such devices are indispensable to the conflicts in which the West is likely to continue to be called upon to act, and urgently to pursue their development.

Non-Lethal Weapons

The devices that have been conceived and found their way to the drawing board are either ultra-high-tech or the imaginative transposition of banal substances. As a group, they tend to remind one of the prescient fantasy world of Jules Verne; and rightly so, since some are actually derived from the early science-fiction products of Janet and Chris Morris. As one-time anti-war campaigners, they began to develop a concept of 'containment of barbarism' as a tool to control disruptive behaviour. This led them to work on applying new technologies which would restrain rather than kill. Many of their devices – and those developed in parallel – have shown promise of being operable, provided their targeting can be accurate and their side-effects controlled. Some of those already in or close to possible deployment are described below. Their full development will take time but, as often happens, it may begin to leapfrog or find unexpected shortcuts, the more so if they are seen also to have a commercial potential.

Tracking devices

Some tracking devices are already with us. The Automobile Association is actively marketing Tracker (based on the US Lolack), a stolen-vehicle location system. Described as 'an arresting idea', it is being operated in collaboration with all Britain's mainland police forces. With the aid of special tracking computers, police are able to read signals emitted by the Tracker radio device fitted to the car, establish its direction of travel and proximity and home in on it. The device itself remains concealed so effectively that vehicles can even carry stickers to warn off intending thieves. If mounted on a helicopter, the detection unit achieves a range of up to 30 kilometres. In the USA, average recovery time is down to two hours.

A similar development is Demon Scan, which allows police both to locate the car and to manipulate its equipment as they close in. From a distance of 500 metres they are able to operate the vehicle by remote control, ordering it to flash its lights, sound its horn and override its accelerator to slow it to a crawl. Before long it will be feasible to achieve the same effect with a signal from a satellite.

Development can be very fast once a commercial incentive is perceived. One of the secret technologies of the Gulf War was the Global Positioning System (GPS). It enabled the smart bombs to find their targets and served as an identification beacon for much of the heavy equipment to be attacked. Now you can buy it to install in your four-wheel drive, to navigate cross country or keep pace with other vehicles. The same process has propelled into the public domain the once top-secret US military project ARPANet (the forerunner of the Internet), which created a network of sensitive computer installations that could withstand a nuclear attack on one or more of its centres. It is now better known as the Internet and is used by hundreds of millions of people the world over.

Tracking technology can be even more sophisticated as well as uncannily swift and accurate. Beady Eye is able to track moving bullets and trace their source. It does so while the bullet is still in the air, by means of a sensor attached to a rifle and a back-pack-sized computer that can retrace the bullet's path within seconds. A successor to the British Army's CLARIBEL, it is an obvious tool for flushing out snipers and removing one of the main hazards to civilian populations.

Electronic interference technology

The first developments in this area have been laser guns to destroy optical navigation or guidance equipment, upon which virtually all modern weapons systems rely. Most of these devices are still undergoing tests. Other types are intended to act directly upon the human operator. Already a decade ago there were reports that several Royal Navy ships were carrying laser guns to dazzle pilots of low-flying aircraft to abort attacks.[3] Although there were no instances of their actual use, fears of blinding the attacker caused the guns to be withheld.

Much more dramatic are 'Magic Bullets', a term used by Senator Sam Nunn when he proposed their use in former Yugoslavia as long ago as 1992. These can take the form of relatively low-intensity acoustic devices, such as acoustic bullets producing an impact similar to being hit by a baseball and now being perfected for in-flight security; microwave projectiles to disrupt military communications; or 'Poobah's Party', which short-circuits switching gear and effectively puts generating stations

out of action, but without destroying them. A hugely more powerful version is the microwave bomb developed in the UK. This is
designed as a travelling wave tube, containing an oscillating
radio wave, surrounded by ordinary explosive. When detonated,
the tube is rapidly crushed along its length, resulting in a gigantic
surge in the pulse to 1 gigawatt. The effect when exploded in mid-
air is to burn out every electronic circuit over an area of many
square kilometres. Telephone communications, computers, guidance
and control systems – whether for military or civilian use –
would be instantly put out of action. While it will not kill, it will
have a temporary disabling effect over the same radius. One
electronics expert has called it 'an outsize stun grenade'.[4]

Electronic 'zapping', the reality of juvenile ray-gun fantasies,
is now becoming deadly (or rather, disablingly) serious. Proposed
applications range from the trivial to the stellar. Its well-advanced
form allows a pursuing police car to generate a mega-volt electromagnetic field which can be 'fired' at the vehicle in front. The
charge will burn out all the computer-controlled functions and
bring the vehicle safely to a halt before it can crash or endanger
persons and property in the chase. Still somewhat into the
future, but already tested for service by the US Air Force, is the
ballistic interceptor. A much simplified version of Star Wars, this
is a patrol plane which can spot the launch of a hostile missile
and, from a distance of 400 kilometres, aim a gigantic laser ray
to destroy it while still at the booster stage.

In between lies the Logic Bomb which employs a mix of surge
technology and electronic hacking to disable distant computer
systems. This can have a devastating effect over a wide range of
civilian installations as well as military command and control
systems. A similar technique could be deployed over hostile
ammunition dumps, using a high-powered microwave to set off
an explosion.

Cyberwar

The use of computers to cause mass disruption is no longer fanciful. Civilian life as well as warfare are increasingly governed by
complex interconnected computer systems. A combination of
hacking, Internet and surge techniques can induce massive
failures. During the bombing of Serbia in 1999, the Pentagon is

thought to have considered an all-out cyber attack on Serb military and civilian services.[5] This would have shut down electricity and water supplies, air and train services and many financial operations. Only the untested legal aspects of such an action served to delay it.

China has shown less restraint. In 1999 it attempted to degrade Taiwanese websites and a short cyberwar actually broke out, with hackers in Taiwan reacting swiftly to the 'aggression'.[6] Serious counter-measures were put in place before the presidential elections in March 2000, which were fully expected to bring a further attack on election centres, financial institutions and military command posts.

Such threats are increasingly real. The US National Security Agency confirms that 'cyber terrorists' have succeeded in penetrating computer systems using devices such as logic bombs, electromagnetic pulses and high-emission radio-frequency guns to unleash an electronic storm through the systems.[7] City of London Police and the US security specialists Kroll Associates in New York confirm that this has become a lucrative field for extortion by specialised international gangs.[8]

Miniaturisation of weapons is now adding to the range of possibilities of such non-lethal interventions. Tiny microsystems being developed could be seeded unobserved into an adversary's communications centres, either to destroy computers or to relay intelligence.

Personnel disablers

While in the microwave bomb the effect on humans is an incidental by-product, a whole group of electronic and magnetic applications is being developed with that express purpose. Physical effects reported from locations as varied as Vietnam, the US Embassy in Moscow, protesters at the former Greenham Common Cruise missile base, and veterans of the Gulf War are consistent with the use of devices based on Extra Low Frequency (ELF) and Radio Frequency Radiation (RFR). Ominously, RFR operates at similar frequencies to power lines, radar, telecommunications and radio transmitters previously considered harmless in their effects upon humans.

Earlier types of frequency weapons based on similar principles were without doubt tested in Vietnam. They will have included the Valkyrie, linked to infra-red frequencies to induce night blindness, and the Squawk Box or Sound Curdler which can be silently aimed at individuals to induce nausea, giddiness and, collectively, disorientation and confusion. Now the armoury has been extended with such additions as acoustic beams causing blunt-object trauma; optical pulsing systems to stun, dazzle or temporarily blind; and electronic stun devices which concuss and rapidly immobilise personnel. Thus the whole field of frequency radiation and electromagnetic (EM) influences is beginning to be exposed.[9]

Even in 1982, the US Air Force noted: 'RFR experiments and the increasing understanding of the brain as an electrically mediated organ suggest the serious probability that impressed electromagnetic fields can be disruptive to purposeful behaviour and may be capable of directing and/or interrogating such behaviour ... A rapidly scanning RFR system could provide an effective stun or kill capability over a large area.'[10] Simon North adds: 'Even though the body is basically an electrochemical system, modern science has [so far] almost exclusively been concerned with the chemical aspects.'[11]

He goes on to cite the work of Dr Ross Adey at UCLA, which shows that cells are able to resist penetration from electromagnetic radiation, *except* at certain frequencies. These are assumed to be the frequencies at which cells communicate with each other. Commenting on this phenomenon, Captain Paul Tyler, USN suggests that EM systems could be used to 'produce mild to severe physiological disruption or perceptual distortion or disorientation'.[12]

The same paper seems implicitly to confirm that such devices have already been used, at least experimentally, by stating: 'The potential applications of artificial electromagnetic fields are wide-ranging and can be used in many military or quasi-military situations. Some of the potential uses include dealing with terrorist groups, crowd control, controlling breaches of security at military installations, and anti-personnel techniques in tactical warfare.'[13]

A further application of frequency projection has been suggested for taking out stockpiles of chemical weapons.[14] Low-frequency vibrations could succeed in breaking down the bonds of lethal chemicals and thus in neutralising them.

Development of such devices is, not unnaturally, to a large extent shrouded in secrecy. Work on them has been taking place simultaneously in the UK, the USA, Russia and elsewhere. No one is anxious to show their hand or share results with others. But the signs are clear that a new generation of dual-use weapons has already taken shape. On the one hand, they may be used in lethal doses to kill; on the other, as non-lethal weapons to disorientate, control or disable crowds or, much more controversially, perhaps to control behaviour.

One of the latest dual-use developments is the scaleable pulse gun developed by the US Department of Energy.[15] It uses high-energy cartridges containing water and aluminium as propellants. An electric impulse causes the aluminium to liquefy and vaporise the water. Unlike gunpowder, the pulse created can be calibrated to stun, disable or destroy. This overcomes the problem of using rubber bullets which lose effectiveness over longer distances but can wound or kill at close range. Another is the Active Denial System, which fires two-second bursts of microwave energy to create a discomforting heat sensation. Crowd dispersal by this means is non-lethal, but longer bursts may have more violent consequences.

A more benign form of dual-use technology are the potential applications of terahertz or T-rays. These electromagnetic pulses, generated at the rate of 1 trillion per second, are destined to substitute X-rays in the medical field. They will be less harmful and more effective in recognising abnormal tissue. By the same token, they could also recognise the chemistry of landmines, reveal whether a person is armed or carrying explosives and serve a variety of other security purposes.[16]

Kinetics

Low-level kinetic devices like blunt-object trauma and entanglements have been available for some years. Research on the higher-technology devices is now well advanced. Among the latter are the Vortex ring generator and the Hurricane simulation of a focused pressure wave.

Of an altogether different order is the High Frequency Active Auroral Research Project (HAARP) run jointly by the US Air Force and Navy, in conjunction with the Geophysical Institute of the University of Alaska. This uses an array of antennae to heat up portions of the ionosphere with powerful radio beams. The 'lenses' created in the ionosphere can be used for many purposes. Great quantities of energy can be harnessed and controlled by manipulating the electrical characteristics of the atmosphere. These can be directed at an enemy or at a moving target such as a ballistic missile. The project would also allow better communication with submarines, or the altering of weather patterns; or disrupting communications. By manipulating the ionosphere it may also be possible to block global communications while transmitting one's own. Yet another application is tomography, X-raying the earth several kilometres deep to detect oil and gas fields or underground military facilities. Over-the-horizon radar would also make it possible to look round the curvature of the earth for incoming objects.[17]

Corroding substances

A good deal of ingenuity has also been devoted to a rather less glamorous field, the adaptation of simple substances to disable both personnel and materials. Much controversy has surrounded the introduction of pepper gas to protect police forces; clearly it, and similar non-toxic substances, would have a place in other than civilian confrontations. The glue guns issued to US marines who returned to Somalia to cover the evacuation of UN contingents were well publicised, but their use and effectiveness as anti-personnel devices has received rather less attention.

Serious consideration has, however, been given to glues and sticky foam as immobilising substances. Tests have been carried out on adhesive rounds, delivered from the air, which are capable of glueing equipment in place. It is easy to see how this might find a ready application against isolated batteries or gun emplacements. More for the saboteur, but against certain targets also capable of aerial delivery, are supercaustics which can eat into bridge girders or the metal of armoured vehicles and weapons systems; and embrittlement agents able to alter the molecular structure of metals. Other essays have involved the development of chemical compounds which consume rubber as in aircraft tyres; inhibit combustion by contaminating fuel and disabling all devices driven by it; and lubricate roads and runways to inhibit mechanical movement.

Biological agents consist of cultured microbes with specifically identified properties and appetites. Some are able to turn jet fuel into jelly; others attack materials commonly used in weapons systems. Many of these may smack of the more simple-minded forms of science fiction or *Boys' Own* exploits. Nevertheless, the list demonstrates the amount of thought and experiment already devoted to finding the means to put adversaries and their equipment out of action before the fighting starts. Among these banal substances are olfactory devices considered by the Pentagon for dispersing human shields planted on strategic installations. These work through the use of pungent smells, forcing people to rush into the open air.

Potentially more dangerous are chemical agents to incapacitate personnel. These include a range of psycho-chemicals and gases – such as CS and BZ – whose function is calmative or sleep-inducing. CS gas was used in Vietnam, BZ by the Serbs in Screbenice. Use of such substances has been greatly contested not only because of their longer-term effects but also because they appear to infringe the Convention on Chemical Weapons.

The critical technologies

A comprehensive view of the fields in which non-lethal weapons development is proceeding can perhaps be gleaned from the US Department of Defense List of Critical Technologies.[18] Many of them are, of course, double use; the Liliput chip is an example of a technology which is critical commercially as well as for its potential defence applications.

Radio-frequency (RF) weapons are already high on the list, together with the RF chip gun. So are other technologies discussed above, such as fibre optics and the transmitters intended to burn out silicon integrated circuits controlling modern weapons equipment, that is everything from precision-guided munitions to radios. Anything relating to advanced computer development and its applications is naturally also to be found there. That includes semiconductor materials and microelectric circuits, software production capability, parallel computer architectures, data fusion, machine intelligence and robotics.

Techniques of computer simulation and modelling are gaining rapidly in importance. Some of their significance lies in the ability to simulate nuclear testing which, while providing a safe alternative to underground tests, also offers a cheap shortcut to the nuclear proliferator. Hyper-sensitive recognition technology – such as photonics, sensitive radars, passive sensors, signal processing and control – also offers insights into the direction of active research and developments.

Pulsed power, as discussed earlier, is to be found on the list, as is weapons system environment. Pointers to other new fields are computational fluid dynamics, air-breathing propulsion, hypervelocity projectiles and, at the frontiers of the new physics, high-energy density materials and superconductors.

The inclusion of biotechnology materials and processes will be principally for commercial reasons and the protection of intellectual property, but also in order to ensure that development remains controlled physically and ethically. However, biotechnology has itself begun to offer interesting possibilities for dealing with some of our graver civil problems. Israeli scientists, for instance, have developed a 'killer seed' that can be used to devastate crops of opium poppies. It is estimated that broadcasting this genetically modified poppy seed can engender a chain reaction which would destroy 70 per cent of the heroin production in a target area.

Lessons From Experience

Non-lethal devices have been progressively used in every US military operation from Vietnam to Panama, Somalia, Haiti, Bosnia, Kosovo and, no doubt, in the current 'War on Terror'. Recent conflicts have therefore already served to assemble a body of experience. Civilian control in Northern Ireland has for many years depended upon devices such as plastic bullets and other kinetic energy weapons, as well as a number of applications in the field of intelligence. More substantial forms of these, among them foam rubber and wooden baton rounds, as well as the bean bag and the 'doughnut gun', were issued to US Marines when they returned to Somalia to protect the withdrawal of the UN contingent. Most famously, they were equipped also with guns which discharged glue to immobilise attackers on impact, or sprayed a mixture of foam and tear-gas. To these have now been added entanglers, sticky nets to ensnare people or armoured vehicles. As a result of Somalia and Haiti, new generations of non-lethal projectiles came into service. One is the 40mm sponge grenade, so called because of its sponge rubber impact head. Both the US Marines and the UK's military in Northern Ireland have come to respect these 'weapons' as effective for their own protection within a hostile environment. Lieutenant-General Anthony Zinni, who commanded the Marines and had asked for non-lethal weapons for crowd control, is quoted as saying that he would never again field a peace-support operation without the aid of such weapons.[19]

Equally positive was the wider-ranging operation against Iraqi power stations. Operation Poobah's Party dropped thousands of spools of carbon-fibre from Cruise missiles to short-circuit switching gear and put generating stations out of action. So impressive was the carbon-fibre bomb over Serbia that the Chairman of NATO's Military Committee declared its use to have been a high point in the whole campaign.[20] The US Commander of the Joint Task Force in Kosovo has also spoken of the value of 'broad, multi-dimensional non-combat theatre ops' and their effects at 'greatly reduced effort, risk and cost'. He specifically praised the system preservation aspects, for instance of road structures within Kosovo for later use by KFOR, the NATO-led international force in Kosovo charged with keeping the peace between the Serb and Albanian populations.[21]

Those most crucially concerned with the type and effectiveness of weapons are the peacekeepers themselves. In *UN Peacekeeping in Trouble,* Wolfgang Biermann and Martin Vadset give the results of a survey of those who were involved in UNPROFOR operations in Bosnia.[22] Interviews were held with key personnel at NATO, WEU and UN headquarters, and with UNPROFOR officers of all ranks in the field in Croatia and Bosnia. Questionnaires were also addressed to 1,200 officers covering a broader spectrum of ranks, nationality and peacekeeping experience. The replies left little room for doubt: 78 per cent agreed with the use of force only in self-defence, even in a civil-war situation. Their comments indicate that they prefer the use of non-lethal force, and the employment of tactics similar to policing operations.

Are They Ethical?

A useful definition of non-lethal weapons (NLWs) describes them thus: 'NLWs are discriminate weapons that are explicitly designed and used to incapacitate personnel or materiel, while minimising fatalities and undesired damage to property and environment. They should have reversible effects and be able to discriminate between targets and non-targets in the weapon's area of impact.'[23] So long as this remains the intention which is enshrined in the doctrine governing their use, there should be few misgivings.

Much will, however, depend on the context. If used as an adjunct to conventional warfare – to smoke hostile pockets out of foxholes or immobilise enemy personnel before killing them – NLWs can lead to vastly increased casualties. Used in the operations covered in this book – that is where pursuit and kill is not the intent, but without their aid could become a necessity – they can clearly be benign.

Published information suggests that all the devices cited here are being actively tested or improved. In some cases the process will be extended and many are unlikely to see service for some years, while others are discarded. One factor to slow down progress may well be the debate as to whether such devices are really ethical or not, and whether some of them may offend against existing international conventions.

Equally legitimate are doubts about their physical effects. Objections were first raised against the Royal Navy's aerial protection laser guns, on the grounds that they permanently blinded the pilots on whom they were trained. As a result, the guns are said never to have been brought into use. Similar protests were raised over the effects of microwave projectiles, which at certain frequencies are thought to risk 'cooking' the target's internal organs.[24] Whether fact or a transposition of kitchen technology, a good deal of research needs still to be done to clarify these issues.

For the moment, they are being studied and discussed in review conferences under the Convention on Prohibitions or Restrictions on the Use of Certain Conventional Weapons, which was concluded on 10 October 1980. This has already succeeded in outlawing the use of riot control agents (as used in Vietnam) in warfare. Specific new protocols covering the use of electro-magnetic weapons have now been introduced.

Other non-lethal technologies must be tested against the Chemical Weapons Convention (CWC) and the Geneva Protocol. The 1925 Geneva Protocol deals principally with 'the use in war of asphyxiating, poisonous or other gases ... ' and therefore with substances which are designed to kill. The CWC, on the other hand, permits the production of toxic chemicals if they are used, among other purposes, for 'law enforcement including domestic riot control purposes'. While the CWC is explicit in limiting their use to domestic riot control and prohibiting it in warfare, the term 'law enforcement' is not defined. Until it is, doubt will remain as to whether it can legitimately be extended to cover UN peacekeeping operations.

It is nonetheless clear that all international conventions have considered the uses of substances and technologies solely in the context of warfare, that is as auxiliaries to offensive operations. No consideration has yet been given to their use either in sub-stitution of warfare or for intentionally non-lethal purposes. Clarity on this issue will be reached only once all devices intended to become operational have been adequately calibrated so as to carry no lethal, maiming or lastingly deleterious effect. In the absence of other reliable international standards for non-lethal weapons, the International Red Cross Committee's SIrUS[25] project could be used, since it has already classified and established mortality, invalidity, necessary treatment and blood supply criteria in respect of conventional weapons.

Some adaptations will be necessary to the current raw tech-nology before such weapons really achieve the purposes of their designers: to restrain hostile personnel, and to destroy or disable the equipment without killing people. All our weapons to date have been designed to immobilise the enemy by killing as many of soldiers – and civilians – as it takes for the rest to capitulate. Modern defence is moving in the direction of achieving the same end by destroying as much equipment as will leave the enemy defenceless. The philosophy of mass destruction has already been displaced by the means of massive disablement.

There is clearly a logical progression in this development. Having once been demonstrated at Hiroshima and Nagasaki – where they certainly achieved the classic objective of inducing capitulation through inflicting unsustainable casualties – nuclear weapons, it can be argued, were of no further practical use other than as a deterrent and an instrument of strong-arm diplomacy. Killing is obsolete, war is no longer the continuation of that diplomacy, and public opinion has become intolerant of either. Soft power rules, OK? Even if on occasion it requires a hard edge to serve as a first deterrent.

Public aversion to force and its consequences gave us the Campaign for Nuclear Disarmament (CND) and the peace movements. Now that world events appear to have justified that mood, to the extent of lifting from us aggression as the major threat to the security of hearth and home, it is predictable that any form of weapon will be contested, and in particular those which have a new and necessarily sinister dimension. The nuclear stand-off itself produced anxieties which went well beyond the realm of reality; Dr Strangelove and Pentagon war games were the exemplars of those hidden fears. Nor have they been stilled with liberation from the threat. There remains a deep distrust of the military–scientific establishment as a manufactury of unspeakable destructive and manipulative devices. Except at times of national euphoria and indignation – such as the Falklands and the Gulf wars, the bombing of Serbia and now Afghanistan – where the awesome splendour of their artefacts is suddenly revealed, public imagination senses the existence of a second world in which the instruments of death continue to be forged for purposes far removed from our own reality. Any device that emerges from this sci-fi Wotan's smithy is bound to become an immediate focus of protest.

Who can say that this is wrong? However irrational such reactions, they are unquestionably based on a grain of truth. Any experts will become so involved in their subject that some corrective needs to be applied before their advice and products can safely be heeded. As far as the defence establishment and its laboratories are concerned, this corrective resides in the political control to which they are subjected. But will this suffice? Where people work in secrecy, deliberately – and unavoidably – separated from the world they exist to serve, objectives can soon become distorted and strange motivations take hold.

It is therefore wholesome to have a body of critics, such as civil society has become, to contest the fruits of this work when they emerge even into the half-light. Whether the criticism is informed, or even rational, matters little in relation to the crucial counterweight it represents. It may even be argued that an element of irrationality and simplicity is required to offset the steely sophistication of the inventors and those who fashion such devices. It is not status quo but the explorative swings of the pendulum that confirm stability.

The answer to the ethical dilemma is therefore not to be found through unquestioning acceptance of one position or the other. 'They-must-know-best' acquiescence is as potentially fatal as instinctively to rally to the ranks of professional protesters. The real answer is to drive back to the utmost the frontiers of secrecy, to insist upon public scrutiny and debate, and to let as much light as possible fall upon the objects of our anxieties. Sustained public pressure to this legitimate end is a *sine qua non* of a civilised society. If eternal vigilance is the price of freedom, the same price is payable for the freedom from nightmare scenarios and excessive zeal.

In the end, the question of whether it is better to blind than to kill belongs to the realm of esoteric theological heresies. Much as we may regret it, the necessity to kill in certain circumstances is unlikely to go away; and, as always, a proportion of the maimed and wounded will also be blinded. The best we can work for is to reduce to the barest minimum the circumstances in which armed conflict becomes necessary at all, progressively substituting it with the non-belligerent techniques advocated here.

The purpose of this chapter has been to show the directions in which parallel weapons research has begun to move. It is clear that, while the rationale is still defensive and belligerent, a new part of its orientation is increasingly towards non-lethal technologies. This is in line with the thesis of this book and supports the strategies advanced by demonstrating that such devices are feasible and to be taken seriously. They are no longer tomorrow's science fiction but the beginning of a set of potentially reliable tools for diplomacy, conflict containment and peacekeeping actions.

The central argument is that peacekeeping missions can 'succeed' only by avoiding open conflict and, where 'weapons' are needed, they must in the first rank be non-lethal. For these purposes, therefore, all those which have anti-personnel consequences more serious than temporary disablement are to be kept in reserve. Only those which neither kill nor maim, nor inflict long-term damage or hidden injury, can be appropriate to this task. As development of these devices progresses, a rigorous selection will have to be made according to these criteria.

In such a context the ethical uncertainty can hardly arise. As in any other test of will, there will be ambiguities about specific applications of these technologies in the field. At some point the wrong people may be disabled, one side or the other of the belligerents may gain an incidental advantage; but at least they will still be alive to redress their own fate once the humanitarian objectives of the peacekeepers have been served.

Among the ethical considerations raised must nevertheless be not only the failures of judgement but the human failings among the peacekeepers themselves. Not all soldiers are able to resist the temptations of war; giving them the means to render individuals defenceless could lead to violations of persons and property. The risks cannot be ignored; but they argue more for discipline, psychological assessment of those chosen for such missions, and their training in the specifics of the application of the devices than for rejecting their benefits for fear of the limited possibility of misuse.

Perhaps of greater consequence is the problem of such devices falling into the wrong hands altogether. What counter-measures are available if peacekeepers become their target rather than their controllers? One part of the answer must follow the same rationale as the deployment of these devices in place of conventional weapons: that they are non-lethal. It follows that an adversary would be more likely to use them to thwart a peacekeeping mission rather than to kill its members. The same would apply if belligerents were to use them against each other: they might become an additional tool to plague their opponents and commit crimes against civilians, but for more murderous designs they would surely prefer their own lethal weapons.

What if non-lethal devices were to become generally available? How would they further the activities of terrorists, drug barons, organised crime, even petty thieves? Would society and the guardians of law and order stand defenceless against them? Would this be a Pandora's box to usher in a new age of lawlessness, gang wars and criminal excesses in our midst? The risks appear undeniable. Throughout history, criminals have appropriated the instruments of personal defence for their own sinister pursuits. Handguns, flick-knives, gelignite, poisons, all manner of lethal tools and materials have been impressed to serve their purposes. But so have wholly innocent substances and equipment. What would the criminal community do without the motor car, the jemmy and women's stockings?

Yet, except for cat burglars in Calcutta and train robbers in Domodossola, criminals do not appear to have been keen to adopt anaesthetising gases and other substances akin to some of the non-lethal devices advocated here. This fact would perhaps repay some Home Office research; for the moment it seems to argue that the risks of enriching the means for malfeasance of the criminal community, though remaining real, are perhaps not as immediate as might be feared.

The Strategic Implications

In great part the secrecy surrounding the development of non-lethal weapons is precisely because they are regarded as weapons. All the awesome and sophisticated systems like the microwave bomb and other Magic Bullets are conceived as offensive weapons to serve strategic ends. They are unlikely to be advertised until a real emergency requires their use, for fear of alerting as yet unknown adversaries and causing them to copy or develop counter-measures. Whole generations of secret weapons, their life-cycle from inception to obsolescence evolving in total obscurity, are thus likely to eat up precious resources. By preparing for *the* great war we are denying those resources to the development of much more modest devices which can protect the lives of our peace-keepers and lend effectiveness to our diplomatic operations.

The time is at hand for the West's weapons research establishments to make a rigorous selection among the technologies they are garnering. Those which are intended to guarantee its national security or that of the alliance should remain embargoed; for if not, the resources with which they have been developed would go to certain waste. Those others, which have a peaceful application in the small-scale conflicts in which the West is most likely to be involved as peacekeeper, should be brought into the open and placed at the service of political decision makers.

A considerable and continuing research effort will be necessary to develop, test and perfect these instruments. Only open inspection and discussion of their potential can lead to rational decisions to allocate the required resources – financial, scientific, technical and academic. This will require political guidance as well as the evidence of experienced commanders in the field. Participation of the latter is considered of extreme importance, for it is they who must judge against the safety of their personnel the real potential of each non-lethal device, as well as make the decisions about its trial in action.

NATO has had the subject under review since 1994. In 1998 it organised a general conference to develop its own concepts. Some of these are contained in its October 1999 policy document on NLWs, whose adoption is confirmed by the statement: 'Relevant concepts of operations, doctrine and operational requirements shall be designed to expand the range of options available to NATO Military Authorities.' NLWs should enhance the capability of NATO forces to achieve objectives such as to:

> (1) accomplish military missions and tasks in situations and conditions where the use of lethal force, although not prohibited, may not be necessary or desired; (2) discourage, delay, prevent or respond to hostile activities; (3) limit or control escalation; (4) improve force protection; (5) repel or temporarily incapacitate personnel; (6) disable equipment or facilities; (7) help decrease the post-conflict costs of reconstruction.[26]

NLWs may be used in conjunction with lethal weapon systems to enhance the latters' effectiveness and efficiency; but they should in no way limit a commander's or individual's right and obligation to use all necessary means available in self-defence. NATO planners are to ensure that the potential contribution of NLWs is taken fully into account in the development of their plans.

With that acknowledgement, the West should now reorder its priorities and put more resources into investing its peacekeepers with a non-lethal capability. All scientific experience has shown that, once a field is given official recognition, the pace of progress – vertical and lateral – is swift. Technological advance in all the pertinent fields has prepared the ground for a decisive leap: electronics and microchip technology, robotics and fibre-optics, neurology, cybernetics, biochemistry, psychology. Once developed, such devices are likely to be far more cost-effective: already computers, sensors and related equipment account for roughly half the costs of the West's weapons. The remainder is likely to become considerably cheaper, if only because many such devices are non-destructive.

In the world of the twenty-first century, cost is as much a strategic component as the system itself. So is the need to safeguard employment and the earnings potential of our already much slimmed-down defence industries. New developments of this kind can give them a fresh impetus. The savings in costs can also be passed down the line, ensuring better logistics and other elements designed to enhance the safety and mobility of our units. All in all, the strategic arguments for conversion to non-lethal weapons are hard to fault.

The New Options

With such an armoury, an international intervention force could more confidently take the field and begin to dominate the situation. Using non-lethal devices, it would retain the standing and impartiality vital to its operations and its own protection. Thus enhanced, intervention will become a more effective tool to achieve political objectives.

The essence of peacekeeping operations is not to cause casualties. The 'CNN factor' brings quick condemnation of any aggressive act for which the intervention force is deemed responsible. Even more compelling than not inflicting them is the need to protect such a force from taking casualties. Public – and therefore political – reactions have been seen to change swiftly once the body count begins. Peacekeeping operations are different in kind from traditional warfare to repel a threat to one's own country. World opinion backs them for humanitarian, not patriotic motives; and if people get hurt, that backing can be swiftly withdrawn.

But it is above all the political dimension which craves the West's concern. It has seen the spectacle of an alliance in danger of disintegrating from within, through mutual recriminations and frustrations because in Bosnia there was, for literally years, no discernible course of action which did not in the end militate against its objectives. The same doubts and stresses were visible over Kosovo and apply in deciding the response to any other humanitarian challenge. Non-lethal means now offer a ground on which all parties can meet. Exercising the non-lethal option, NATO's political leaders could be spared some of their differences as well as regaining the respect of their public.

Western leaders, and the peoples they are aiming to help, would still need to agree on a valid set of peace aims. Even if all that takes time, at least they will know how to act effectively wherever in this real world of nationalist banditry rather than nuclear shadow the next barbarian chooses to strike. They would have freed themselves from a future paralysis which undermines the role of the peacekeepers at the same time as risking the unity of the alliance. There can hardly be a more compelling political imperative.

A US Council on Foreign Relations study concludes: 'It is important to close the options gap between a Gulf War type response on the one hand and, on the other, typical economic sanctions of often limited effect.'[27] It is precisely in that gap that both politicians and military commanders will find a new capability to confront the challenges of our time.

No generals or politicians will allow their personnel to enter into ground operations without the backing of massive conventional force. But non-lethal weapons can and should be the first line of operational capability, with lethal force held in reserve and acting principally as the deterrent.

General Zinni, former Commanding General of the US Marine Expeditionary Force in Somalia, has described the force continuum of modern operations:

Deterrence → Show of Force → Riot Control → Use of Non-lethal Weapons → Combination of Non-lethal and Lethal Weapons → Lethal Conflict.

He shares the view of the gap to be filled:

> The addition of non-lethal weapons not only adds a new category in the force continuum but also fortifies other categories previously regarded as having limited value. In the past, we typically would move directly from deterrence to combat; with the addition of non-lethal weapons we strengthen the potential of show-of-force and riot-control tactics.[28]

Notes

1. As quoted by Christy Campbell, *Sunday Telegraph*, 27 September 1992.
2. Peter Scholl-Latour, *Im Fadenkreuz der Mächte: Gespenster am Balkan,* Bertelsmann, Munich, 1994.
3. See Michael Evans, *The Times*, 7 January 1993.
4. See Christy Campbell, *Sunday Telegraph*, 27 September 1992.
5. See Michael Evans, 'War Planners Warn of Digital Armageddon', *The Times*, 20 November 1999.
6. See *The Times*, 8 March 2000, p. 22.
7. Evans, 'War Planners Warn of Digital Armageddon'.
8. *The Sunday Times*, 2 June 1996.
9. See Simon North, 'Field of Nightmares: War in the Desert – Electronic Weapons', *Guardian*, 2 February 1991.
10. *US Air Force Review of Biotechnology*, 1982.
11. See North, 'Field of Nightmares'.
12. Paper by Captain Paul Tyler USN, published by Center for Aerospace Doctrine, Research and Education, Alabama, 1986.
13. Ibid.
14. See Matthew Campbell, 'Pentagon turns to Fred Flintstone', *The Sunday Times*, 4 July 1999.
15. Defense Press Service, USA, 3 January 2000.
16. See Robin McKie, 'T-rays Take Over from X-rays', *Observer*, 2 July 2000.
17. Resolution on the Environment, Security and Foreign Policy, European Parliament, A4-0005/99, 26 January 1999, EP/159.
18. The Militarily Critical Technologies List, Office of the Under-Secretary of Defense (Acquisition and Technology), Washington DC, Part I, June 1996; Part II, February 1998.

19. Lieutenant-General Anthony Zinni and Colonel Gary Ohls, 'No Premium on Killing', *Defense News*, Proceedings, US Naval Institute, December 1996.
20. Addressing a West-West Agenda meeting at NATO Headquarters, 5 November 1999; see also Michael Evans, 'Graphite Bomb Short-Circuits Power Stations', *The Times*, 4 May 1999.
21. Admiral James O. Ellis USN, 'A View from the Top', Briefing notes 1999.
22. Wolfgang Biermann and Martin Vadset (eds), *UN Peacekeeping in Trouble: Lessons Learned from the Former Yugoslavia*, Ashgate, Aldershot, 1998.
23. Nick Lewer, 'Non-Lethal Weapons: A New Dimension', *Bulletin of Arms Control*, Centre for Defence Studies, King's College London, 3 September 1996.
24. Liesl Graz and Shyam Bhatia, 'Hi-Tech Booby-Traps targeted by Landmine Campaigners', *Observer*, 2 August 1998.
25. The Superfluous Injury or Unnecessary Suffering (SIrUS) project to study the effect of weapons. See Robin M. Coupland and Peter Herby, 'Review of the Legality of Weapons: A New Approach – The SIrUS Project', *International Review of the Red Cross*, No. 385, June 2001, pp. 583–92.
26. NATO Press Statement, 'NATO Policy on Non-Lethal Weapons', 13 October 1999.
27. *Report of an Independent Task Force on Non-Lethal Technologies: Military Options and Implications*, Council on Foreign Relations, New York, 1995.
28. Zinni and Ohls, 'No Premium on Killing'.

8 Taking the Lead

'I hope our wisdom will grow with
our power, and teach us that the less
we use our power, the greater it will be.'
Thomas Jefferson[1]

A Political Base for the Silent Strategies

The components and parameters of a strategy for the non-belligerent management of crises have been adequately explored. We have examined the techniques of dealing with adversaries peaceably but effectively, traced the building blocks which can enable diplomacy to do its work and measured these against some of the world's most complex areas of hostilities, including the Middle East. What remains to be provided is the political impetus for a deliberate changeover to these strategies, and an appropriate framework within which this can take place.

Consideration of the growth of authority around zones of pacification has shown how such frameworks are capable of developing organically. We have seen how the European Union came to crown the Franco-German reconciliation by bringing stability, economic progress and prosperity to all of Western Europe. The breaking down of once fought-over frontiers and the scrambling of the industries of war brought unexpected dividends of growth and profit. It took another 30 years to extend the single market to all goods and services, and to expand the Community of six into a Union embracing virtually the whole of Western Europe.

No longer faced with the necessity of fighting periodic hot wars, Europe generated a degree of wealth which not even the defence demands of the Cold War were able to restrain. The economies of the West as a whole continued to grow despite the costs of the most expensive arms race in history, which was eventually to lay low its adversary. Where wars produced an artificial surge in domestic production, only for it to collapse from exhaustion once the conflict was over, peace has brought real and sustained profit. Even if some of that profit is still derived from defence industries, it is small wonder that most of the countries of the West, and particularly those formerly most aggressive, have turned against warlike acts; and that the European Union as a whole has found it so hard to decide on violent means.

Individual member countries like Denmark and those traditionally neutral – Austria, Finland, Ireland, Sweden – would no doubt embrace the new doctrines and strategies set out here. So might Germany, whose path to military assistance outside NATO has been one of embarrassed reluctance. More importantly, these instruments should commend themselves to the UK and France, which continue to make the most important European contributions wherever Western military intervention is required. Their patent economy should enable both countries to continue to play a significant role in world leadership, and to 'punch above their weight'.

However, making these strategies effective will require a political weight far greater than that of any individual country, unless it be the United States itself. For the time being, it seems unlikely that the USA would adopt such a role, since its reliance on armed might is too profound to allow it to change course on political grounds. On strategic grounds also, it is desirable that the deterrent role of its armadas should not appear to be in any way diminished or its resolve to strike lessened. Thus the only equivalent political power, even if still in its infancy, is the European Union as a whole.

The EU has indeed a natural role to play in this area. It was born out of a late recognition of the tragic and destructive consequences of war and with the mission to secure a lasting peace. The development of a non-belligerent capability is a highly appropriate role for a union which stands for the rule of law and came into being to put an end to an era of force as an instrument for the settlement of domestic and international disputes. Now, rather than seeking to don the traditional military panoply of a superpower, or to shadow what is more efficiently done by NATO, it would seem a natural destiny for the EU to establish the rules, means and practice of peacekeeping. Such a role is already inherent in the EU's assumption of the Petersberg tasks (see later in this chapter).

There are strong practical grounds why such a role should be adopted by the EU. By many indicators, the EU is the Western world's biggest civil power. Its economic weight has made it an important player on the world stage. Its actions and achievements in this area, such as its determinant role in global trade negotiations, have already overlapped into the political field. The beginnings of political co-operation have shown both solidarity and results over several of the more pressing issues, including South Africa, the Middle East, Iraq and China. Some of its joint actions have proved effective, notably in negotiations for the unlimited extension of the Nuclear Non-Proliferation Treaty.

There is now wide agreement on building up its political reach by giving substance to its Common Foreign and Security Policy (CFSP); but as yet there is little consensus or idea on how to set about it. Nevertheless, the implicit recognition that security is an element of diplomacy is already a significant step towards the adoption of non-belligerent strategies. It also implies an uncoupling of security from defence which, far from being one and the same thing, have often militated against each other. The security of empires has failed because their need to defend conquered territories outgrew the capacity of the core. The Soviet empire was only the most recent to suffer collapse from an unsustainable arms race. The Republic of South Africa, too, was to discover that its nuclear defiance had prejudiced its real security.

Future security will certainly depend on keeping shields in place against the ultimate emergency. But the challenges to the EU's foreign and security policy are more likely to involve the conflicts of *others* rather than direct challenges to the EU members themselves. Some, like Serbia, Macedonia and various Kurdish lands – or indeed Cyprus – may still have the potential to become uncontained and ultimately to involve the EU or its allies. Most, however, will challenge the EU because they are violations of human decency which civilised people cannot watch without being impelled to act. These are likely to be small conflicts – at least at the beginning – to which EU members will not be party. If the EU acts judiciously, they may remain localised and without involving the big powers as active and opposing combatants. The EU's part will be as a largely self-appointed umpire, aiming to bring succour to the affected populations and employing diplomatic and civil pressures rather than the force of arms to procure peace.

Such a stance will be even more important in combating terrorism. If its attacks are ever more likely to be in the EU's midst, there will be no room for firepower or massive responses. Even the pursuit of its perpetrators overseas is unlikely to yield to force concentrations. On all fronts, therefore, the EU's future security needs to be assured by the silent means of shrewd policing, intelligence and commercial counter-operations.

Civil wars and civil assault need in the end to be met with civil power. For these tasks the EU's forces will require not firepower but riot gear. At issue will be the EU's *security*, as members of a family of nations which it intends shall remain peaceful. As member states have to refrain from becoming combatants, they shall rarely be required to use their *defence* capacity, even if deterrent capability needs to be kept well in sight. Where, as in Bosnia and Somalia, the EU has instinctively confused the two, it has reaped only grief and casualties without serving its real objectives.

The concept of the EU itself engaging in warfare is still far off, if only because the time taken to reach common decisions rules out the instant reply demanded by a real emergency. That does not, however, mean that it should not begin to perfect its instruments for dealing with such extreme situations if called upon. Politically, the EU's decision-making processes will need to be defined and improved. Strategically, the EU's Military Committee will need to perfect its dual vocation to serve as the EU's military co-ordinator in matters of both security and defence and as the European pillar of NATO. For the foreseeable future, however, NATO itself will remain an inextricable part of any EU defence policy, if only because of the inability to undertake all but the lightest military tasks independently of US logistic and intelligence support.

A further compelling reason for the EU to adopt the strategies of peaceful conflict prevention and resolution are the pledges made to the traditionally neutral member states at the time of their joining. These assurances of comfort are at risk of being infringed by the development of the CFSP and the absorption of the WEU, as much as by the confusion of security with defence. For internal reasons, therefore, it will become increasingly necessary for the EU to choose a role in line with the humanitarian and non-belligerent precepts of Austria, Finland, Ireland, Sweden and increasingly also Denmark. That this coincides with the stance required for any foreseeable EU security operations, as well as with the EU's innate purposes, provides a strong basis for the adoption of the 'silent strategies'.

If prompt and effective defence is therefore likely to remain the province of NATO (no doubt through successive adaptations of its reach and role), the EU's foreign and security policies should nevertheless be enhanced with speed. One of their primary tasks needs in any event to be the development of techniques, equipment and doctrines for the new challenges of policing, peacekeeping and counter-terrorism. As we have seen, there is in this a substantial role for psychological and non-lethal 'weapons', and a consequent need for a sustained effort to perfect and press them from the experimental stage into service in the field. Conceptually, they need to become the tools of diplomacy and of over-arching strategies without which the EU cannot take on the new responsibilities required of it.

This complex of strategies, and the effort to develop its tools, must therefore become a strong support for a modern CFSP which is no longer only an aggregation of national foreign policies but provides some additionality to them. Responsibility for it could usefully be incorporated in a capability development centre, established in co-operation with NATO and charged with the planning and direction of these tasks, and with the co-ordination of the scientific, academic and military inputs required for their achievement.

If outsiders have a role at all in conflicts like Bosnia, it must depend upon the strictest impartiality. If the EU has to fight, it is not to join the warring factions but to oppose force, subjection and inhumanity. It is surely the vocation of the EU's foreign and security policy to establish itself firmly in that non-partisan role.

Taking the Decision

There is no doubt that these of all policies will need time to develop, mature and achieve their aim. Strategically that time is granted them so long as all parties can be persuaded to stand back from major conflict. Politically, however, the steadfast pursuit of coherent policies has become more and more vulnerable. Political leaders and decision makers are exposed to a triple hazard: the electoral cycle, events on which the media focus, and the almost daily opinion poll. The media demand action *now*, public opinion cries out for it so long as the media focus remains, and the political party needs it in time to redress its ratings. Wisely considered strategies for mankind will have to wait until tomorrow.

Media, opposition and pressure groups will make common cause to vilify government inaction and press for a change of course. Whatever the outrage, we have already seen it perpetrated and no time for reflection can be granted. 'Action Now' is the slogan, and woe to the politician who refuses to adjust to the situation. The air is heavy with recrimination. 'The crisis of leadership', rather than any reasoned response, becomes the focus of debate. Sabre-rattlers, demagogues, extremists of right and left take the stage, bask in their brief hour of attention and demand their chance to right the world. All manner of the darker urges press to the fore, presenting instant remedies for every world problem.

The fundamental contradiction is not only between reason and reaction; it is between the veil of discretion needed by policy makers, and those who regard the existence of any veil as provocation, and ripping it apart as their principal mission. Disclosure, exposés, investigative journalism are the techniques to capture attention against all other distractions. Too frequently they become not the scourge of hidden guilt but the tools of media competition. Exposing evil for the good of society becomes a respectable cloak for offering dramatised trivia for the sole benefit of circulation.

In field operations, this can have even more dire consequences. Speaking for the USA, Carnes Lord points out that, although the media acknowledge a responsibility not to risk lives, 'they do not recognise an obligation to refrain from publicising information

188

that demoralises US troops, reveals aspects of US intelligence or military planning, undermines US diplomatic initiatives, or gives psychological aid and comfort to the enemy'.[2]

The best crisis is the one that never happens. Averting a threat and preventing the ember from becoming a conflagration is the best of all outcomes. That invariably needs diplomacy, and diplomacy needs discretion. Diplomacy is the search for a bargain, and a bargain rests on compromise. Part of the bargain is that the parties are given time to present that compromise without losing face with their own followers. Exposing such a process to the glare of premature publicity is not to advance the interests of society but to destroy the chances of peaceful resolution.

All of these pressures militate against calm and coherent efforts of policy makers and diplomatists. The silent strategies and their instruments above all others need space, time and tolerance for their success. To burst into a darkroom and turn on the light does not serve the process of exposure, nor that of the task in hand. All diplomacy is like a laboratory experiment; shattering the test-tube will not lead to the truth, nor to a successful outcome.

For a political leader it already requires supreme courage to postpone the quick surgery and satisfaction of a punitive strike, trusting instead to the intangible means of quiet diplomacy. Politics may well be the art of dissimulation, and its practitioners well-schooled illusionists. But peaceful conflict resolution requires them to operate in a fourth dimension of time and patience, at odds with political time and imperatives.

It is a dilemma which can be resolved only within another new dimension: multilateral diplomacy. The political equation becomes soluble with the introduction of additional external functions. Widening the frame of reference brings two benefits: it avoids I. L. Janis's[3] 'groupthink' – the impairment of decision making through overconcern for cohesion of a small group – and the growing obsession with the defence of a 'higher interest' within an international system perceived as anarchic. The multilateral frame enlarges the 'group', bringing in fresh intellectual power at the same time as confirming the outside world in a co-operative rather than antagonistic state.

For these purposes also, the European Union offers itself as a useful frame. It is multilateral, co-operative and – at specific levels of foreign policy – non-competitive. Its procedures are deliberative and referral to them legitimately buys domestic time, more tolerantly granted outside the precincts of party sparring. Lastly, since the EU itself is effectively free from the electoral cycle, any failure to act or inability to make its decisions prevail will not be considered as damaging to its constituent governments. Although its members are individually elected at home, the Council of Foreign Ministers is a privileged body. Pointing the finger at 'bureaucrats' in Brussels somehow ignores their involvement. Nor has trial by media as yet reached the Brussels foreign-policy area.

These calmer waters should provide more ample scope for reflection. They are somewhat more conducive to discussion of long-term intentions, the kind of world we wish to see, and a progressive plan of action designed to bring us towards it. Decisions can more easily be made to adopt the silent strategies within a coherent intellectual approach, then to apply them, gauge their effects, modify and adapt according to their success. Above all, the EU can avoid the political trap of committing itself to a course of action which cannot subsequently be changed without loss of face.

A European Security and Defence Identity

To understand the foundations which would have to carry the silent strategies, it is important to look at the origin and implications of the European Security and Defence Identity (ESDI). At the outset, ESDI was essentially an attempt to provide a structure for implementing the tasks confided to the Western European Union (WEU) by the 1992 Petersberg Declaration (since defined in the Treaty of European Union): conflict prevention, crisis management and humanitarian operations. This involved a search for practical ways of using European defence capabilities within NATO for purposes other than NATO operations, yet with the ability to draw on NATO assets. This complex formula was first agreed in Berlin in 1996, on condition that ESDI was to be developed within NATO.[4] There would be regular consultation between NATO and the WEU, also at the level of their councils. In recognition of the European political commitment to make a more effective contribution to the Alliance, NATO would also take the requirements of the WEU-led operations into its defence planning system, and provide HQ facilities and command positions for them.

By the time of its 1998 Madrid summit, NATO had developed the Combined Joint Task Force (CJTF) concept, originally agreed in 1994 to permit the WEU to draw on NATO assets. It put more flesh on the Berlin principles but, most importantly, approved the creation of forces capable of operating under the political control and strategic direction of the WEU.

Some of these premises changed when, in Helsinki in late 1999, an EU summit decided to absorb the WEU into the EU.[5] At the same time it agreed the creation of a European Rapid Reaction Force of up to 60,000 troops by 2003 for peacekeeping operations as well as the original Petersberg tasks. It approved appropriate decision-making structures, including a Standing Committee on Political and Security Affairs, a Military Committee and a Military Staff. What seemed a logical step to simplify EU–NATO relations has, however, led to certain doubts over the EU's intentions, particularly on the US side.

There may indeed be possibilities for divergence. The EU's primary concern will be regional crisis management; for NATO this is only an ad hoc concern. The EU embraces four states which are not members of NATO, and enlargement is likely to make this number grow. Formalising an EU–NATO relationship might not be an improvement on continuing representation by individual EU states. EU strategic decisions could be influenced by its neutral members and could prove difficult to amend in discussions with a militarily better-qualified NATO; and they would not automatically embrace European NATO members not in the EU.

In other respects, procedures which had been traced out for relations with the WEU lend themselves almost equally to those with the EU direct. Joint sessions of their respective councils can be retained and there might even be some double-hatting among members of the two military committees. The fact that the EU's High Representative for the CFSP, Javier Solana, is the former Secretary-General of NATO should facilitate the strategic dialogue with his successor, and preferably also involve the European Commissioner for External Affairs. These co-ordinating arrangements are now in place, as is machinery for regular consultations with NATO members and applicants not within the EU.

More intricate will be to keep step between NATO's Defence Capabilities Initiative and the development and operation of the EU member states' collective capability in the areas of command and control, reconnaissance and lift capacity. The extent to which these are separate but still enhance NATO's overall capabilities will have to be closely monitored by both sides. This will apply even more strongly to the HQ command centres created for any EU operations.

A strong undertow to these practical adaptations is that the term NATO in this debate is synonymous with the United States. The extent to which they are seen to serve the interests of NATO is therefore a prime determinant of the future transatlantic relationship.

The same is true of the trend in European defence expenditures. The USA is keeping one jaundiced eye on their continuing decline and another jealous one on any diversion of those resources into duplicating NATO (that is US) assets in intelligence and heavy lift capacity. Advancing US understanding of the motives of ESDI, and demonstrating its additionality for NATO, will be a major EU responsibility.

It is crucial that ESDI, as well as any new tasks proposed here, should not be seen by the USA simply as a demonstration of European self-will, a beginning of superpower pretensions and a flight towards independence from US leadership. Instead, they should present themselves as vital parts of a new transatlantic security structure and the basis of a fair and sensible sharing of responsibilities with the USA.

Fundamental to this will be a proper and agreed definition of security which encompasses not only defence but the whole gamut of policies examined in this book. Only a full understanding of the interaction and relevance of all these factors can bring about an adequate system to safeguard our common security into the long-term future.

A Transatlantic Security Structure

The European contribution to security has seen a half century of largely unquestioning support for NATO, proud military participation in a number of post-war campaigns, and both peace enforcement and peacekeeping operations, often alongside US troops. But the contribution has been even more marked in other fields. The classic EU way to security is the progressive integration within itself of countries which presented, or are still likely to present a risk. Two examples will suffice.

The first is the enlargement process. The EU has been a pole of attraction for those who lived under dictatorship and those recently emerged from it. It began with Greece, then Spain and Portugal. Almost immediately after the end of the Cold War, the EU began discussions on association with the freed countries of East and Central Europe. There are currently 13 applicant countries and actual accession negotiations are already at an advanced stage with Poland, Hungary, the Czech Republic and Slovenia. The Head of the German Delegation to the North Atlantic Assembly, Klaus Francke, judges the effect: 'The EU may currently be less able than NATO to fulfil the security aspirations of applicant countries. However, I am convinced that in the long term, EU membership and hence participation in the European area of prosperity, will offer as much stability, and therefore security, as the guarantees contained in Article 5 of the North Atlantic Treaty.'[6]

A second example is the Stability Pact for South Eastern Europe,[7] which has established a framework for bringing the Balkan countries onto a path of progressive political and economic development. While rather further into the future, this is hoped also to be a prelude for eventual membership of the EU, and possibly even NATO. The pact has created three 'working tables' (similar to those used in the one-time Helsinki process with the USSR) addressing democratisation and the promotion of civil society, economic development, and matters of internal and external security. Bearing in mind the fractious nature of the countries involved, the road will be long. For that reason the EU-sponsored pact has brought together a broad-based membership including the Group of Seven (G-7) industrialised countries, Russia, the countries of the region, NATO, OSCE, the

UN, Council of Europe, major financial institutions headed by the World Bank, the European Investment Bank and the European Bank for Reconstruction and Development, as well as many NGOs.

The drawing of recalcitrant states into a framework of democracy and co-operation, with its rewards becoming obvious at each stage, and at the same time involving the international community on the widest possible scale, is patently a powerful formula for consolidating peace and security.

These examples illustrate that the EU is capable of operations at three levels of security: participation in classic military operations and force projection; low-level security operations like the Petersberg tasks; and using its political and economic weight for much more advanced and durable solutions. Producing new amalgams of states and converting breeding grounds of historic conflict into potential zones of peace is a unique function which no other agency could achieve. Rightly, this should be one of the major roles confided to the EU under a transatlantic security structure.

But the European contribution can also be demonstrated in terms of conventional defence. The EU's Rapid Reaction Force of up to 60,000 troops, even if not enhancing the number of troops assigned to NATO, will bring a significant gain in their efficiency through the practice of field operations under a joint command. Better preparedness and operational skills will strengthen NATO's overall capability. At the same time the EU is also seeking to make its conflict intervention operations embrace the civil, post-conflict dimension by simultaneously creating a Rapid Reaction Facility. This will contribute to operations run by international bodies through mobilising police and other non-military personnel for crisis management and re-establishing civic structures to reassert political, social and economic stability.

The EU's major value for future Atlantic security thus lies predominantly in the projection of 'soft power'. At the same time, however, its member states will be perfecting their 'hard-edge' contribution to NATO by building up a European capability based on common assets and command structures.

The US contribution to the transatlantic security structure will clearly continue on more classic and robust lines. Undoubtedly the USA will remain the single most powerful country in military terms, delivering the most important input for the common defence in both the conventional and the nuclear field. That is the fate to which its physical, economic and political weight has predestined it.

Yet even the US defence effort is not immune from being undermined by change. Economically, there are signs of strain. The arsenal of smart bombs threatened to run low by the end of the Kosovo campaign. Admiral James O. Ellis warned that, although the USA is the only nation in the world with all the tools, the process is very expensive in terms of investment required to maintain and improve capabilities; and he wondered whether the USA was not embarking on 'self-inflicted asymmetric warfare'.[8] Yet current intolerance of casualties by the Pentagon as well as US public opinion means increasing the use of capital intensive forces with the lowest possible exposure. The effect, as Edward N. Luttwak has pointed out, is that 'the distinction between forces that are only theoretically available and those that are in fact politically usable in real-life confrontations is still largely disregarded'.[9] The paradox of deterrence is that military forces are most useful when they are not used at all.

It is clear that calls for the 'rebalancing' of Atlantic security are well founded and timely. They are not unique, nor will the need remain confined to this particular juncture or cause. Change and transition are permanent features of a relationship which is in any event traditionally ambivalent. The USA has consistently and from its very beginnings given generous support to the process of European integration. That has not prevented it from voicing dislike of some of its practical emanations where they hurt American toes. ESDI is only the latest in that process, hitherto confined largely to matters of trade, with intermittent calls for military 'burden-sharing'. It demonstrates that the USA instinctively prefers the 'hub-and-spoke' dynamic in which it continues to deal with EU member states bilaterally while hammering out the more important bargains at the EU or NATO centre.

In any event, there is as little likelihood of overcoming the contradictions in US opinion as arriving at a uniform European consensus. Both sides are too large, and as societies too open, not to be strongly influenced by competing views. On the US side, the Pentagon tends to reflect one view, the State Department often quite another. Within the EU this is mirrored by tensions between the Commission and the Council, the EU executive and the member states. Democrats and Republicans are as legitimately divided as, for instance, the good Atlanticists in Britain and the more sceptical French.

Yet at the end of the day, NATO and the EU, that is the USA and Europe, are condemned to an inextricable destiny. However far the EU integration process advances in the military sphere, the EU will for the foreseeable future have to rely on NATO infrastructure. With its dominating position in technology, the USA will continue to be at the leading edge of assets essential to any demanding military task. And as the leaders in the industrial and democratic world, the two powers share vast economic and political interests which it will remain vital for them jointly to protect.

Nor should the current emphasis on European and transatlantic issues make us overlook the substantial US contribution to security on a global scale. Its alliances and bases throughout Asia and the Pacific, the southern Atlantic and the northern approaches are a bulwark of deterrence. In a steadily shrinking world, they are a protection for everyone whose interest lies in living on in peace.

A New Basis for Transatlantic Understanding

The forward march of US technology means that for all of us the costs of defence are moving on a steep escalator. The US economy may well be able to absorb the costs of research and development, since it can live amply on the spin-off technologies. Customers, allies and others required to share the burden find it harder. Yet interoperability effectively ties other NATO members to these flying coat-tails, requiring them to buy upgrades to existing technologies or acquire new ones at frequent intervals. There are also charges levied on those who live under the protection of US systems, such as the request to Kuwait for 'depreciation' on aircraft carrier groups steaming in the Gulf.[10]

Much has been made of the technology gap between the USA and its allies, particularly that revealed by the Kosovo combat experience. But do asymmetric campaigns really call for Uncle

Sam's finest? Or was it in truth needed only to avoid the exposure of low-level missions?

Admittedly, there is much that the Europeans need to attend to. NATO Europe spends only 60 per cent of what the USA does on defence. As a percentage of GDP, the proportion is roughly similar. Within those sums, however, are interesting divergences. Europe's standing forces total 2.4 million, fully 1 million more than those of the USA. Yet each US soldier is kitted out with equipment and firepower amounting to $36,000 against the European fighter's $11,000.[11] The figures show how much room there is for improving the efficiency of European defence spending, as well as for economies through pooling their key capabilities. ESDI may well achieve what NATO has so far done with only limited success. Lord Carrington, a former NATO Secretary-General, once famously said: 'The only thing the NATO armies have in common is the air in their tyres.' We have come a long way since then, but clearly not far enough.

It may still be questionable whether vastly greater sums are really needed. European troop levels are adequate for regional defence and peace enforcement as well as wider peacekeeping missions. Returning to Luttwak, for these tasks it should be perfectly feasible for the Alliance to deploy 'usable' EU troops equipped with standard weapons (but including non-lethal ones), backed by scarcer highly equipped but 'usable' US forces. This after all was the way that NATO strategy was designed for the Cold War and, lest we forget, explains why the Americans still flew most of the bombing missions over Serbia and Kosovo.

Political dynamics within the US Congress also ensure that the only yardstick used to measure the heft of the US allies' security contributions is the size of their defence budgets. In recent years the gap has been further increased by the Republicans' tendency to foist handfuls of billions of dollars onto every defence appropriations bill.

This is clearly a contest which the Europeans cannot win. Yet they should not allow themselves to be intimidated and made to feel second-class nations or warriors, let alone submit to jibes of being 'free riders'. It is a contest which they should not permit themselves to be coerced to enter.

It has been demonstrated that the EU has the ability to deliver impressive contributions within an appropriately broadened definition of security. It alone has the ability to offer gradual integration into its zone of prosperity to all the remaining countries of Europe. It has shouldered £4 billion worth of the reconstruction assistance in the Balkans and established, by the 1995 Barcelona Declaration, the Euro-Mediterranean Partnership to create a shared area of peace and security to the South, which over time will contribute also to the Middle East peace process. Beyond that, the EU and its members account for 55 per cent of all official international development assistance and some 66 per cent of all grant aid.[12] In specific cases, such as the demobilisation and reintegration programmes in Uganda, they are providing an even higher percentage. Together with support for regional organisations in Latin America, the Caribbean, South-East Asia and Africa, this reaches out to most of the poorer countries where security is often most endangered.

A major contribution to the security debate, and to a fuller understanding with the USA on the respective standing of their physical contributions towards it, would be to draw up a Security Purchase Index (SPI). In effect, this would be a balance sheet not solely of classic defence budgets but of expenditures on the totality of the security effort. It would include comparative expenditures on defence-linked departments such as the intelligence services, civil defence and the appropriate portions of foreign affairs and police budgets, border guards and customs services and the civil structures responsible for their management and oversight; in short, all those with authority to use or support the use of force. It would track official aid programmes, voluntary sector aid transfers and subscription payments to the UN and other multilateral organisations. It would include contributions to peacekeeping and relief operations, to the extent that these are not included in other items; and those to post-conflict operations such as restoration of the civil functions and reconstruction of damaged infrastructure. And it would take account of the costs of major political initiatives such as the ACP and other conventions embracing virtually the whole of the troubled developing world. On the European side, it would aggregate the EU's central expenditures with those of the member states.

Naturally, the USA would also register an impressive contribution on the soft security side. Since 1992, for instance, it has spent $2.3 billion to promote democratic development and market reforms in Russia.[13] It is ready to disburse substantial sums to underwrite an Arab–Israeli peace settlement: tens of billions of dollars will be required to assist Israel to enhance security of new borders and settlements, while even greater amounts will be needed in Palestine and Jordan finally to stabilise the refugee problem. Support for substitution of North Korea's nuclear reactors and the reconciliation between North and South are also falling heavily upon the USA.

There is little doubt that such accounting would show a very different balance of effort between the Atlantic partners. It should then be possible for each side to regain a better respect for the other, and for the benefits it has to offer for the common good. The SPI would also perhaps promote a better understanding by the rest of the world of the totality of the West's contribution to the global community.

To Each His Own

A new basis of respect and appreciation can offer a rational and emotionally appropriate sharing of responsibilities between the USA and EU, capable of becoming a new paradigm for transatlantic security relations. Both the USA's armadas and its natural responses favour the punitive might which the world needs to keep in reserve. The EU, on the other hand, has shown its ability not only to provide effective auxiliary forces within the Alliance but also to deal with the more subtle requirements of remaking and administering the peace. The investment required to develop those capabilities, rather than duplicating US assets, will also go a good way to answer US concerns about shrinking European defence budgets. A formal acknowledgement of these complementary roles should do much to reduce current frictions and misinterpretations in transatlantic relations.

To give its rightful place to 'soft power' in this way will also allow the silent strategies to be viewed in a more positive light. While the USA has indeed adopted and implemented some of them, they are still unlikely to commend themselves there as a holistic and reliable instrument. The American psyche, with its belief in the intrinsic right to defend oneself, arrives more quickly than the European at the point of reaching for its gun. Yet it was an American, Henry Kissinger, who from the wealth of his experience concluded wistfully: 'The fulfilment of America's ideals will have to be sought in the patient accumulation of partial successes.'[14]

Europeans, raised with ten centuries of invasions and accustomed to living with vulnerability, have well-founded misgivings about the US quest to achieve 'total security' through unassailable technological advance. To many, it appears as a return to the Vietnam fallacy that carpet bombing and superior artillery can defeat a barefoot rebel army. Worse, it may directly lead to the 'Revolution in Military Affairs of the Poor', encouraging development of crude and clandestine weapons of mass destruction by those who feel threatened by overwhelming and unanswerable technology.

The obverse of techno-war may well be terrorism. 'The more we allow ourselves to ignore proportionality or minimum use of force, the more certain we can be that opponents will do the same and that the level of background violence will escalate', says Paul Schulte.[15] By contrast, President George W. Bush has announced his goal as seizing the chance 'to project America's peaceful influence, not just across the world, but across the years. This opportunity is created by a revolution in the technology of war ... The best way to keep the peace is to redefine war in our terms.'[16]

The West as a whole has clearly still to come to terms with the need to moderate its objectives. Not to strive for dramatic victories, but to develop 'soft security' with all its mutations from deterrence through non-lethal and non-partisan self-protection, to pacification and gaining full co-operation. That is the essence of the silent strategies. It does not imply the abandonment of Western armed forces, but instead to enlarge dramatically the room for manoeuvre before – if ever – they need to be deployed.

In the pursuit of that goal, it will not be sufficient to think only in terms of conflict prevention and peacekeeping. The West must outgrow the notion of conflict altogether and begin to fix its eyes on expanding co-operation. It must transcend the concept of containment of whatever is not to its liking and exchange it for the positive one of bringing even its enemies ultimately into a fruitful circle of amity and co-operation.

As so many times in the past, before and after their fateful invention of gunpowder, the West might take a lesson from the Chinese. Very informally, they have let it be known that their response to deployment of the US national missile defence would not be a symmetrical one. Instead, they might, for instance, prefer to act against US commercial interests in space. Their concept of 'alternative war' is a return to the wisdom of Sun Tzu and his 2,500-year-old precept, 'Don't respond directly'. Some of us at least should join him while we still have a free choice.

The world is as we find it; there is no other starting point. It is up to us to make it better; and there are no more effective means on offer than the silent strategies to answer today's challenges from inside as well as out. This is the real mission for the USA and for NATO; but above all for the EU and its new foreign and security policy: to adopt them, and with them the stance of an enlightened twenty-first-century power. Not to soften the toughness of their collective responsibilities, but to lead all of us into a future that is more secure than our bloody and tumultuous past.

Notes

1. Jefferson to Thomas Leiper, 1815, ME 14:308.
2. Carnes Lord (ed.), *Political Warfare and Psychological Operations*, National Defense University Press, Washington, DC, 1989.
3. I.L. Janis, *Victims of Groupthink*, Houghton Mifflin, Boston, MA, 1982.
4. Communiqué of the Ministerial Meeting of the North Atlantic Council, Berlin, *NATO Review*, Vol. 44(4), June 1996.
5. 'Presidency Conclusions', European Council Meeting Helsinki, 10–11 December 1999, Council of the European Union, Brussels, 1999
6. Klaus Francke, 'Rebalancing Transatlantic Relations', *NATO Review*, Vol. 45(5), September–October 1997, pp.17–20.
7. Chris Patten, 'A European Vision for the Balkans', *NATO Review*, Summer–Autumn 2000, p. 13.
8. Admiral James O. Ellis USN, 'A View from the Top', Briefing notes, 1999.
9. Edward N. Luttwak, 'A Post-Heroic Military Policy', *Foreign Affairs*, 75 (4), July/August 1996.
10. James R. Holmes and Toshi Yoshihara, 'The Puzzling Failure of America's Counter-Proliferation Policy in the Middle East', *Strategic Review*, Fall 1999, p. 44.

11. IISS, *The Military Balance 1999/2000*, IISS/Oxford University Press, London, 2000.
12. Highlights of the Report of the Senior Level Group, EU–US Summit, Queluz, 31 May 2000, Council of the European Union, Brussels, 100/193, p. 7. International Development Statistics 2001, OECD Development Assistance Committee, Paris, 2001.
13. *The Military Balance 1999/2000*.
14. Henry Kissinger, 'How to Achieve the New World Order', *Time*, 14 March 1994, pp. 73–7.
15. Paul Schulte, 'Ethics and Counterinsurgency – The UK Approach', lecture prepared for IISS Conference in Moscow, April 1998.
16. Remarks by the President at US Naval Academy Commencement, Annapolis, 25 May 2001, The White House, Office of the Press Secretary.

Bibliography

Albright, D. and Hibbs, M., 'Hyping the Iraqi Bomb', *Bulletin of the Atomic Scientists*, 47 (2), 1991.

Allen, P. M., 'Evolutionary Theory, Policy Making and Planning', *Journal of Scientific & Industrial Research*, 51, August–September, 1992.

Axelrod, R., *The Evolution of Cooperation*, Basic Books, HarperCollins, New York, 1984.

Baranyi, S., *The People's Peace: Civil Society Organisations and Peace Processes in the South*, CIIR, London, 1998.

Biermann, W. and Vadset, M. (eds), *UN Peacekeeping in Trouble: Lessons Learned from the Former Yugoslavia*, Ashgate Publishing, Aldershot, 1998.

Boniface, P., *La Volonté d'Impuissance*, Editions du Seuil, Paris, 1996.

Brown, M. E. and Rosencrance, R. N. (eds), *The Costs of Conflict: Prevention and Cure in the Global Arena*, Carnegie Commission on Preventing Deadly Conflict, Washington, DC, 1999.

Bull, H. and Holbraad, C. (eds), *Power Politics*, Leicester University Press, Leicester, 1978.

Bundy, M., Crowe Jr, W. J. and Drell, S., 'Reducing Nuclear Danger', *Foreign Affairs*, 92(2), Spring, 1993.

Cahill, K. M. (ed.), *Preventive Diplomacy: Stopping Wars before they Start*, The Center for International Health and Cooperation, Basic Books, New York, 1997.

Clark, W., *Waging Modern War*, Perseus Books, Oxford, 2001.

Clausewitz, C. von, *On War*, Book I, W. Hahlweg, Bonn, 1952.

Comité d'études de défense nationale, *Défense Nationale*, February 2000.

CSIS, *Defense in the Late 1990s: Avoiding the Train Wreck*, Center for Strategic and International Studies, Washington, DC, 1995.

Deutsch, M., *The Resolution of Conflict: Constructive and Destructive Processes*, Yale University Press, New Haven, CT, 1973.

Dyer, M., *The Weapon on the Wall*, Johns Hopkins University Press, Baltimore, MD, 1959.

Eggenberger, D., *A Dictionary of Battles*, George Allen & Unwin, London, 1967.

Elliot, G., *The Twentieth Century Book of the Dead*, Allen Lane, Penguin Press, London, 1972.

Fisher, R., *Beyond Machiavelli: Tools for Coping with Conflict*, Harvard University Press, Cambridge, MA, 1994.

French, C. C., *Psychological Aspects of the Gulf War*, SANA, Washington, DC, 1992.

Gabrielli, F. (ed.), *Storici Arabi delle Crociate*, Einaudi, Turin, 1957.

Goldstein, F. L. et al., *Psychological Operations: Principles and Case Studies*, Air University Press, Maxwell Air Force Base, AL, September 1996.

Human Rights Watch USA, *Needless Deaths in the Gulf War,* Human Rights Watch, New York, 1991.

Huntley, J. R., *Pax Democratica: A Strategy for the 21st Century*, Macmillan, London, 1998.

Ignatieff, M., *Virtual War: Kosovo and Beyond*, Chatto & Windus, London, 2000.

IISS, *Strategic Survey 1999/2000*, IISS/Oxford University Press, London, 2000.

IISS, *Strategic Survey 2000/2001*, IISS/Oxford University Press, London, 2001.

IISS, *The Military Balance 1999/2000*, Brassey's, London, 2000.

IISS, *The Military Balance 2000/2001*, IISS/Oxford University Press, London, 2001.

Klare, M. T., 'Lessons of the Gulf', *The Nation*, Vol. 252, 1991.

Lewer, N., 'Non-Lethal Weapons: A New Dimension', *Bulletin of Arms Control*, Centre for Defence Studies, King's College London, 3 September 1996.

Lord, C. (ed.), *Political Warfare and Psychological Operations*, National Defense University Press, Washington, DC, 1989.

Luttwak, E. N., 'A Post-Heroic Military Policy', *Foreign Affairs*, 75 (4), July/August 1996.

Maddison, A., *Monitoring the World Economy 1820–1992*, OECD, Paris, 1995

Massie, R. K., *Dreadnought: Britain, Germany and the Coming of the Great War*, Random House, New York, 1991.

Mathews, D., *War Prevention Works: 50 Stories of People Resolving Conflict*, Oxford Research Group, Oxford, 2001.

Quinlan, M., *European Defense Cooperation: Asset or Threat to NATO?*, Woodrow Wilson Center Press, Washington, DC, 2001.

Rauschning, H., *Gespräche mit Hitler*, Zurich, 1940.

Report of an Independent Task Force on Non-Lethal Technologies: Military Options and Implications, Council on Foreign Relations, New York, 1995.

Roetter, C., *Psychological Warfare*, B.T. Beresford, London, 1974.

Rose, M., *Fighting for Peace: Bosnia 1994*, Harvill Press, London, 1998.

Scholl-Latour, P., *Im Fadenkreuz der Mächte: Gespenster am Balkan*, Bertelsmann, Munich, 1994.

Schramm, W. von, *Sprich von Frieden wenn du den Krieg willst*, Mainz, 1973.

Stein, J. G., *Psychology and Deterrence*, Johns Hopkins University Press, Baltimore, MD, 1985.

Stoltenberg, T., *The Management of Intractable Conflicts: Bosnia Hercegovina*, Wyndham Place Trust, 1995.

Streetley, M., 'The Weird Stuff', *Flight International*, 3–9 August 1994.

The Strategic Defence Review Presented to Parliament by the Secretary of State for Defence, HMSO, London, 1998.

Topitsch, E., 'Psychologische Kriegsführung – einst und heute', ASMZ, 7.8.86.

UNDP, *Human Development Report*, New York, 1991.

US Air Force Review of Biotechnology, 1982.

Watson, P., *War on the Mind: The Military Uses and Abuses of Psychology*, Hutchinson, London, 1978.

Weeks, A. L., 'Psy-War: Persuading the West to Lose', *Journal of Defense and Diplomacy*, 4 (12), December 1986.

White, R. K. (ed.), *The Malignant (Spiral) Process of Hostile Interaction: Contributions to Psychology and the Prevention of Nuclear War*, New York University Press, 1986.

Williamson, R. (ed.), *Some Corner of a Foreign Field: Intervention and World Order*, Macmillan, London, 1998.

Index

Note: Page numbers in *italic* type
refer to figures; those in **bold** refer
to tables.

ABC (atomic, biological and chemical)
weapons 40
ABM (Anti-Ballistic Missile) Treaty
27, 32, 139
Act of Union 10
Adey, Ross 166
Aegean 23
aerial mapping 62; reconnaissance
89
Afghanistan 6, 24, 37, 49; airliner
hijack 28; bombing 136, 174; Soviet
invasion 113; withdrawal 77
Africa 3, 153, 198; Africans 12; Armed
forces training 37; arms control
151; Great Lakes 56; NEPAD (New
Partnership for African
Development) 154; terrorist attacks
in 36
agitators: anti-globalisation
movement 29; demonstrations 29;
Internet 29; 'virtual groups' 29
Albania 27, 37, 38, 171
Algeria 54, 98; FMLN (Farabundo
Mart' National Liberation Front) 54
Allen, Peter 19, 125
alliances 10, 12, 15, 46, 48, 113
al-Qaeda 12, 29

Alsace 5
alternative war 23, 201
alternative weapons 10
American Council for Economic
Priorities 57
Amnesty International 56
Angola 21, 32, 46, 113
Annan, Kofi 63, 67
annexations 5
anti-terrorist skills 14
Arabs 12, 23, 25, 32, 85, 88, 119; Arab
brotherhood 25; Arab–Israeli
relations 30, 32, 118, 120; culture
118, 119; guarantee of Israel
security 121; historians 87; Pan-
Arabism 118; peace settlement 199
Argentina 55, 127
armed forces 36; availability 38, 39;
deployment 37; dual and multiple
roles 37; level of 37; mobilisation
and training 39; preparedness 40;
reductions in 36, 40
Armenia 27
arms control: Annual Report on
Strategic Export Controls 134;
Arms Control Conventions 138;
Auditor General 134; Biological
Weapons Convention 156; black-box
technology 149; Chemical Warfare
Convention 156; compliance 142,
149; Comprehensive Test Ban

Treaty 156; defence industries 134, 136, 148; Eastern Africa and the Horn 151; ECOWAS moratorium on small arms 151, 156; European Union Code of Conduct 141, 156; heavy weapons 29; intelligence gathering 150; interdiction technology 137, 138, 143; interoperability 142, 155; Landmines Convention 142, 149, 156; limitation on production 115; long-range guidance systems 136; Missile Technology Control Regime 156; multilateral controls 138; new manufacturers 136; Nuclear Free Zone Treaty for South-East Asia 156; Nuclear Non-Proliferation Treaty 156; nuclear quadruple lock 137; Permanent UN Conference on Disarmament 156; precision locating 147; remote instruction weaponry 138; satellite technology 150; Scott Inquiry on exports to Iraq 135; Select Committee on Defence 134; small arms 29, 151; Southern Africa Action Programme 151, 156; START II Treaty 139; surplus weapons 135, 136; track-and-immobilise technology 147, 149, 150; Tracker 138, 162; UK–Scandinavian embargo 141; UN Action Programme on Small Arms 142, 156; UN enforcement 142, 150; UN register of conventional arms 139, 156; unguided weapons 146; University research 138; US alert system 138; verification 150; Wassenaar Agreement for disclosure of arms deliveries 156; weapons of mass destruction 29, 155
arms sales 34, 140, 141, 147; Airbus A-3XX 148; employment 148; IISS study 148; KONVER programme 148; re-export 147
Asia 20, 21, 26, 34; terrorist attacks in 36
Atlantic world, partnership 12
atrocities 17, 18, 88
Australia 6; Australasia 12, 75; and North Korea 30
Austria 184, 187; Austro-Hungary 107

Axelrod, Robert 122, 123
Azerbaijan 24, 27

Baghdad 87, 102; Cruise missiles over 103
Balkan conflicts 1, 2, 15, 24, 37, 38, 45, 75, 84, 100, 107, 112, 118, 158, 160, 193, 198; *see also* individual countries
Ballistic missiles 94, 114, 127, 138, 155, 156, 168; Code of Conduct 156; interceptors 94, 155, 164; Technology Control Regime 156
Baltic states 27, 112
Basque separatists 12, 36; *see also* ETA
BBC 91; Soldatensender Calais 92
Beijing 53
Belgian interests 3
Belgrade 103
Belize 37
Berlin 58, 126, 190; airlift 46
Biafra 46
Biermann, Wolfgang 171
biological weapons: blackmail 29, 31; proliferation 30
bipolarity 113, 114, 117, 119
Black Sea 24
bluff and deception 39
Boer War 4
Bosnia 6, 17, 27, 37, 38, 40, 47, 70, 72, 74, 76, 78, 106, 112, 143, 151, 159, 160, 170, 180, 186, 187; UNPROFOR (UN Protection Force) 171
Brazil 55, 136, 147
Bretton Woods institutions 15; *see also* World Bank, IMF
British: interests 3, 4; military history 4, 11; Navy 4
Brunei 37
Brussels Treaty 116
buffer states 5, 126
Bulgaria 27
Bundeswehr 10
Bundy, McGeorge 26
Burma 24, 46; *see also* Myanmar
Burundi 23, 53; Hutus and Tutsis 23
Bush, President George (Sr) 44; to American Legislative Exchange Council 44; and Iraq 65, 71, 97
Bush, President George W. 200

Cambodia 20, 21, 24, 46, 51, 59, 77
Canada 37
Caribbean 21, 198
Carrington, Lord 197
Caspian 56
casualties: Afghanistan 77; Agincourt
    2; American Civil War 2; Balkan
    conflicts 2; Bosnians 2; civilian and
    collateral 1–3, 13, 97; Coalition 1;
    Croats 2; First World War 2; Gulf
    War 1; Iraqi 1, 2; just number 47;
    Norman Conquest 2; own casualties
    14; Second World War 8; Serbs 2,
    97, 108; US intolerance of 195
Caucasians 12; Caucasus 56
Cavell, Nurse Edith 83
ceasefires 48, 56, 114
Central America 21
Central Asia 16
Central and Eastern Europe 61, 62;
    Force integration 62;
    interoperability 62; and NATO 117;
    nuclear security 62
CFE (limitation of Conventional
    Armed Forces in Europe) Treaty
    115
Chechnya 17, 24, 27, 46
chemical and biological weapons:
    Chemical Weapons Convention 110,
    156, 169, 173; First World War 31;
    Iraqi use on Kurds and Iranians 31;
    napalm and Agent Orange 31;
    proliferation 30; terrorist blackmail
    29, 31
Chile 55
China 9, 12, 17; arms exports 148
    (fissile materials 129); challenge to
    western supremacy 23, 33, 63;
    confrontations 46; economic reforms
    22, 34 (growth rate 34); and
    European Union 185; food deficit
    20; Hong Kong 22; insurgents in
    South-East Asia 22; Maoist ideology
    22; maritime power projection 23;
    missile technology for Iran, Libya,
    Syria 23; and National Missile
    Defense 201; and North Korea 30;
    nuclear capacity 26, 39 (no first use
    declaration 26; Non-Proliferation
    Treaty 139); peace initiatives in
    Cambodia and Korea; regional
    security 17, 29; and Russia, Japan,

USA 22; Sun Tzu philosophy 23,
    201; Taiwan 23 (cyber attack 165);
    UN Resolutions 67; World Trade
    Organisation 48
Christian ethic 87; *see also* Judaeo-
    Christian
Churches 58; Chaldean 59;
    communications network 58;
    monitors 58
Churchill, Winston 93
CIS (Commonwealth of Independent
    States) 27, 33, 112, 116; *see also*
    Soviet Union successor republics
City of London 29
Civilian populations 83
civil institutions 15, 74, 194
civilisation 88, 125
civil society organizations 29, 57, 59,
    175; *see also* NGOs
civil wars 46, 76, 172, 186
Clausewitz, C. von 83
coalitions: with business 57;
    international 59, 67, 78; of the
    willing 16, 48
Cold War 3, 16, 22, 36, 40, 41, 46,
    84, 96, 99, 113, 115, 121, 126, 131,
    134, 137, 142, 148, 154, 159, 184,
    193
Colombia 21, 36, 48, 57
colonialism 22
Command and Control Warfare
    (C2W) 85, 103
Command, Control Communications
    and Intelligence (C3I) 105
commercial interest 17
Commonwealth 32, 61
communist expansion 46
compliance 88, 115
confidence-building measures 50, 56,
    115
conflict: escalation 17, 47, 76, 144;
    management 43, 78, 143, 176
    (*see also* Harvard techniques);
    number of post-Second World War
    conflicts 69; prevention 17, 40, 43,
    48–50, 57, 61, 78, 200 (cost of 49,
    144, 156) (sanctions 64); resolution
    43, 189
Conflict Prevention Network 68
Congress of Berlin 15, 107
Congress of Vienna 15, 107
Constituencies for Peace 56

containment 31, 34, 127, 129, 200; hegemony 129

co-operation strategy 88, 110, 111, 113, 115, 118, 119, 200; bipolarity 113, 114, 117; deterrence and reassurance 119; frame of stability 119, 120, 128; frequency of contact 120; Middle East 121; proximity 114, 120

co-operation theory 122, 124, 125; diplomacy and deterrence 126; It Pays to be Nice 126; Non-Punitive Deterrent 123, 131; Prisoner's Dilemma 122; Tit-for Tat 122, 123

Council of Europe 194

Coventry Cathedral International Centre for Reconciliation 58, 59

Critical Technologies 169, 170; air-breathing propulsion 170; biotechnology 170; computer simulations 170; fibre optics 169; fluid dynamics 170; high-energy density materials 170; hyper-sensitive recognition 170; Liliput chip 169; hyper-velocity projectiles 170; micro-electric circuits 169; pulsed power 170; radio-frequency weapons 169; semiconductor materials 169; superconductors 170; weapons system environment 170

Croatia 27, 107, 112, 114, 171; Krajina 160

Crusades 25, 87, 88, 119

CSIS (Center for Strategic and International Studies) 38

CTBT (Comprehensive Test Ban Treaty) 26, 139; US stance 26, 139

Cuba 21; in Angola 24, 32; missile crisis 46, 126, 127 (Kennedy 128; Khrushchev 127; US blockade 128); and UN 67

Cyprus 23, 37, 52, 54, 59, 69, 185

Czechoslovakia 5, 126; Czech Republic 27, 148, 193

Dalmatia 107

Dark Ages 5

Darwinian evolution 6

David and Goliath 41

D-Day landings 94; Kent, Pas-de-Calais, Boulogne 94; Le Havre,

Isigny 94; Normandy Beaches 94; Operation Fortitude 94; Operation Titanic 94

defence: budgets 44 (rebalancing 14); European 15, 197–9 (standing forces 197); expenditure 7, 36, 197–9 (opportunity cost 9; bases in Germany 10); Germany and NATO 7, 36; industries and procurement 18, 184; Italy 36; needs 36; policy 9, 18 (post-Suez 9); reviews 18; Third World 7; UK 7, 36, 37; *see also* defence diplomacy

defence diplomacy 61; civilian control of armed forces 61; cost 62; reform 61

defensive software 40

democracies 12

Democratic Republic of Congo (former Zaïre) 16

Denmark 184, 187

Desert Storm, Operation 1, 43, 65, 89

deterrent 41, 47, 61, 84, 126, 127, 184, 200; balance of terror 126; deterrence 98, 126, 131, 132, 180, 184, 195, 196 (lessons from 131); economic effects 126; level of tolerance 128; Mutual Assured Destruction 130

Deutsch, Morton 122, 123, 131

diplomacy 34, 174, 176, 185, 189; megaphone 63; multilateral 189; pressures 60, 102, 177; preventive 36, 40, 110, 117, 125; versus propaganda 91; restoring peace 18, 99; silent 63, 183

disaster relief 106

discovery 6

domestic world 11–13, 20, 26, 40

Dresden 58

Dual Code 6

Dyer, Murray 95

Eastern Europe 11, 75; EU association agreements 116, 193

East Germany 91

East Timor 6, 16, 57, 58, 75, 77, 114

EBRD (European Bank for Reconstruction and Development) 194

Ecole Nationale d'Administration 53

economic development 16, 50, 57

economic pressures 40, 60
economic sanctions 64, 65, 73;
    international monitoring 64;
    proceedings against individuals 65;
    smart sanctions 66
Ecuador 51, 55; President Jamil
    Mahuad 55
Egypt 4, 28; fundamentalists 120; and
    Israel 98, 119, 128
Ellis, Adm. James O. USN 171, 195
El Salvador 48, 54, 77
Ennals, Martin 56
Eritrea 23, 49, 62, 77
escalation 63, 129, 144
ETA (Euzkadi ta Askatsuna) 23
Ethiopia 21, 23, 46
ethnic cleansing 44; strife 69, 144
Europe: military history 11
European Union 11, 116, 184; ACP
    (African, Caribbean and Pacific
    countries) 50, 62, 198; Capability
    Development Centre 187; CFSP
    (Common Foreign and Security
    Policy) 50, 185, 187, 201 (High
    Representative 191, Policy
    Planning Unit 50); conflict
    prevention 50, 186, 189 (Conflict
    Prevention Network 68); Cotonou
    Convention 50; Council of Foreign
    Ministers 190; development co-
    operation 57, 68, 198; enlargement
    62, 116, 191, 193; Euratom 116;
    Euro-Mediterranean Partnership
    198 (Barcelona Declaration 198);
    European Coal and Steel
    Community 116; European
    Commission 68 (Commissioner for
    External Affairs 191); European
    Security and Defence Policy 62;
    European Council, Nice 62;
    European Economic Community
    116, 183; European Investment
    Bank 194; European Parliament
    68; European Rapid Reaction Force
    144, 160, 191, 194 (HQ command
    centres 192); immigration policy 28;
    European Security and Defence
    Identity 190, 192, 197; European
    Single Market 183; Gibraltar
    autonomy 69; KONVER
    Programme 148; Lomé Convention
    50 (and human rights 68); and

Middle East 121, 185; Military
    Committee 186, 191; Military Staff
    191; neutral Member States 187,
    191; non-lethal weapons 187, 197;
    non-state bodies 50; Petersberg
    tasks 185, 187, 190, 191, 194
    (peacekeeping 185, 197,
    impartiality 187, regional defence
    and crisis management 191, 197);
    political and economic integration
    50; Rapid Reaction Facility 194;
    Schuman Plan 116; security vs
    defence 185, 186; Security Purchase
    Index 198, 199; Stability Pact for
    South-Eastern Europe 193, 198;
    Standing Committee on Political and
    Security Affairs 191; workforce
    projections 28; and USA (balancing
    and sharing effort) 62, 199
evolutionary theory 124–6, 131;
    possibility space 124

Falkland Islands 37, 127; campaign
    84, 174; HMS *Invincible* 127
Far East 17, 39
Finland 184, 187
flexible response 160
food security 28; China 20
force reductions 18
France 6, 62, 98; defence diplomacy
    61; deployment in Africa 38; Force
    contributions 16, 184; Force
    reductions 36, 37; Franco-German
    relations 112, 113, 116, 119, 183;
    Franco-UK forces in Bosnia, Kosovo
    72; French interests 3; French
    Revolution 112; and Middle East
    118; nuclear deterrent 37, 139
Francke, Klaus 193
French, Christopher C. 97
front-line states 21
fundamentalism 24, 31, 59; Arab 118;
    Egyptian 28

G7 (Group of Seven industrialised
    countries) 193
Game Theory 99
Geneva Protocol 173
Genoa 29
Georgia 27; President Sheverdnaze 54
Germany 59, 111, 116; Atlantic Wall
    96; Balkans 107; Blücher 112;

economy 8; export controls 141; force reductions 36; Frederick the Great 112; High Command 93; Navy 4 (naval communications 93); overseas possessions 15; participation in NATO operations 38, 184; prisoners of war 93; RAF bases 37; rehabilitation 116; reunification 10; and former Warsaw Pact countries 61; and USA 114
Gibraltar 37, 69
Glasnost 84, 113
Glaspie, Amb. April 87
globalisation 20
Goebbels, Joseph 83, 91
Goldstein Col. Frank L. 85
Gothenburg 29
governance 11
Great Depression 8
Great Game 16
Great Powers 5, 71, 107, 143
Greece 193
ground forces 14, 39, 134
groupthink 189
Guatemala 57, 58
guerrillas 31
Gulf Co-operation Council 155; regional missile defence 155
Gulf War 1–3, 16, 40, 45, 46, 52, 67, 84, 85, 89, 90, 93, 94, 97, 103, 136, 140, 151, 163, 165, 174, 180; Coalition 44, 73, 89, 90, 94, 160

Haiti 6, 71, 106, 170, 171
Hanish Islands 62
Hanoverians 11
Harvard conflict management techniques: African Union 53; Algeria 54; Boston 54; Camp David 54; Cyprus 54; El Salvador 54; FMLN (Farabundo Martí National Liberation Front) 54; Hague initiative 54; Iran 54; mediation 51; Peru–Ecuador dispute 51; South Africa 54 (Constitution 52); Springfield, Mass. 54; tools 51, 53, 79 (counter-analysis test 53, four-quadrant analysis 52, 53, messages 52, one-text formula 54); workshops 53 (Chinese–US diplomats 54; Ecole Nationale d'Administration

53; RUC–New York Police Department 54)
Healey, Lord 134
Helsinki Process 115, 193; *see also* OSCE
historic analysis 19
Hitler 4, 91
Holocaust 2, 91
humanitarian actions 14, 18; aid 78; challenges 180; consensus 13; principles 45, 185
human rights 7, 13, 17, 24, 56, 63; basic needs 35; economic freedom 35; Helsinki agreements 115; monitoring 68; violations 44, 70
Hungary 27, 126, 193

Idaho 6
immigration 28
India 4, 6, 12, 16, 59; Calcutta 177; India and Pakistan 17, 23, 29 (superpower support 129)
Indo-China 21
Indonesia 23, 35, 68, 114, 135, 148; Suharto 35
infrastructure rebuilding 49, 178
instability 33
Institute of Communications Studies, Leeds University 97
insurgency 18
intelligence and peacekeeping operations 36, 150, 185
interdiction 31, 74, 86; programme of 63, 65, 69, 70, 90
International Action Network on Small Arms 56
International Alert 56, 57
International Atomic Energy Agency (IAEA) 40, 77, 143, 150; inspections 77
International Committee of the Red Cross 173; SIrUS (Superfluous Injury or Unnecessary Suffering) Project 173
International Court of Justice 48
International Institute of Strategic Studies, USA 58
international law 45
International Monetary Fund (IMF) 15, 67, 68, 154
Internet 60, 105, 150, 163, 164
Intervention 7, 17, 40, 46, 47, 49, 70,

179; intrusive 63, 70, 77, 89; legitimisation 71–73
investment in non-military security 49
Iran: Ayatollah Khomeini 118; EU 121; Hezbollah 120; Iran–Iraq War 77; missiles 23; nuclear proliferation 29, 32, 34; regional stability 17; revolution 24
Iraq 3, 7, 17, 24, 44, 119, 127, 160, 171, 185; arms sales to 35, 135, 141; Kurds 70; Kuwait invasion 87; nuclear proliferation 29, 34, 89, 97, 139; religious communities 59; sanctions 65, 66, 73; Scud missiles 29, 129; Shias 70; and UN 67
Ireland 184, 187
Islam 16, 118; fundamentalism 16, 25, 118; Stans (Islamic Republics) 24; teachings 118, 119 (Quranic 25); terrorist groups 36
isolation 32, 56, 130
Israel: Arab–Israeli relations 30, 119, 120; demographic change 121 (Orthodox populations 25); killer seeds 170; Messianic Jews 59; nuclear proliferation 29; outside threat to peace process 121; Palestinian Christians 59; Patriot missiles 137; regional stability 17, 23, 24; settlers 120; Suez 120; US support 120
Italy: Domodossola 177; Force reductions 36; and North Korea 30; RAF bases 37; and Slovenia, Dalmatia 107

Jackson, Lt-Gen. Stonewall 93
Janis, I.L. 189
Japan 12, 17, 26, 56, 111
Jefferson, Thomas 183
Johnson, Douglas 58
Jordan 65, 119–21, 199; King Abdullah 121
Judaeo-Christian ethic 45, 87, 88; New Testament 45; Old Testament 45, 83
Just War 3, 45, 46; criteria 45, 47; St Thomas Aquinas 45

Kaiser 4
Kant, Immanuel 12
Kashmir 23, 30

Kenya 26, 59, 68
Kiel 58
Kissinger, Henry 200
Korean War 3, 16, 121, 127
Kosovo 1, 2, 6, 16, 18, 27, 37–40, 43, 70–2, 117, 143, 144, 154, 160, 170, 171, 180, 195–7; Joint Task Force Noble Anvil 108; KFOR (International Force in Kosovo) 171; KLA (Kosovo Liberation Army) 160; Operation Allied Force 108; Rambouillet negotiations 44
Kurds 6, 23, 36, 70, 185
Kuwait 25, 71, 160, 196; annexation of 25, 87, 94

Laos 20, 21, 24, 46
Latin America 20, 12, 198
law and order 11; civil order 13
League of Nations 15, 145
Lebanon 98, 119, 120, 143
Liberia 23, 48, 56, 75, 151
Libya 23, 141; nuclear proliferation 29; Rabta Chemical Plant 30
Lord, Carnes 188
Luttwak, Edward N. 195, 197

Macedonia 27, 48, 160, 185
Madagascar: French protectorate 4; tribal tensions 23
Mafia 9, 35
Malaya 51; Emergency 3
Mali 151; Tuareg rebellion 151
Marines 6
Médecins sans Frontières 48
Medellin 58
media reporting 83, 103, 188–90
Mediterranean 24
mercenaries 5
merger of forces 10
Metz 111, 112; Cross of Lorraine 112; Foch, Maréchal 112; Haeseler, F.-M. von 112; Roland 111, 112
Middle East 6, 25, 88, 128, 183; anti-Americanism 118; arms sales 140, 152; bipolarity 119, 121; co-operation 117; nuclear proliferation 29; regional rivalries 129; two-basket approach 121; water politics 25
migrants 9, 11, 28, 35; asylum seekers 35; freedom of movement 35

military reprisals 18
Moghuls 6
Moldova 27
Montenegro 27, 112
Moravia Conflict Resolution Centre 58
Mozambique 21, 48, 59, 77
Muslims 87; *see also* Islam
Myanmar 24, 51, 117; *see also* Burma

Namibia 26, 48, 77
Napoleon 3, 5, 10, 15, 112, 116
national elites 57
national interest 4, 16, 48, 100, 135
nation-state 5, 10; nationalism 24, 84, 88, 180
Native Americans 6
NATO (North Atlantic Treaty Organisation) 15, 16, 187, 193; Alliance 44, 46, 71, 75, 108, 113, 116, 180, 199; Article 5 of Treaty 193; Berlin summit 190, 191; civil and military co-operation 70; Cold War strategy 197; Combined Joint Task Force concept 191; credibility (Kosovo) 44; Defence Capabilities Initiative 192; deterrence 16; duplication of assets 192, 199; enlargement 27, 62, 116 (Czech Republic, Hungary and Poland 61; Russia 116); European defence capabilities 190; European pillar 186; expenditure reductions 36; flexible response 160; Helsinki summit 191; interoperability 196; intervention options and strategies 51; KFOR 171; Madrid summit 191; and Mediterranean 120; Military Committee 171; mobilisation and training 39; NATO military authorities 178; non-lethal weapons policy 178; and OSCE 144; Partnership for Peace 61, 62, 117; public information 108; Rapid Reaction Force 37; rebalancing Atlantic security 195; Serbia bombings (cost of) 49; technology gap 196; troop availability 38, 39; WEU-led operations 191
Nazis 92; Neo-Nazis 12
Near East 6

negotiating processes 48, 51; techniques 58, 78
Netherlands 16
New Guinea 6
newscasts 13, 83, 103, 108, 158; CNN factor 179
new states 12, 31
Newton, Isaac 130
NGOs (Non-Governmental Organisations) 50, 56–8, 78, 79, 143, 194
Nicaragua 77
Nigeria 6, 23, 56, 68, 75
non-belligerent techniques 96, 110, 121, 184, 185; *see also* peace-making
non-lethal weapons 40, 110, 159, 161, 162, 172, 173, 180, 181, 200; acoustic bullets 161, 163 (beams 166); Active Denial System 167; ARPANet 163; Automobile Association Tracker 162; ballistic interceptors 164; Beady Eye 163; biological agents 169; blunt-object trauma 167; carbon fibre bomb 161, 171 (Poobah's Party 163); Claribel 163; corroding agents 168 (supercaustics 168); cost 179; counter-measures 161, 176, 177; crowd control 166 (riot squads 161, 173, 186; pepper gas 168; tear gas 161, 171); CS and BZ gases 169; cyberwar 164, 165; Demon Scan 162; disabling technologies 159, 160; dual-use weapons 167; electromagnetic pulses 165, 166; electronic interference technology 163 (hacking 164); electronic stun devices 166; electronic zapping 164; embrittlement agents 168; entanglements 167, 171; extra-low frequency radiation 165; Global Positioning System 163; glue guns 168, 171 (adhesive rounds 168, doughnut gun 170, sticky foam 168, 170, 171); HAARP (High-frequency Active Auroral Research Project) 168; hurricane focused pressure wave 167; kinetics 167, 170; laser guns 161, 163, 172; logic bomb 164; Lolack 162; low-frequency devices 161; magic bullets 163, 167;

microwave projectiles 161, 163, 172 (microwave bomb 164, 165, 177); micro-systems 165; Morris, Janet and Chris 162 (containment of barbarism 162); olfactory devices 169; optical pulsing systems 166; plastic bullets 170 (bean bag 170); psycho-chemicals 169; radio-frequency radiation 165, 166, 169; research 161, 177, 178; rubber bullets 167; scaleable pulse gun 167; sponge grenade 171; Squawk Box/Sound Curdler 166; surge technology 164; terahertz rays 167; Valkyrie 166; wooden baton rounds 170

Noriega, Gen. Manuel 7, 93

North, Simon 166

North Atlantic Assembly 193

Northern Ireland 18, 23, 36, 37, 54, 59, 161, 170, 171; Commission on Policing 55; Royal Ulster Constabulary 54

North Korea: enriched uranium production 30, 199; ideological disarmament 21; isolation 24, 32; and South Korea 17; weapons development 17, 26, 30, 34, 89, 117, 139 (Nodong missile 29); US and EU negotiations 139

Norway 48

nuclear threat 14, 17, 23; CND (Campaign for Nuclear Disarmament) 174; confrontation 46, 84, 96, 174; defence 33; deterrent 41; Hiroshima, Nagasaki 174; Iraq 97, 129; missiles 29; narcotics for plutonium 129; NPT 26, 139, 140, 149, 150, 185 (Review Conference 26); nuclear blackmail 28, 130 (nuclear suitcase 28); pre-emptive action 30, 32, 130; proliferation 26, 29, 33, 34, 77, 129, 139; Soviet response 130; Dr Strangelove 137, 174

Nunn, Senator Sam 163

observer forces 69; monitoring 69; preventive deployment 69

oil: Caspian 16, 57; Crises 1973, 1980 25; Middle East 97, 118; US dependence 25; for weapons 34

O'Neill, Tip 98

OODA (Observation, Orientation, Decision, Action) 62; satellite surveillance 162

options and strategies 46, 57

Organisation of African Unity (OAU) 48, 50

Organisation of American States 68

organised crime 35, 36, 150, 177; arms dealing 65; cross-border operations 35; nuclear materials 35; vice and drugs 35

Orissa 6

Osama bin-Laden 28

OSCE (Organisation for Security and Co-operation in Europe) 50, 75, 115, 144, 145, 193; Charter for European Security 144; crisis management, peacekeeping, post-conflict rehabilitation 144; delegation of enforcement functions to 144; membership 145; Paris Charter 144; Platform for Co-operative Security 144

Ossetia 24; Georgia-Ossetia 54

Ottoman Empire 24, 118

Owen, David 48

Oxford Research Group 49

Pacific Islands 23

Palestine 119, 120, 199; Hamas 120; Hezbollah 120; independent state 121; *intifada* 120

Pakistan 17, 106, 148

Panama 6, 7, 93, 170

patriotism 47, 180

peace-making 18, 193; fear reduction measures 59, 79; non-belligerent means 96; peace agreements 48, 58; peace aims 111, 132, 180; peace-building 56–9, 62, 79; peace enforcement 161; peace processes 57, 58; peace settlements 107; stabilisation 60

peacekeeping missions 37, 47, 144, 161, 176, 178–80; availability of forces 38; equipment 40; Kosovo 37

Peace of Westphalia (1648) 15

Perestroika 84, 113

Perry, William 101

Persian Gulf 24, 37, 38

Peru 51, 55; border dispute 55;

President Fujimori 55; Rio de
Janeiro Protocol 55
Philippines 23, 59
Poland 27, 112, 193
police action 43
policing, international 7, 40, 144, 146,
172, 186
political action 40; sanctions 66, 68;
suspension of memberships 67
political interest 17
population growth 20
Portugal 193
post-war malaise 45
poverty 12, 20; *see also* Third World,
economic development
Powell, Gen. Colin 103
preventive diplomacy 30, 40, 47, 51
Prince of Wales Business Leaders
Forum 57
principalities 10
proximity test 114
proxy wars 3
psychological warfare (psywar) 41, 82,
83, 96, 97, 99, 100, 102, 104, 105,
107, 110; Agents of influence 91,
104; behaviour control 88;
Broadcasting C2W (Command and
Control Warfare) 85, 103; C3I
(Command, Control,
Communications and Intelligence)
105; civil disobedience (*satyagraha*)
89; clarification techniques 87;
communicative measures 86, 95;
covert operations 103; deception 95;
decoys and feints 89, 94, 103;
disorientation 86, 89, 103; domestic
policies 98; ethics 99; historical
data analysis 101; information
gathering 89, 100, 101 (Services
91); information operations 90, 92,
108; imaging and listening devices
105; instruments 83, 85, 86, 90;
intelligence monitoring and
analysis 101, 102; intercepts 91;
mechanical measures 86; mental
judo 95, 96; messages and delivery
102, 105; mind games 105;
misinformation 83, 89; orientation
86; passive measures 86, 87; plants
92; poison drip (sibs) 92; political
communication 90, 95; political
warfare 86, 96; propaganda 83, 85,
90, 91, 98; psychological analysis
95, 100 (mapping 89); spin doctors
96; truth 104; wedges 102
psychology 5, 83; causes and effects of
war 99; depersonalisation 99;
manipulation 97; pressure points
48, 98, 102; psychological tools 34,
36, 40, 78, 87, 88, 95; withdrawal
and isolation 33
public opinion 13, 44, 63, 84, 85, 92,
97, 174, 179, 180, 188
public relations 96, 97

racial antagonisms 35
Rapid Reaction Forces 40, 158
reconciliation 48, 56, 58, 59, 78, 79,
113, 121
Reformation, the 118; Martin Luther
118
refugees 3, 28
regional development banks 68; Africa
68; Asia 68; Caribbean 68; EBRD
(European Bank for Reconstruction
and Development) 68; EIB
(European Investment Bank) 68;
Latin America 68
regional organisations 145, 146, 150;
ANZUS (Australia, New Zealand,
USA) Treaty 145; ASEAN
(Association of South-East Asian
Nations 50, 145; Asia-Pacific
Economic Council 51; Baghdad Pact
145; conflict resolution 145;
ECOWAS (Economic Community of
West African States) 75; human
rights 145; international policing
146; OAU (Organisation of African
Unity)/African Union 50, 53; OSCE
(Organisation for Security and Co-
operation in Europe) 50, 57; SEATO
(South-East Asia Treaty
Organisation) 145; *see also*
NATO
regional stability 17
relief operations 40
religion 58, 100
religious tensions: Indian
subcontinent 22; Indonesia 23;
Nigeria 23; Pacific Islands 23;
Philippines 23; Serb Church 58;
Sudan 23
risk assessment 18, 33; Eastern

Europe 69; perspective 36; sketch
  map 20
Roetter, Charles 83, 93
rogue states 17
Romania 27
rule of law 6, 45, 141, 184
Russia 9, 112, 116, 140, 161, 167, 199;
  and Cuba 21; and India 29; and
  Kosovo 67, 117; and N. Korea 30,
  34; Russian Federation 27; and
  UN 67
Russo-Turkish War 15
Rwanda 6, 17, 23, 46, 59, 70, 154;
  Hutus and Tutsis 23, 76

sabotage 90
Saddam Hussein 7, 35, 66, 85, 87, 93,
  138
Saferworld 57, 141
sanctions 60
Sarajevo 41
Saudi Arabia 25, 130; arms purchases
  140; political fragility 25
Scholl-Latour, Peter 158
Schramm, Wilhelm von 83
Schulte, Paul 60, 200
Seattle 29
Second World 26
security 185, 192, 193, 198–200;
  needs and objectives 18
Security Purchase Index 198, 199
self-defence 10, 47, 75; vigilantes 11
Serbia 27, 37, 39, 58, 107, 114, 165,
  185, 197; bombing 44, 49, 52, 97,
  117, 136, 144, 161, 164, 171, 174;
  Pale 106; sanctions 66; Screbenice
  169; Serbs 2, 12, 112, 114
Shias 59
Sicily Landings 94; Operation
  Mincemeat 94; Spain, Sardinia,
  Southern Greece 94
Sierra Leone 6, 21, 37, 38, 48, 75, 151
Silesia 5
Sinn Fein 12
Slavs 112
Slovak Republic 27
Slovenia 27, 107, 193
small-scale aggression 43, 186
smart bombs/weapons 1, 146, 195
soft power 33, 174, 194, 197–200
Solana, Javier 191
soldiers: cost of equipment 13

Somalia 21, 48, 70, 74, 76, 98, 99,
  159, 161, 168, 170, 171, 180,
  186
South, the 20; belligerence 28;
  revolution of unfulfilled
  expectations 20; *see also* Third
  World
South Africa 23, 26, 32, 57–9, 70, 77,
  147, 185; ANC (African National
  Congress) 32, 54; apartheid 32, 70
  (anti-apartheid movement 21);
  Constitution 52; Inkhata Freedom
  Party 54; nuclear deterrent 32, 33,
  129, 185; sanctions 66
South China Sea 4, 23
South-East Asia 198
South Korea 17, 30, 127; US
  withdrawal 127
sovereignty 7, 15, 45, 49, 55, 70, 140,
  145
Soviet Union: aerial broadcasts 93;
  buffer states 27; confrontation 46;
  conspiracy theories 92; Daniloff,
  Nicholas 92; destruction of economy
  126, 155, 185; détente 85;
  dissolution of 115, 116; *Glasnost,
  Perestroika* 84, 113; Helsinki
  Process 193; KGB 84, 92, 113; and
  Middle East 120; Mitrokhin Archive
  92; MO (International Department)
  84; nuclear war 84; OP
  (Propaganda Department) 84;
  Pavlovian techniques 85; political
  warfare 92; psywar system 84; spy
  episodes 84, 85; successor republics
  11, 16, 23, 24, 26, 27, 54, 113, 115
  (*see also* CIS); and UN 67; Warsaw
  Pact 116
Spain 55, 69, 193
Spencer, Herbert 6
spheres of influence 17; Cuban 21;
  Soviet 21
Sri Lanka 48, 56
stand-off bombs 14
START (Strategic Arms Reduction
  Treaty) I and II 27, 115, 139
Stein, Janice Gross 98
Stilwell, Gen. Richard 98
Stoltenberg, Thorvald 47, 50
strategic interests 13, 17
Suez 98, 120
Sunnis 59

Sun Tzu 22, 88, 93, 201; alternative war 22
superpower confrontation 7
supply routes 13, 16, 17, 25, 34, 47
surgical air strikes 3, 30, 41, 97, 160, 161, 189; cost of 49
Sweden 8, 184, 187
Switzerland 8
Syria 23; and Israel 52, 119, 120

Taiwan 17, 23, 127, 165
Tajikistan 24
Tanksley, Col. David USA 103
terrorism 9, 14, 18, 29, 31, 35, 106, 129, 160, 170, 177, 200; attacks 36, 186; cyber-terrorists 165; groups 36, 166; World Trade Center bomber 106
Teutons 112
Third World 7, 20, 36; African socialism 21; Aid 21, 60, 152, 153 (good governance, human rights 68); Alliances for Progress 154; ban on export credits 154; corruption 153; debt cancellation 154; economic support 154; migration 35; military expenditure 67, 152; military support 22, 152–4; NEPAD (New Partnership for African Development) 154; political pluralism 153; poverty reduction 153; privatisation 21; proxies 34; revolution in military affairs of the poor 200; solidarity 66; terrorist attacks on USA 69; threat to peace 69, 200; trade 21; tribal and ethnic divisions 21–3; vulnerability 50
Thirty Years' War 15, 83
threats to security 9
Tibet 24
Tigreans 23
Tolstoy, Leo 5
tomography 168
Topitsch, Ernst 83
Tornados 1, 37
Toynbee, Arnold 88
Trafalgar 4
transatlantic security structure 192, 194, 199
Treaty of Utrecht (1713–14) 15
Treaty of Versailles (1919) 15, 107
Troy 41; Trojan Horse 93

Tungsten 26
Turkey: force contribution 16; Islamic leadership 24; Orthodox movement 112
Tyler, Capt. Paul USN 166

U2 flight 46
Uganda 46, 59, 198
United Kingdom 4, 59, 85; armed forces 37, 38, 184 (deployment 37, 38, force contributions 16); Brixton riots 161; City of London police 165; debt cancellation and export credits 154; Defence Assistance Fund for Central and Eastern Europe 62; Defence Intelligence Staff 101; economy 4, 8; Farnborough Air Show 61; and Gibraltar 69; Greenham Common Cruise missile base 165; Gulf patrols 38; Home Office 177; Hong Kong and China 114; Information Research Department 91; Middle East 118; miners' strike 161; nuclear deterrent 37 (upgrades and the NPT 139); overwhelming force 73; police and administrative reserves 75; Royal Navy 61, 172; SAS (Special Air Service) 89, 94; SOE (Special Operations Executive) 96; Strategic Defence Review 61; terrorist target 28; Wellington House Publicity Department 92
UN (United Nations): arms control 143, 150 (UN Register of Conventional Arms 139); budget and resources 39, 49, 77; Charter 6, 71, 74, 141 (Art. 2(7): non-intervention 71; Ch. VI: peacekeeping and building 71; Ch. VII: enforcement operations 71; Article 51: self-defence 71); civil administration, policing, election monitoring 75, 77; civil and military co-operation 70; conflict resolution 49; delegation to regional bodies 75; disarmament, demobilisation, rehabilitation 75; dual mandate 78; early warning system 48; establishment 15, 46, 77, 111; faults and capacities 74, 75; General Assembly 26, 66; global

security system 16; Group of 77 Non-Aligned Countries 66, 67; legitimisation 16, 71, 73, 74, 78, 90; humanitarian interventions 76; Human Rights Commission monitoring 77; independence assistance 77; management structure 67, 76 (executive committees for core areas 76; Senior Management Group 76); observer forces 69, 70, 76, 77, 143 (security of 70); peacekeeping operations 16, 37, 76, 142–4, 173 (numbers of 76); peace settlements 77; police force 16, 142; preventive deployment 48, 69; preventive diplomacy 48, 77; preventive disarmament 48; relief operations 16, 70; Secretary-General 48, 49, 63, 67, 76; Security Council 17, 26, 30, 40, 49, 67, 73, 76, 114, 143, 150, 154 (Permanent Members 49, 63, 67, 76, 143; Resolutions 70, 71); and Somalia 171; and South Africa 32; Strategic Planning Unit 67, 76, 143; Task Force on Humanitarian Intervention 49; UNPROFOR (UN Protection Force in Yugoslavia) 70, 73, 171; UN Rapid Reaction Force 72 (command structure 72–4; enforcement missions 72; equipment 78; mandate for peace enforcement 73; Military Staff Committee 72, 143, 151; monitoring, planning and analysis capability 72, 143; permanent or national units 72, 142, 143; rules of engagement 78); UN Reform 75, 76; Virtual Intellectual Resources Group 49

UN Specialised Agencies: FAO (Food and Agriculture Organisation) 66; IMF (International Monetary Fund) 15, 67, 68, 154; UNCTAD (UN Conference on Trade and Development) 66; UNDP (UN Development Programme) 28, 56, 152–4; UNESCO (UN Educational, Scientific and Cultural Organisation) 82; World Bank 15, 57, 152, 154, 194

USA (United States of America) 59; Air Force 166, 168 (Special Operations Command 106); Air National Guard Volant Solo aircraft 93; Arab states, involvement in 87; and Barbary pirates 114; 'black programs' 105; bombing of N. Vietnam and Serbia 52; Boston 54; and China 33, 114; CIA (Central Intelligence Agency) 92; Civil War, General Stonewall Jackson 93; Commanders for US Forces 73; Congress 94, 197; Cooperative Threat Reduction Program 62, 199; Council on Foreign Relations 180; CTBT (Comprehensive Test Ban Treaty) 26; defence programme 14; Department of Defense List of Critical Technologies 169; Department of Energy 167; EC130 Commando Solo 105; EC130 Compass Calls 106; and Egypt 120; European integration, support for 195; forces in Europe 37; funding agencies 56; global security 196 (Total Security 200); Grenada invasion 71, 106; Haiti 106; hegemony 16; Iran 121; Iraq, punitive air strike 71; Joint Task Force in Kosovo 171; President Kennedy assassination 92; King, Martin Luther 92; Kroll Associates, New York 165; leadership 13, 16, 75, 82, 184, 192; Libya, Rabta Chemical Plant 30; marines 168, 170, 171 (Expeditionary Force 180); Moscow Embassy 165; National Guard 38; National Missile Defense (NMD) 24, 27, 32, 155, 201; National Security Policy 85 (Agency 165); Navy 168; New York Police Department 54; Nicaragua, aid to Contras 71; North Korean reactors 30; and Pakistan 29; peace-support operations 171; Pentagon 85, 93, 94, 164, 169, 174, 195; police and administrative reserve 75; preventive defense 61; renewal of military assets 38; self-inflicted asymmetric warfare 195; shuttle diplomacy 120; meeting with Soviet defence ministers 61; Springfield, Mass. 54; State Department 195;

Strategic Defense Initiative (SDI, or Star Wars, Stellar Shield) 32, 85, 94, 137, 164; Strategic Information Operations (SIO) 106; terrorist target 28; UN subscriptions 39; University of Alaska 168; redefining war 200; joining world wars 92, 114

Vadset, Martin 171
Vanadium 25
Vance, Cyrus 48
verification 58, 115, 116; Dragon-Eye 60; media 60; microverification 60; mobile communications 60; monitoring 60 (on-site 58); NGOs (Non-Governmental Organisations) 60
Verne, Jules 162
Versailles 107
Vietnam 20, 21; Boat people 70; Syndrome 44
Vietnam War 3, 52, 97–9, 121, 161, 165, 166, 169, 170, 173, 200; Viet Cong 44, 98
virtual war 13
Vistula 112
Volksarmee 10

Wahabism 24, 36; xenophobia 25
water 25, 28, 121
war: brush-fire 57; economic cost 7, 8, 10, 13; expansionist 16; last resort 47; obligatory and discretionary 14; operations other than war 158; political cost 13, 14; reasons for 3, 47; techno-war 200; total war 134
war aims 4, 44, 107, 111
War Crimes Tribunals 60
warfare: conventional 13, 36, 172; countering aggression 9, 10, 125; future lies with technology14; military action 9; nuclear 14; reaction against 13; tactical 166; total 13

Warsaw Pact countries 136, 148
War of the Spanish Succession 15
Washington DC 29
weapons: ABC (Atomic, Biological and Chemical) 40; assessment 18, 47; clean 3; conventional 40; counter-proliferation 155; dual-use 167; heavy 57; hi-tech systems 44; of mass destruction 31, 84, 155, 200; micro-systems 165; miniaturisation 165; non-lethal 40, 175; parallel weapons research 175; too powerful 47; smart 43
Weeks, Albert L. 95
Western European economy 8, 183
WEU (Western European Union) 116, 171, 187, 190, 191
Wight, Martin 91
Wilde, Oscar 47
Wolfram 25
World Bank 15, 57, 152, 154, 194; security sector reform 50, 67, 153
world management 9
world population 28; pressures 28
World Wars 3, 4, 8, 15, 40, 41, 46, 58, 82, 91, 92, 111, 113; First 5, 8, 92, 107; Western Front 5
WTO (World Trade Organisation) 48, 66

xenophobia 6

Yemen 62, 67
York, Archbishop of 1
Yugoslavia 5, 7, 23, 144; former 27, 38, 62, 67, 114, 163; International Conference on 48

Zaïre 49
Zambia 42
Zanzibar 4
Zimbabwe 148
Zinni, Lt-Gen. Anthony 171, 180, 181
zones of conflict 11
zones of peace 11, 183, 194, 198